Glory to the Three Eternal

Monographs in Baptist History

VOLUME 13

Ours is a day in which not only the gaze of western culture but also increasingly that of Evangelicals is riveted to the present. The past seems to be nowhere in view and hence it is disparagingly dismissed as being of little value for our rapidly changing world. Such historical amnesia is fatal for any culture, but particularly so for Christian communities whose identity is profoundly bound up with their history. The goal of this new series of monographs, Studies in Baptist History, seeks to provide one of these Christian communities, that of evangelical Baptists, with reasons and resources for remembering the past. The editors are deeply convinced that Baptist history contains rich resources of theological reflection, praxis and spirituality that can help Baptists, as well as other Christians, live more Christianly in the present. The monographs in this series will therefore aim at illuminating various aspects of the Baptist tradition and in the process provide Baptists with a usable past.

Glory to the Three Eternal

Tercentennial Essays on the Life and Writings of
Benjamin Beddome (1718–1795)

Edited by
Michael A. G. Haykin
with *Roy M. Paul*
and *Jeongmo Yoo*

PICKWICK *Publications* · Eugene, Oregon

GLORY TO THE THREE ETERNAL
Tercentennial essays on the life and writings of Benjamin Beddome (1718–1795)

Monographs in Baptist History 13

Pickwick Publications
An Imprint of Wipf and Stock Publishers
199 W. 8th Ave., Suite 3
Eugene, OR 97401

www.wipfandstock.com

PAPERBACK ISBN: 978-1-5326-6612-4
HARDCOVER ISBN: 978-1-5326-6613-1
EBOOK ISBN: 978-1-5326-6614-8

Cataloguing-in-Publication data:

Names: Haykin, Michael A. G., editor. | Paul, Roy M. , editor. | Yoo, Jeongmo, editor.

Title: Glory to the three eternal : tercentennial essays on the life and writingf od Benjamin Beddome (1718–1795) / edited by Michael A. G. Haykin, Roy M. Paul, and Jeongmo Yoo.

Description: Eugene, OR: Pickwick Publications, 2019 | Series: Monographs in Baptist History | Includes bibliographical references.

Identifiers: ISBN 978-1-5326-6612-4 (paperback) | ISBN 978-1-5326-6613-1 (hardcover) | ISBN 978-1-5326-6614-8 (ebook)

Subjects: LCSH: Beddome, Benjamin, 1718–1795 | Baptists—Biography

Classification: BX6493 G44 2019 (print) | BX6493 (ebook)

Manufactured in the U.S.A.   AUGUST 23, 2019

With thanks for the witness of a faithful Christian and dear friend,
Eric Hugh Lindsay (1951–2018)

Contents

Contributors | ix

Preface | xi

1. Being Benjamin Beddome: A Biographical Study | 1
   Gary Brady

2. "Glory to the Three eternal":
   Benjamin Beddome and the Teaching of Trinitarian Theology | 34
   Michael A. G. Haykin

3. Benjamin Beddome's Christology | 51
   Jeongmo Yoo

4. The Pneumatology of Benjamin Beddome | 89
   Daniel S. Ramsey

5. "Such wondrous grace demands a song":
   The Hymns of Benjamin Beddome | 118
   R. Scott Connell

6. Benjamin Beddome and the Modern Question:
   The Witness of his Sermons | 142
   Jason C. Montgomery

Bibliography | 173

Contributors

A published author, **Gary Brady** has pastored Childs Hill Baptist Church, London, since 1983. After earlier studies in Wales and London, he gained a ThM from Westminster Seminary. He is a proud grandfather.

R. Scott Connell holds a PhD in Christian Worship from the Southern Baptist Theological Seminary where he is a faculty member and was the program coordinator for the undergraduate program for Music and Worship Studies for six years. He and his wife Mary have seven children and currently reside in Jacksonville, Florida, where he is the Pastor of Worship and Music at the historic First Baptist Church.

Michael A. G. Haykin (ThD, Wycliffe College, University of Toronto) is chair and professor of church history at The Southern Baptist Theological Seminary and director of The Andrew Fuller Center for Baptist Studies.

Jason C. Montgomery (PhD, Southwestern Baptist Theological Seminary) serves as Pastor of the Faith Community Baptist Church in Fort Worth, Texas, and Adjunct Professor of Church History at the IRBS Theological Seminary, Mansfield, Texas.

Roy M. Paul (BA, BSc, MTS) is Executive Research Assistant at the Canadian office of the Andrew Fuller Center for Baptist Studies.

Daniel S. Ramsey is a Baptist historian who earned his PhD in Historical Theology from the Southern Baptist Theological Seminary in Louisville,

Kentucky. He currently serves as an International Trainer in Systematic Theology with Training Leaders International. Daniel and his wife Denise live in Minneapolis, Minnesota.

Jeongmo Yoo (PhD, Calvin Theological Seminary) is assistant professor of Church History at Torch Trinity Graduate University in Seoul, Korea, and a senior fellow of the Andrew Fuller Center at the Southern Baptist Theological Seminary.

Preface

ON AUGUST 7, 1776, John Sutcliff (1752–1814) was ordained to the Baptist church at Olney, Buckinghamshire. Benjamin Beddome (1718–1795), the pastor of the Baptist cause in Bourton-on-the-Water in the Cotswolds, did not take part publicly but was present and was prevailed upon to preach in the evening. He preached on Zechariah 11:12. John Newton (1725–1807), then vicar of Olney, was present and wrote in his diary, "He is an admirable preacher, simple, savoury, weighty." Newton had also heard him fourteen months earlier, in June of 1775, when Beddome preached on 2 Corinthians 1:24. The sermon "gave me a pleasure I seldom find in hearing," Newton wrote in his diary that June evening. "It was an excellent discourse indeed, and the Lord was pleased to give me some softenings and relentings of heart." This is high praise indeed given that Newton had heard many of the great preachers of the day, including George Whitefield (1714–1770) and John Wesley (1703–1791).[1]

Today, though, Beddome is relatively unknown. The occasion of the bicentennial of his birth in 2018[2] presents a golden opportunity for those who appreciate his life and ministry to make him better known to the Evangelical world. Beddome's ministry in Bourton-on-the-Water was very much a ministry between the times—those times of Baptist advance in the seventeenth century and those of revival in the final couple of decades of the eighteenth century. Yet, the example of his faithful ministry, which sought to pass on the lineaments of orthodox Christianity, his encouragement of

---

1. John Newton, "Diary (1773–1805)," entries for June 27, 1775 and August 7, 1776.

2. Beddome's birth is often given as 1717, but he was born on January 23, 1717, Old style, which is actually 1718 according to our modern reckoning.

younger men like John Sutcliff,[3] who played a central rôle in the revival, his evangelical catholicity—he was not afraid to associate with men like George Whitefield when a good number of his fellow Baptists had grave doubts about the Anglican evangelist—and his hymns all helped to clear away stumbling-blocks in the pathway of revival. The essays in this volume are designed to reveal the solidity and fruitfulness of his ministry. They encompass a substantial overview of his life (by Gary Brady), examination of his teaching on the Trinity (by Michael Haykin) and on the free offer of the gospel (James Montgomery), and studies of his Christology (Jeongmo Yoo), pneumatology (Daniel Ramsey), and hymnology (Scott Connell). His life and ministry are an eloquent example of the truth of those concluding lines in George Eliot's *Middlemarch*: "That things are not so ill with you and me as they might have been, is half owing to the number who lived faithfully a hidden life, and rest in unvisited tombs."

This volume of essays is the realization of a personal dream, which gripped me sometime in the early 1990s. I had gone to Bourton-on-the-Water to see the scene of Beddome's labours. Many of the houses date from the eighteenth century and one can still see Beddome's own home, now the Old Manse Hotel in the centre of the village. That first time in Bourton taught me how to pronounce Beddome's name (like Beddam) and gave me a desire to do further study of this faithful pastor in the long eighteenth century. Over the past twenty-five years or so others have come to study Beddome and this present collection of essays is a partial fruit of this study. I am deeply thankful to all of the contributors to this volume, and especially for the help of Roy Paul and Jeongmo Yoo in editing. I am also deeply indebted to the proofing skills of Ian H. Clary. I could not have done this without them.

May this volume of essays not only make Beddome better known but also bring glory to the great God he strove to serve with all of his strength!

Michael A. G. Haykin

Dundas, Ontario
August 1, 2019.

---

3. For Beddome's influence on Sutcliff, see Haykin, *One Heart and One Soul*, 58, 95–97, 120.

1

Being Benjamin Beddome

A Biographical Study

Gary Brady

THERE IS NO PORTRAIT of Benjamin Brandon Beddome (1718–1795) in existence or even a silhouette and no written description of his physical appearance. However, a brief anecdote he once told and a piece of doggerel poetry from his own hand that has survived give us a good picture of the man. Beddome was minister of the Baptist cause at Bourton-on-the-Water, Gloucestershire, his sole charge, from about 1740 until his death in 1795. Nevertheless, he was often criss-crossing the roads of Gloucestershire and beyond, from Somerset to Oxfordshire, north to south from Worcestershire to Hampshire. In an undated anecdote we read:

> The late venerable Mr. Beddome, of Bourton-on-the-Water, in Gloucestershire, in a conversation I had with him, some years ago, informed me, that journeying from Bourton to Devizes, in his way, he stopped at an inn at Wootton-Basset, a small borough town in Wiltshire,[1] where he was quite a stranger, to take some refreshment. The person who kept the house, a widow woman, from his appearance, supposed him to be a clergyman of the Church of England, and was willing to do him a pleasure:

1. Wootton Bassett—now Royal Wootton Bassett, since 2011—is a few miles west of Swindon.

therefore, after serving him herself with what he called for in a very obliging manner, said to him, "Sir, the inhabitants of this place are a very happy people," "I am glad," replied Mr. Beddome, "you are so." "Yes," added the widow, "we do I assure you, Sir, think ourselves some of the most happy people in the world." "For what reason, Madam?" said Mr. B. "Why, Sir," answered his hostess, "*we have but one Dissenter in the town, and he is a Roman Catholic; and you know, Sir, they are the best of them!*" The good man, not willing to confound her, pleasantly passed off the matter, without making himself known.[2]

The printed doggerel poem is found in a manuscript book compiled by Beddome's grandson, Samuel Beddome, and headed "Original poetic epistle." It is addressed to John Collett Ryland (1723–1792), one of his early converts, and was written from Tewkesbury, Gloucestershire "the Day after he had left Bristol, his friend Ryland having accompanied him about ten Miles from Town."[3] The poem begins,

DEAR BROTHER, WHEN of your company bereft,
I turn'd a little to the left;
I spurr'd my mare, and made her go
Thro' thick and thin, thro' hail and snow:
But she (alas!) is aged grown,
As by her pace may well be known.

Having left Bristol very early he arrives in Tetherington "at nine o'clock, or somewhat past" "wet thro' " and spends an hour there in front of an open fire, drying his coat and stockings. He has breakfast and makes sure the horse is fed ("the charge was small, the diet coarse"). He had hoped the snow would ease but,

Large flakes of snow came down apace,
And still the wind was in my face.

2. It is likely that Beddome was wearing a white cravat and dark clothing, suggesting his clerical status.

3. The poem must be from the 1740s, after Ryland went to Bristol and before the death of Sarah Evans (1751). It may relate to a record in Ryland's diary (Saturday, May 25, 1745): "At 2 I rode with Mr. Benja Beddome about 9 miles onward of his journey to Horsely, it was very wet. he told me substance of his sermon, Rev 19:8. . . . He writes 5 sides 8vo—for a morning sermon and about half so much for an afternoon. Mr. Benja Beddome told me the following texts to think up, viz. Jer 1:6, Job 36:22—and he advis'd me to go to Jesus the great Prophet of the Church." See Hayden, *Continuity and Change*, 77.

"With feet benumb'd and spirits down" he arrives next at Newport, then Cambridge,[4] where again, "wet to the skin" he took a meal, fed the horse and dried out.

On the next leg of the journey, the snow is gone but it is still raining. He says he thought of Ryland, "and Bristol friends" and, "you know who" which could fit a number of people, but probably refers to his father. He hoped they were thinking of him passing through the storm. He also thought of God's showers of blessing,

> 'The Lord' (said I) 'with gentle show'rs
> Visit these barren souls of ours,
> Till ev'ry plant of grace within
> Be like the earth more fresh and green!

He arrived at Gloucester around 5:15 pm where he stayed with a Mrs. Smith, whose identity is unknown. Tired but thankful for her kindness, he still had another eleven miles or so to cover. He eventually arrived in Tewkesbury at eight in the evening. There he put up for the night, still more than twenty miles from Bourton and home or a lesser distance from Horsley, if that was his destination. The next morning he finished the poem with these lines:

> The Lord be with you, my dear friend,
> And me to those I know commend,
> To parents dear be love expressed,
> And then to Mrs. Evans next[5]
> First read, then burn these doggerel lines.
> But I must haste—day brightly shines.
> Then think of me as I of you,
> My dearest friend once more adieu.

These items perhaps reveal something of Beddome's character. He knew the eighteenth-century roads well and he looked like a minister to the casual observer. He was approachable, a good listener, a gentleman, a man of God. He had a certain sense of humor. He did not seize every opportunity to cry up his own cause.

---

4. This Newport is in Gloucestershire, halfway between Bristol and Gloucester.

5. That is Sarah Evans (1714–1751), née Browne, the first wife of Hugh Evans, mother of Caleb Evans, who died July 8, 1751, en route to Pershore, where she was buried.

Earliest Days in Warwickshire

Beddome was born in 1718, the son of a Baptist minister called John Beddome (c. 1674–1757). Beddome senior was probably born in Shakespeare country, in Stratford-upon-Avon, but moved to London when young, becoming a member of the Baptist church in Horsley Down, Southwark, the church that called him to the ministry.[6] In 1697 John moved back to Warwickshire where he began to work in Alcester Baptist church. He purchased a large property, a former inn, in nearby Henley-in-Arden, called Holmes House. It served as a home to him and his family and others and as a meeting place for the church. He also had a school there, it seems.[7]

Perhaps the source for the financial outlay necessary was his wife, Rachel Brandon. She was the daughter of Mercy Neckless (1673–1726) and Benjamin Brandon (1666–1702), a London silversmith said to be in an illegitimate line from Charles Brandon (1484–1545), first Duke of Suffolk and brother-in-law to Henry VIII.[8] She received a good education at a boarding school in Nantwich, Cheshire, due to the generosity of an aunt Rachel, for whom she was named and from whom she later inherited a fortune. The author of a nineteenth century memoir describes Rachel Beddome as "amiable and accomplished."[9] John Beddome was said to be "remarkable for his spiritual winning discourse, especially to young converts and enquirers."[10]

John and Rachel had at least five children who survived infancy. Benjamin, their firstborn, arrived on January 23, 1717,[11] and spent his first seven years in Warwickshire, where his father ministered from 1697 in Henley, Alcester and Bengeworth, near Evesham, Worcestershire.[12] According to Beddome's grandson Samuel, whose genealogical notebook is preserved in the archive of the Angus Library, Regents Park College, Oxford, Benjamin's brother Joseph 1718–1794, was an American merchant in Bristol. He died a Quaker in Philadelphia, leaving at least three daughters. Two sisters (Martha, wife of Christopher Ludlow from 1757 and Mary, wife of Moses Brain

---

6. The minister at Horsley Down (the church mentioned in connection with Rippon) was Benjamin Keach (1640–1704).

7. Eadkins, "Beddome Family."

8. Haykin, "Benjamin Beddome (1717–1795)" 169; Rippon, "Rev. Benjamin Beddome," 314.

9. Beddome, "Memoir," x.

10. Hayden, *Continuity and Change,* 113–14.

11. Beddome, "Memoir," ix.

12. Beddome Senior originally assisted John Willis (d. 1705), a blacksmith and Alcester's first Baptist minister (from 1660). See "History of the Baptist Church," 293.

from 1740, then Edward Bright from 1753) lived in Bristol. Respectably married, both had families. A third sister, Sarah, it seems did not marry.

Growing up in Bristol

In 1724, the family moved to Bristol, where John became assistant to William Bazley (1673–1757), pastor of the Pithay Baptist Church, 1723–1736. Broadmead was the smaller of the two Particular Baptist churches in Bristol at the time. Its meeting place was just 200 yards from the Pithay building. Bernard Foskett (1684–1758) had previously worked with John Beddome in the Midlands but had moved to Bristol four years before, in 1720, to teach in the Academy and co-pastor the Broadmead Church with Peter Kitterell (d. 1727). Foskett and Beddome had been together both in London and in Warwickshire, 1711–1720. They were now reunited and their friendship was again strengthened. The two apparently lived in the same house once more. Foskett remained a close family friend and Benjamin eventually named one of his sons Foskett. Beddome senior and Foskett eventually shared the same grave in Redcross Street.

Thus, at an impressionable age, Beddome came to live in the bustling seaport of Bristol, Britain's second city at the time. In his *Tour Through England and Wales*, c. 1720, the dissenting journalist and author Daniel Defoe (1661–1731) speaks of Bristol as, "the greatest, richest and best port of the trade in Great Britain, London only excepted. The merchants of this city not only have the greatest trade, but they trade with a more entire independency upon London, than any other town in Britain . . . the Bristol merchants as they have a great trade abroad, so they have always buyers at home, for their returns and that such buyers that no cargo is too big for them." This was the end of the era of men such as Edward Colston (1636–1721) and John Pinney I (1686–1720) whose wealth came chiefly from the flourishing slave trade.

Following schooling in the city, Beddome completed an apprenticeship to a surgeon-apothecary. He seems to have taken to this well and it is said that he never lost his love for things medical. Two sons trained in the same field and he himself, it seems, later carried on some form of medical practice in Bourton. It is said that he would often turn to the world of medicine for an apt illustration in his preaching.[13]

---

13. Beddome, "Memoir," xi.

Conversion

Benjamin and John were clearly close. Benjamin continued to sit under his father's ministry through his teenage years but made no profession of faith until he was twenty. *The Baptist Register* speaks of how, "the bent of his mind affected and afflicted his parents several years."[14]

The visiting minister on August 7, 1737, was Mr. Ware of Chesham, Buckinghamshire.[15] He preached on Luke 15:7, "I say unto you that likewise joy shall be in heaven over one sinner that repenteth more than over ninety-nine just persons which need no repentance." Beddome wrote that it was with that, "sermon I was, for the first time, deeply impressed." It made him weep, not just then but, it would seem, for some weeks afterwards. He would often hide himself away in a quiet corner of the chapel gallery, making the excuse that he wanted to sit somewhere where he could slip in or out easily, which he sometimes had to do in his capacity as a medical practitioner.[16]

Beddome was later to write,

> Lord, let me weep for nought but sin,
> And after none but thee
> And then I would—O that I might—
> A constant weeper be.

He found relief in reading the Scriptures and was soon brought to Christ.

Preparation for the ministry

No sooner was he converted than Beddome felt called to the Christian ministry. His medical apprenticeship was at an end and he began studies at the Baptist Academy, not only based in Bristol but under Bernard Foskett's stern but effective leadership. For some reason the arrangement lasted only a year or so before Beddome moved to London to study at the Fund Academy, an Independent academy at Tenter Alley, Moorfields under the leadership of John Eames (d. 1744).[17]

Beddome began to attend the Baptist church, Little Prescott Street, Goodman's Fields. Perhaps strange to say, Beddome was still unbaptised but this was remedied when the pastor Samuel Wilson (1702–1750) baptised

14. Rippon, "Rev. Benjamin Beddome," 316.

15. Joshua Ware (d. 1739) was a gentleman, perhaps a knight, and it seems, another medical doctor.

16. Rippon, "Rev. Benjamin Beddome," 316; Haykin, "Benjamin Beddome," 170.

17. Beddome, "Memoir," xii.

him, September 27, 1739, in the baptistery of a church in the Barbican.[18] Thomas Brooks quotes a letter sent from father to son at the time.

> I am pleased to hear that you have given yourself to a church of Christ, but more, in that I hope you first gave up yourself to the Lord to be his servant, and at his disposal. And now I would have you remember that when Christ was baptized, how soon he was tempted of the devil; and I believe many of his followers, in that, have been made conformable to their head. So also may you, therefore, of all the evils you may find working in your heart, especially beware of spiritual pride and carnal security.

The following year, on January 9 and February 28, Beddome preached before the church and was soon called by them to gospel ministry. Another letter from Beddome Senior expressed concern that Wilson was acting with too much haste but added, "The Lord, I hope, will help you to make a solemn dedication of yourself to him, and enter on the work of the Lord with holy awe and trembling."[19]

Just a letter from home

An interesting item exists in the Library at Bristol Baptist College. It is a letter dated "May 26, 1740 Munday [sic]" and addressed to Benjamin Beddome at "Mr. Wards, Bookseller at the Kings Arms in Little Brittain."[20] It was written when Beddome was a student in London and is from his parents back home in Bristol.[21]

Part of the fascination is that both parents have written something in their own hands. John Beddome starts by talking about cloth for a suit that he hopes to send (not realizing, typical of husbands no doubt, that his wife has already taken care of it). He digresses, however, to more spiritual matters: "I am sorry Mr. Willson[22] is in such a hurry to call you to ye ministry it would have been time enough just before you came Away but seeing it must be so I think you must not preach in public above once or twice at most at

18. Haykin, "Benjamin Beddome," 170.

19. For this and the previous quotation, see Brooks, *Pictures of the Past*, 23.

20. John Ward (d. 1758), son of Aaron Ward, London printer and bookseller (c. 1721–24) until his death (1747). Based at the sign of the King's Arms, Little Britain, London, John Ward later printed the first edition of Beddome's catechism.

21. John and Rachel Beddome, Letter to Benjamin Beddome, May 26, 1740 (Bristol Baptist College).

22. Samuel Wilson (d. 1750), pastor and writer, under whose ministry at Prescott Street, Goodman's Fields in London, Beddome then sat.

your own place & no where else except Mr. Stennet or his people ask you & if ye latter do it you may serve them as offt as their requiairs." He then comes back to the suit before going over to preaching in places mentioned in a previous letter. He hopes the Lord "will help you to make a solemn dedication of yr self to God & enter on ye work of ye lord with holy awe & trembling." He also promises to urge people to pray for him.

Rachel Beddome takes up where her husband leaves off with, "My dear Child I can't Inlarge now by Reason your fathers hand & mine is so different that it will make you pay double postage so I shall only add that I Received ye wig paid Carriage 1s 6d your father don't know but it came in the Box I have sent the paper parcel of cloth this day by Mr. Biddell att the kings arms Holborn Bridge about two o'Clock I hope my dear the lord will be with you & help you in the ensuing work."

News follows—Foskett has gone to the annual Baptist association meetings in Birmingham, returning in a week's time.[23] Then comes a sequence in which we learn that Mr. Moor is better, Mrs. Beers about to die and Mr. Poynting is dead! John Trotman the glazer "is in a consumption" and may already be dead. As the end of the paper and the time for the post loom, she closes, "but I must add no more but conclude with kind Love to yourself & service to all enquiring friends your truly affectionate mother Rachel Beddome." She adds that "the carriage of the parcel is paid" (the parcel of cloth for the suit). Presumably the letter survives because of its power to remind Beddome of his parents, who he surely loved, even when they were gone.

Early preaching at Bourton

It was in the spring of that same year, 1740, on his way back to Bristol that the younger Beddome first preached at Bourton-on-the-Water. Lying in the Cotswolds, near the Roman Fosse Way, it is just south of Stow-on-the-Wold. In Beddome's time there were more sheep than people. The houses huddled either side of the River Windrush formed what really was a remote place.

Puritans had been meeting in the southern Cotswolds from earlier times.[24] A congregation seems to have been gathered before 1655 and came to be pastored briefly, on an open membership basis, by the local clergyman, Anthony Palmer (1618–1678), who left the established church in 1660. Later pastors may have included a John Dunce, also known as Wolgrave. At

---

23. The annual association meetings were an important part of Baptist life at this time. Beddome, like his father, was very much involved in them throughout his life.

24. Holmes, "Early Years (1655–1740)," 1–19.

one point there may have been two ministers, John Collett, a Paedo-baptist, and Joshua Head (d. 1719), a Baptist ejected from the Church of England in 1662. A chapel was built in 1701 for the Baptists, the Paedobaptists having left to form their own congregation. Head was succeeded by Thomas Flower Senior, who led the congregation to constitute itself as a baptised church. Some fifty people, twenty-four men and twenty-six women, signed the covenanting document on January 30, 1720.

By 1740, Flower was dead and the church was eagerly seeking a new pastor. Before his coming to the village in 1740, Beddome described the church as one that had been "for a long time . . . unsettled and divided."[25] The church wanted Beddome to preach regularly for them, which he agreed to do. For some time, however, he also continued to preach in Warwickshire. One Sunday Beddome was preaching in Maze Pond Baptist Church (probably in 1739) when a deacon unfriendly to the preferred candidate (Benjamin Wallin, who became the next pastor) "without having even consulted his brethren in office or the church, stopped the members after the sermon, and proposed Mr. Beddome as a suitable person for the pastoral office." No one was willing to second this proposal and so the idea was dropped.[26]

It was during this period, in 1741, before he accepted a full call that, according to William Newman (1773–1835), there was "a great awakening in Beddome's congregation at Bourton. Forty persons were brought to repentance at the same time, and Mr. Ryland was among them."[27] This Mr. Ryland is John Collett Ryland (1723–1792), a young man who, despite his godly forbears, had shown no interest in the things of God until this point, preferring card playing to hearing sermons. However, the Lord saved him and he himself went on to be a leading Baptist minister. In October, 1742, he joined the church and in February, 1744, he began training for the ministry in Bristol. Ryland wrote in his diary for June 25, 1741:

> Surely Mr. Benjamin Beddome is an instance of the existence of God and the truth of the Christian Religion. What could change his heart and induce him to leave his profession or trade—what could have him to stay at Bourton rather than to go to Exeter to which he was strongly solicited—what is it that moves him to preach, pray and be so active? Is it not the delight he finds in the work—'Tis plain that it is not worldly interest.[28]

---

25. Haykin, "Benjamin Beddome," 168.

26. Ivimey, *History of the English Baptists*, 1:476.

27. Newman, *Rylandiana*, 3.

28. Ryland quoted in Robinson, "Baptist Student," 25.

Ryland began to pastor at Warwick in 1746.[29]

There were around seventy or eighty members at Bourton when Beddome first preached there, many coming in from the neighbouring villages, some from as far as fifteen miles away, quite a distance to travel in inclement weather. Under this enthusiastic, if still immature, young preacher the congregation and membership grew markedly. In May, 1743, some 48 new people joined the church, bringing the membership to 113. Shortly after, the travelling backward and forth between the Cotswolds and Warwickshire came to an end and Beddome agreed to be the regular "teaching elder" at Bourton.

He was ordained on September 23 that year. Bernard Foskett preached the charge, from 1 Timothy 4:12, and one of the most eloquent preachers of the day, Joseph Stennett II, preached to the church from Hebrews 13:17. Messers Haydon, Cook and Fuller prayed.[30] Beddome's father was unable to be present but wrote promising his prayers and good wishes. The week before, the church had produced a formal written call to their "beloved brother Benjamin Beddome, to the office of teaching elder to us."[31] They also made quite clear that they would not stand in his way should there be a call from elsewhere. His duties included supplying the nearby Stow church, which had recently come under the Bourton oversight when its membership had fallen below 25. According to Brooks, there were soon a hundred members coming into Bourton from at least twenty parishes in the neighbourhood.[32]

Association meetings and early calls to other churches

Brooks comments that 'it was not a light thing, in a secluded village, to have secured for so many years the service of Benjamin Beddome.'[33] In 1743, Beddome preached for the first time at the Midland Association meetings in Leominster. He went on to preach another sixteen times at such gatherings over the next 46 years. He probably authored the circular letters both of 1759 and 1765. He was association moderator in 1761 and 1771. *The*

29. His ordination took place on July 26, 1750. John Brine (1703–1765), High Calvinist pastor from Cripplegate, London, gave the charge, which appears in his printed works. John Haydon of Horsley, preached to the people. Beddome himself, John Overbury (1729–1764) of Alcester and Thomas Craner (1716–1773) of Blunham, Bedfordshire, prayed.

30. This was John Haydon (1714–1782), Edward Cooke (d. 1746/1747) from Pershore, and William Fuller (1671–1745) of Abingdon.

31. *Bourton Church Book 1719–1802*, 67.

32. Brooks, *Pictures of the Past*, 29.

33. Brooks, *Pictures of the Past*, 31.

Midland Association of Baptist Churches was founded in 1655 and continued to meet annually throughout Beddome's lifetime and beyond. The churches were united in holding to the stated Calvinistic doctrines of the Trinity; election; original sin and man's depravity; particular redemption; free justification by the imputed righteousness of Christ; efficacious grace in regeneration and final perseverance, and the unstated Baptist doctrines as found in the 1689 Confession.

From Ryland's diary we know that there had been a request for Beddome to pastor in Exeter. In October, 1748, his father had the idea of Benjamin coming to Bristol as his assistant. Benjamin knew Bristol well and his father employed many arguments, including the emotive "It would be a great comfort to your mother to sit under your ministry" to try and entice him back to the big city.[34] But he was unpersuaded. This was not to be the last time he was asked to leave Bourton.

Marriage and family

In 1642, when Beddome was aged 25, he wrote a letter proposing marriage to his contemporary Anne Steele (1717–1778). There is no record of her reply but she seems to have firmly rejected her earnest suitor and, unlike Beddome, she happily remained single all her days. She too was later to be a celebrated hymn writer. At this time he wrote the following lines, under the heading "The Wish":

> Lord, in my soul implant thy fear,
> Let faith and hope and love be there;
> Preserve me from prevailing vice,
> When Satan tempts or lusts entice.
> Of friendship's sweets may I partake,
> Nor be forsaken, or forsake.
> Let moderate plenty crown my board,
> And God for all be still adored:
> Let the companion of my youth
> Be one of innocence and truth
> Let modest charm adorn her face
> And give her thy superior grace
> By heavenly art first make her thine

---

34. Dix, "Thy Will Be Done," 9. This article occupies the bulk of the *SBHS Bulletin* and is lacking pagination.

Then make her willing to be mine
My dwelling place let Bourton be
There let me live and live to thee.[35]

Whether Beddome made any other proposals we do not know, but over the next few years he came to fall in love with a member of the congregation. Elizabeth Boswell (1732–1784) was the second daughter of Richard and Hannah (née Paxford) Boswell. Richard was a deacon and a stalwart of the Bourton church. Baptised in 1733, he was a wealthy jeweller.

While still single, Beddome lived outside Bourton, in the nearby village of Lower Slaughter, in the home of a Mr. Head. With the announcement of his marriage and there be nothing suitable found for them elsewhere, work began in 1748 on a fine new and commodious manse just the other side of the Windrush, in Bourton itself. The cost was £324.17s.6½d, quite a sum at the time. However, the Bourton congregation raised the bulk of it.[36] The chapel was also extended the same year. Benjamin moved into the manse in September, 1749, and on December 12 of the same year, aged 32, he married 17-year-old Elizabeth. She was a girl of good Nonconformist stock and a help-meet to him for more than thirty years to come. Rippon records that "she was a person of strict piety; sincere in her friendships; affectionate in all her relations, scarcely ever seen out of temper."

Adding further to his happiness, on January 7, just over a year after their wedding, Elizabeth gave birth to a son, John Reynolds. There seem to have been two more boys who died in infancy and, after that, seven more children, six boys and a girl. Benjamin was born October 10, 1753, Samuel (1756), Foskett (1758), Boswell Brandon (1763), Elizabeth (1765), Richard (1769) and lastly, Josephus (1779). What hopes and fears must have been wrapped up in this growing family. What joy the children must have brought. However, the domestic bliss was not to remain undisturbed.

Earlier trials and troubles

"The Wish" was certainly answered but from 1750 onwards Beddome had to face various new trials. Shortly after marrying, he became seriously ill and for six weeks was at death's door. "Languor seized" his "feeble frame." He "mourned and chattered like a dove."[37] The church was much in prayer and

---

35. Rippon, "Rev. Benjamin Beddome," 318. It is in a notebook in the Angus Library.

36. Brooks says that subscriptions were all carefully recorded by Beddome.

37. See Beddome, *Hymns Adapted to Public Worship*, #741, #742, both headed "Recovery from Sickness."

did all they could to help him. Eventually, in the goodness of God, he made a full recovery. As he himself wrote of the Lord,

> He spake, and lo, afflicting pains
> My wasted limbs forsook;
> Death threw his poisoned dart in vain,
> For he repelled the stroke.[38]

It was a distressing time for Beddome and his new wife. Always writing poetry, he wrote doleful verses dreading his demise but later added more confident verses in the following vein.

> "If I must die"—O let me die
> Trusting in Jesus' blood;
> That blood which full atonement made
> And reconciles to God.[39]

The lines quoted before, have not been dated. They also say,

> When sore diseases threatened death,
> 'Twas he restrained their power,
> Did then prolong my fleeting breath,
> My feeble frame restore.[40]

As in so many dark providences, there was a beautiful outcome to this one. It served to endear the people to their pastor who they had so nearly lost with more than ordinary bonds of love.

This factor was to have immediate effect in a trial of a different sort. On October 6, 1750, Samuel Wilson died in London. The next month Beddome and his church received letters strongly urging that he come to pastor the Little Prescott Street church.[41] That church feared its congregation would soon scatter unless someone of Beddome's stature came to them soon. It was London's largest Baptist church at the time and to receive a unanimous call from such a church must have tempted Beddome to leave what was, despite many advantages, something of a backwater, to return to his father's church and the place where he himself had been baptised and set apart to

---

38. Beddome, *Hymns*, #741:4.

39. Beddome, *Hymns*, #778:1 under the heading "Death Inevitable."

40. Beddome, *Hymns*, #741:3.

41. Written copies are preserved in the archive of the Angus Library. They are reproduced in Dix, "Thy Will Be Done."

the ministry. However, he declined to move unless the people at Bourton, most of whom had been converted under his ministry, were willing.

For their part, the church unanimously felt that they could not comply. 'Our great love and esteem for this our learned and faithful pastor would make the parting stroke very severe and unsupportable' they argued. They were strengthened in their resolve not only by their pastor's recent recovery from illness but also by the thought "that we were destitute for many years, and not withstanding our many cries to Almighty God, he was pleased to withhold direct answers to prayers until at length he graciously raised up, eminently qualified, and unexpectedly sent, our dearly beloved and Rev. pastor, Mr. Beddome, to become our pastor." Also the fact that "his endeavours have been wonderfully blessed for restoring decayed religion, the increasing of our church . . . and the raising up of gifts for the help of other churches, some of which are fixed as pastors."[42] weighed heavily. They felt it would be ungratefulness to God to allow him to go.

Such a firm refusal should have put an end to the matter but in February, 1751, the London church wrote again, imploring the Bourton folk to reconsider. The Cotswold folk were unshaken and immediately responded negatively, urging their brothers to reconsider where God's Providence was leading them. Beddome also wrote acquiescing and quoting John Owen's view that without the free consent of both churches involved it is unlawful for a minister to move from his charge. He also felt John Gill (1697–1771) was on his side. He wrote:

> If my people would have consented to my removal though I should have had much to sacrifice on account of the great affection I bear to them, yet I should then have made no scruple in accepting of your call; but as they absolutely refuse it, the will of the Lord be done. I am determined I will not violently rend myself from them; for I would rather honour God in a station much inferior to that in which he hath placed me, than to intrude myself into a higher without his direction.[43]

Apart from a last-ditch attempt from a small group within the London church who wrote to Beddome at the end of 1751, that was the end of the matter. As Kenneth Dix observed, the whole incident reveals a man who was not concerned about himself and his own reputation.

It must have been an unsettling time for Beddome and his new wife. However, his singular commitment to his congregation impressed itself

42. All quotations from Dix, "Thy Will Be Done." The letter is signed by three deacons and thirty-seven male church members.

43. Dix, "Thy Will Be Done."

upon the members and led to a fresh appreciation of their pastor. This came to expression in increased material comforts for him and his family and the paying off of a debt of nearly £100 outstanding on their meetinghouse.

As well as the deaths of at least two infants in the early 1750s, further sadness in the earlier part of his ministry include the deaths of an older generation. On July 8, 1751, Sarah Evans, first wife of Hugh Evans (1712–1781) and mother of Caleb Evans (1737–1791), died. She was buried in Pershore and Beddome, her most intimate and esteemed friend took the funeral, preaching from Matthew 3:12. The sermon was not printed. Over the next few years, four family members died: his father in 1757; his mother in 1758; Foskett; and his mother-in-law.

There is evidence that in 1762 Beddome went through a time of spiritual darkness. A letter exists written to this effect from fellow hymn writer and younger contemporary Daniel Turner of Abingdon (1710–1798). The letter is accompanied by some verses and a note saying:

> You may possibly think it strange, my good brother, that I who have so little personal acquaintance with you, and know so little particularly, of your case, should give you the trouble of so long a letter, as the enclosed—and I confess it a liberty I am not sufficiently warranted to take. Nevertheless, I having myself once felt so much from a situation not perhaps much unlike yours, I was, more than I should else have been, affected with the short hints of your case in your last favour with the association Letter, that I could not easily rest the inclination I found in my mind, to say something that might administer to your comfort through the Divine blessing, though I confess I had no thought when I set out of going half this length. If I have been impertinent, I did not design to be so, and the rectitude of my intention, and your goodness, I trust, will plead my excuse. I am however, wishing to see you.[44]

Progress and decline at Bourton

The Bourton church continued to grow after 1750 but with some variation. Referring to the church books it is observed that although by 1751 there were 180 members, the next 14 years were variable. Association Letters speak in 1751 of "decay" despite the "large auditory," in 1753 of languor and

---

44. Daniel Turner, Letter to Benjamin Beddome, September 4, 1762 in "Spiritual Darkness," 9.

in 1755 of "coldness yet a little strength."[45] None were added between 1752 and 1754, bringing numbers down to 162. Then in 1755, some 22 were baptized. By 1759 there were 160 members. This too was followed by a dearth until 1764, when some 28 were added. Over two hundred baptisms had taken place since Beddome's coming by 1766 and the number of members had again risen to 196. It had been necessary to undertake a major enlargement of the premises in 1764 and 1765.

Over the next thirty years there was a relative decline, with only 53 added by baptism and six by letter. Some 105 died, twelve moved to other churches, two were excluded. One notes in the 1780s references in the church book to poorly attended church meetings and the need to revive the midweek meeting, suggestive of a measure of spiritual languor. At the prompting perhaps of former member John Ryland, in 1784 the church did agree to follow the example of the Northamptonshire Association and join in the concert for prayer but little seems to have come of this, as far as Bourton itself is concerned. In over half of the thirty years after 1765, there were no additions to the membership. Brooks says that by 1786 they were down to a hundred members.[46] By the time of Beddome's death there were 123 members on the roll, although congregations apparently continued to be large with five or six hundred attending.

There is evidence that Beddome was continuing to have influence right up to the end and beyond. In 1848, *The Baptist Magazine* recorded the death of a 91-year old Bourton deacon called Richard Cooper (1757–1848). He had been an Anglican for many years but, "became a hearer of the Rev. Benjamin Beddome, and was united to the church at Bourton-on-the-Water at the commencement of the present century."[47]

Deacons

Bourton, like most Baptist churches, was led by the minister and deacons. In 1789 there were eight deacons. Prior to this, Richard Boswell (Beddome's father-in-law) and Joseph Strange had served. Other earlier deacons included John Reynolds Senior (d. 1758), Jeremiah Cresser (d. 1768), John Wood and John Reynolds Jr. (1731–1792), who became a minister. In *Pictures of the Past,* Brooks also refers to James Ashwin (1710–1801) and William Palmer (1725–1807). He quotes from the Church Book concerning Ashwin:

45. *Bourton Church Book 1719–1802.*

46. Holmes, "Early Years (1655–1740)," 62.

47. "Recent Deaths," 428.

September 3, 1801, departed this life, an honoured and beloved brother in the Lord, James Ashwin, aged ninety-one. An honourable member and deacon of this church, of a savoury spirit in the things of God, a humble Christian, often afflicted, and greatly comforted in his affliction. A constant attendant on the means of grace, when able, and an admirer of the grace of the means, saying, 'why me, such a sinner as I have been, to have hope toward God, my Redeemer?' He cherished an ardent desire for the good of souls, and for the peace and prosperity of Zion. He was calm and composed in his last affliction, though in great pain. Though not destined to enjoy the ministry of Mr Coles,[48] he felt much interest in the prospect of his coming, and requested that he would preach at his funeral, from Jeremiah 31:3, which was done on the eighth of that month.[49]

Brooks also noted the death of Palmer on August 28, 1807. He had been a deacon for 26 years. As for the other six, Edward Reynolds (d. 1811) and Thomas Cresser (1738–1808), both from Little Rissington, became deacons, with Ashwin and Palmer, in April, 1781. The other deacons in 1789 were Richard Dolby, Joshua Perry, William Collett from Lower Slaughter and Samuel Fox , father of philanthropist William Fox (1736–1826).

Troubles and joys in the mid-sixties

At this point we record some of the joys and troubles Beddome faced in the 1760s and the grace of God that he knew. He observed that

Unnumbered trials, doubts and fears
Attend us in this vale of tears;
But through the grace of God our friend
They shall in lasting triumphs end.[50]

The year 1765 was, in many ways, encouraging. In this year the new enlarged chapel was erected and the August Association met in Bourton, Beddome's association letter receiving publication. By January, 1766, Nathaniel Rawlins (1734–1809), a Bourton member, was settled as pastor at the Back Street Chapel, Trowbridge.

However, tainting such joys was the death on February 4, 1765, of Beddome's first son, John Reynolds, aged only 15. Despite his youth he

48. Thomas Coles (1779–1840) was pastor from 1801.

49. Brooks, *Pictures of the Past*, 69–70.

50. Beddome, *Hymns*, #550:1, under the heading "Trials over-ruled for Good."

apparently died well, giving evidence of genuine faith in Christ. This must have been a comfort to Benjamin and Elizabeth as they committed themselves to God.

Collections and fast days

It is evident from the Church Book that Bourton was not parochial in its thinking. Several fast days were kept to pray about international wars and numerous collections took place for needs elsewhere. In April, 1767, the Church Book notes that, "Having previous notice, the Revd Messers Whittaker and Occam came when we had a meeting at which they both preached . . . after which there was a collection taken for the support of the Indian schools under the care of Mr. Wheelock of Lebanon, Connecticut, also New England. The collection amounted to £30." This refers to Eleazar Wheelock (1711–1779), Nathaniel Whitaker (1730–1795) and the native American Samson Occom (1723–1792). Eventually, Wheelock founded Dartmouth College. A college history reveals that the £30 donation from Bourton was made up of ten guineas from Beddome's strong supporter, William Snooke, Esq. (1730–1779) and nineteen guineas "collected at the Rev. Mr. Beddom's."

Final trials and troubles

In 1777, Beddome turned sixty. He was suffering increasingly from the painful arthritic condition of gout, which sometimes prevented him from carrying out his duties. It was decided that he should have an assistant. A number of men were considered but in the end it was William Wilkins from Cirencester who was chosen. He had trained for the ministry in Bristol and in Scotland. He remained for at least the next 15 years. This move was designed to ease Beddome's burdens but, as we will see, served in some ways to increase them.

Beddome's son Benjamin had moved to Edinburgh to pursue the study of medicine. A gifted linguist and an all-round scholar he had been accepted into the Edinburgh medical society at a young age. Later that year came news that he had gained a doctorate from the University at Leyden in Holland for a thesis on the human variation and its causes.[51] What an excellent future seemed to lay before him. But it was not to be. At the turn of the year, he took ill with "a putrid fever" (typhus) and on January 4, 1778, he quite

51. Beddome Jr., *Tentamen Philosophico-Medicum*. The Angus Library has a second edition.

suddenly died. He was only 25 years old. He died in Edinburgh so news of the untimely death did not reach the family immediately. However, it so happened that the day before the death, Beddome preached aptly on Psalm 31:15, "My times are in thy hand." The congregation had also sung Beddome's hymn "My times of sorrow and of joy."[52] It includes the appropriate closing fifth verse:

> Here perfect bliss can ne'er be found,
> The honey's mixed with gall;
> Midst changing scenes and dying friends,
> Be thou my all in all.

It was Beddome's practice to begin next Sunday's preparation on the previous Sunday evening and he had also already made plans to preach the following Sunday on "full of eyes" from Ezekiel 10:12. It is salutary to note his comment, "But alas! How much easier is it to preach than practice! I will complain to God but not of God. This is undoubtedly the most affecting loss I have ever yet sustained in my family. Father of mercies, let me see the smiles of thy face, whilst I feel the smart of thy rod (Job 14:13). Thou destroyest the hope of man."[53]

On December 9, 1779, William Snooke died. To lose such a strong supporter would undoubtedly have been a great blow to Beddome. In the following year, Wilkins married a Miss Alice North, a Presbyterian from Overthorpe, near Banbury, Oxfordshire.[54] This seems to have been the catalyst in the church for an easing of the previously strict requirements regarding qualifications for communion. There is evidence that Wilkins took an open view of communion rather than the strict view held in the church until this period.[55] There continued to be some tension over the matter. It was not the only source of unhappiness and on December 13, 1781, Wilkins angrily resigned his post. This led to something of a crisis, which is described over several pages in the church book.[56]

The main cause of contention seems to have been Wilkins's belief that, although very much Beddome's junior, he should be given equal footing. A

---

52. Beddome, *Hymns*, #222, headed "Resignation," begins: "My times of sorrow and of joy / Great God, are in thy hand; / My chief enjoyments come from thee, / And go at thy command."

53. Beddome, "Memoir," xxiv.

54. According to one of the Bourton Church books, she died May 8, 1798. Samuel Beddome's notebook notes that Wilkins later married Letitia Field in Hackney in 1800.

55. See Holmes, "Early Years (1655–1740)," 3, 73, 81; Naylor, *Picking Up a Pin*, 60.

56. *Bourton Church Book 1765–1920*, 44–47.

certain amount of envy, on Wilkins's part, appears to be at play here. It is clear that the sympathies of the congregation are very much with Beddome in this crisis, although they want to keep Wilkins. Beddome clearly seeks to be magnanimous but is hurt by Wilkins's behavior. Eventually, Wilkins is brought to see that an equal financial split was not possible, as certain benefits had been given to Beddome in person. The crisis dragged on into 1782 and flared up again in 1784. Wilkins finally resigned in 1791. A Mr. Reed appears to have assisted Beddome following Wilkins's departure.

From the beginning of 1783 Beddome was confined to his home by gout. In one week, early in April 1783, his brother-in-law and father-in-law both died. Then, early in 1784, a fever was prevailing in the village and on January 21 his beloved wife Elizabeth died. She was only 51. Contemporaries spoke of her as being "eminent for her unobtrusive piety." They spoke also of the "amiableness of her tongue and the sincerity and permanence of her attachment; while her patience under suffering excited the admiration of all."[57] The church book says that "no person could be more beloved or their loss more lamented."[58] After some 34 years of happily married life she must have been sorely missed.[59] To add sorrow to sorrow, on October 20, 1784, his son Foskett drowned at Deptford as he was about to board ship. Like his brother Benjamin, and Beddome himself, he had been trained in the medical line. He was just 26 years old. The other children appear to have lived to a good age.[60]

Thus, in his later years Beddome had to face many trials that drove him back to the God of all grace.

> The trial, awfully severe,
> Will have a gracious end;
> And though no helper now is near
> The Lord will be thy friend.
>
> Then will I humbly wait, till he

---

57. Beddome, "Memoir," xxiv.

58. *Bourton Church Book 1765–1920*, 57.

59. Early in 1784, Beddome composed the four-verse Hymn #324, "If loads of guilt oppress," sung according to a ms notebook, January 11. Verse 3 runs thus: "Supported by his arm,/ I need no other aid;/If he but look on my distress,/I will not be afraid" and verse 4: "To him myself,/ my all I cheerfully resign;/Thankful, if smooth the path I tread,/If rough I'll not repine."

60. In Samuel Beddome's notebook, he notes that Richard died, 1795; Samuel, 1815; Boswell Brandon, 1816. Eliza married a Samuel Fawell and Josephus married a Sophy Petrie. Their deaths are not recorded but by 1834 Josephus was dead as Thomas Coles mentions his widow, living in Leamington. See *Bourton Church Book 1719–1802*, 20.

His kindly aid afford;
To his kind arm for succour flee
And trust his Holy Word.[61]

It was not all trouble by any means. There were many opportunities for fellowship with other ministers at Association meetings and ordinations and, although never a great one for preaching away from home, he would still visit Bristol, Warwickshire, Abingdon and London to preach and to renew acquaintance with family and friends.

Entrance to the Universities of Oxford and Cambridge was still very much barred to Nonconformists at this time but in 1770 Beddome received an honorary Master's degree from the *Senatus Academicus* of faraway Providence College, Rhode Island (now Brown University). A backwater Bourton may have been, but news of its distinguished pastor had travelled far and wide.

The Double Lecture

From 1774–1788 a double lecture was established among six churches, namely Abingdon, Fairford, Wantage, Cirencester, Cote and Bourton. In the six summer months there would be a double lecture (an older and a younger minister preaching) at each of the churches in turn.[62] A typical list is the one from the first year, 1774:

> Fairford: [James] Biggs [Wantage] and [Daniel] Turner [Abingdon] [April]
> Wantage: Caleb Evans [Bristol] and Joseph Stennett [London] [May]
> Cote: Beddome and Biggs [June]
> Cirencester: [Samuel] Dunscombe [Cheltenham] and Turner [July]
> Bourton: Biggs and Turner [August]
> Abingdon: [Thomas] Davis [Fairford] and Beddome [September]

Beddome usually preached twice a year at these gatherings. We know from Snooke's diary that in August, 1774 the order of service at Bourton was:

1. Mr. Stanwell (Cirencester) prayed

2. Singing

3. [Samuel] Dunscombe (Cheltenham) prayed

---

61. See Beddome, *Hymns*, #548, headed "The Christian in a Storm."
62. See Hayden, *Continuity and Change*, 88.

4. [James] Biggs (Wantage) preached on Rom 5:3–5

5. [Thomas] Davis (Fairford) prayed

6. Singing

7. [Daniel] Turner (Abingdon) on Mark 9:50

8. Singing

9. Mr. Pindy (sic) prayed [probably Thomas Purdy, Chipping Norton]

Snooke had all the ministers back for a meal afterwards and put some up at his home. Some went on to Bengeworth. Stanwell stayed to preach in Bourton on the Sunday and Beddome went to preach for him in Cirencester. Snooke gives a similar order for the double lecture in Abingdon, September 28, where we know Beddome was one of the speakers. Something similar happened in August, 1775. This time Snooke notes that the meeting began at 10:45 am and ended at 1:45 pm, a length of three hours.

Final years and death

For the last eight years of his life Beddome lived frugally and apparently adopted the policy of giving away his entire stipend to charity. It is clear from his will[63] that he had grown quite a wealthy man with several thousand pounds at his disposal as well as property. In 1789, in his seventies, he attended his last Association meeting, at Evesham, and preached for the last time. To hear this man of God preach, even in his declining years, must have been a great privilege. In these final years he would preach sitting down and had to be carried to meetings in a chair.

He had the habit of composing sermons, many of which were never preached. He began the general practice of destroying his sermon notes on the Monday after he had preached, perhaps to prevent him from preaching them again. In 1792 he made a final visit to London to preach and to see his remaining children and friends. On October 25 he amended his will, rescinding his previous decision to provide for poor members of the Bourton congregation and poor ministers in nearby congregations. He also revoked his intention to leave part of his library and certain furnishings in the manse for the use of future ministers. The reason given is "the irritating Conduct I have met with after 52 years service"!

It was at this time that William Carey's (1761–1834) *An Enquiry into the Obligation of Christians to Use Means for the Conversion of the Heathen*

63. The original document of 1791 or 1792 is in the archive of the Angus Library with a photocopy and a typed record.

(1792) was published and the *Particular Baptist Society for the Propagation of the Gospel* was just about to be formed.[64] In a 1793 letter to Andrew Fuller (1754–1814), the first secretary of this missionary society and the theological driver behind Carey's mission, Beddome expressed his doubts as to the wisdom of mounting an overseas mission. "Considering the paucity of well qualified ministers" he believed it had a "very unfavourable aspect with respect to destitute churches" in Britain, where, "charity ought to begin."[65] He lined up with the negative viewpoint found in Haggai 1:2, candidly confessing that the problem was perhaps his own lack of faith. He expressed the view that Carey might have succeeded him at Bourton but he realized that was now impossible. Beddome certainly cannot be accused of a complete lack of vision. Compare these lines:

> Where'er the sun begins its race
> Or stops its swift career
> Both east and west shall own his grace
> And Christ be honoured there.

Also:

> Thus shall spread the glorious gospel,
> To the earth's remotest bound.
> Distant empires, lands and nations,
> Soon shall hear the solemn sound;
> Darkness fleeing
> Light shall everywhere abound.[66]

The truth is that a new era in God's work was dawning and Beddome would not and could not be part of it. He was destined for another world.

He died, as was his wish, "in harness," missing only one Lord's Day's preaching before falling asleep in Jesus on September 3, 1795. Right to the very last he had continued not only to preach but also to write hymns. Six hours before he died he was composing a hymn. Its final unfinished lines include these,

> God of my life and my choice

64. William Carey preached at Bourton on August 24, 1787, according to the *Bourton Church Book 1765–1920*, 67.

65. Beddome, "Letter to Andrew Fuller," October 2, 1793.

66. Beddome, *Hymns*, #702:2 under the heading "Triumphs of the Saviour"; #707:2, under the heading "Rapid Spread of the Gospel." David Breed also cites Beddome, *Hymns*, #705, which begins "Ascend thy throne, Almighty King" (Breed, *History and Use of Hymns*, 150).

> Shall I no longer hear thy voice?
> O let that source of joy divine
> With raptures fill this heart of mine!
>
> With various and malignant storms,
> With ugly shaped and frightful forms
> Thou openedst Jonah's prison door
> Be pleased O Lord to open ours.
>
> Then will we to the world proclaim
> The various honours of thy name
> And let both Jews and Gentiles see
> There is no other God but thee.

He had left a note saying there should be no funeral discourse but this was only discovered later so Benjamin Francis (1734–1799) of nearby Horsley in Shortwood preached. His text was Philippians 1:21. The body was laid to rest in the yard outside the meetinghouse near the door. A large plaque on the wall of the present Baptist church in Bourton remains as a memorial to Beddome and his wife. William Palmer, a deacon, recorded the death of his pastor.

> On Thursday morning about Three O Clock September the third 1795 departed this life after fifty five years faithfull labours and unblemisht carracter and useful Services both to saints and sinners, In the Seventy Ninth year of his age That Great and Worthy man of God and Minister and Pastor of the Baptist Church and Congregation of Dissenters at Bourton on the Water the Revd Benjamin Beddome of Blessed Memory. . . . Some of his last words were In my Father's House are many mansions & Also Is not this a Brand pluckt out of the Burning; Then fell a Sleep Aged 79 years.[67]

Following Beddome's death, there was a split over whether to call Wilkins back or for Reed to become the main pastor. Eventually, it was agreed that it was better to go for an outsider and in April, 1797, Thomas Uppadine (1768–1837) was called.[68] Wilkins's name continued to be promoted, however, until in October 1801, they called their own former member, Thomas Coles.

67. See Holmes, "Early Years (1655–1740)," 82–83.

68. Thomas Uppadine from Cannon Street, Birmingham, was baptized there at the end of 1787. He had been a buckle manufacturer by trade but began to prepare for the ministry from 1795. He went on to serve in Hammersmith, 1801.

His character and influence

The eloquent and scholarly Robert Hall Jr. (1764–1831) wrote about Beddome in his preface to the collected hymns. We should bear in mind that
this is a young man's description of an eminent man of an older generation.
Hall speaks of his personal acquaintance with Beddome but he was only 31
when Beddome died, there being an age gap of near fifty years. No doubt the
input of Hall's father, Robert Hall Sr. (1728–1791), was significant.

> Mr. Beddome was on many accounts an extraordinary person.
> His mind was cast in an original mould; his conceptions on
> every subject were eminently his own; and where the stamina
> were the same as other men's, (as must often be the case with the
> most original thinkers) a peculiarity marked the mode of their
> exhibition. . . . Though he spent the principal part of his long life
> in a village retirement, he was eminent for his colloquial powers,
> in which he displayed the urbanity of the gentleman, and the
> erudition of the scholar, combined with a more copious vein of
> attic salt than any person it has been my lot to know.[69]

As for Beddome's abiding influence, besides his later published hymns and
sermons and his immediate influence on the Bourton congregation and beyond, there was that which came in the shape of men converted under his
ministry who later became ministers themselves.

Richard Haynes (d. 1768) was converted, shortly before Ryland, whom
we have mentioned, in the 1741 awakening. He began to preach in 1747
and went on to pastor at Bradford-on-Avon from 1750. John Ryland Sr.
became "a master preacher" and "a giant in the land."[70] He was set apart to
the ministry in 1746. There were several others. Richard Strange (d. 1768)
became pastor at Stratton, Wiltshire, 1752. Little is known of him. John
Reynolds from Farmington, baptized in 1743 at the age of 14, studied in
Bristol and for several years often deputised for Beddome. In this period his
more settled ministry appears to have been at Cirencester, Cheltenham and
Oxford.[71] In 1766 he became minister at Cripplegate, London.[72]

Nathaniel Rawlins has been mentioned. He was probably from More-
ton-in-the-Marsh and was baptized in 1750. Another Bristol student, he

69. Hall, "Recommendatory Preface." By "attic salt" he means elegant and delicate
wit.

70. Naylor, "John Collett Ryland" 200–1.

71. Holmes, "Early Years (1655–1740)," 46.

72. He succeeded the High Calvinist John Brine and is buried next to him in Bunhill Fields.

became pastor in Trowbridge in 1765. Alexander Payne (1742–1819) was a former Methodist preacher who joined the Bourton church in the autumn of 1775, the same year that he was baptized at Fairford by Thomas Davis (c.1730–1784). His name first came before the Bourton church in 1778 but there was no call until 1780. The church at Bewdley considered calling him for some while but he eventually became minister first at Bengeworth, from November 1780.

Thomas Coles, Beddome's eventual successor, was baptized and joined the church at the age of 15 or 16. He headed off to study at Bristol ten days before Beddome died. His youth does not rule out Beddome's influence. Even at the age of 11 he was taking extended notes of Beddome's sermons and at 13 was reading them back at the midweek meeting. He went on to gain an MA from the Marischal College, Aberdeen, in 1800. He eventually succeeded Beddome the following year and pastored the church until 1840.

Beddome's interest in young men coming into the ministry went beyond his own congregation. On July 28, 1779, he was one of the preachers (with Caleb Evans of Bristol and Robert Hall Senior) preaching at the induction of the Devonshire born Bristol student Thomas Skinner (1752–1795) to Clipstone, Northamptonshire. It appears that although Beddome had been due to preach he forewent his evening opportunity so that people could have the opportunity of hearing the 15-year-old Robert Hall Jr.

His Library

During his lifetime Beddome amassed a sizeable library. Perhaps he built on what was left by previous ministers or his father's collection or both. He acquired books on a regular basis, presumably keeping them at the manse. At some point after his death, the library was moved to the attic of a member of the Bourton Church and passed on to his succeeding family. Sometime in the 1940s the library's existence came to the attention of Ernest Payne, then Principal of Regent's Park College, Oxford, who managed to have it transferred to the college on permanent loan.

The library has now been properly catalogued and is what American historian Pope A. Duncan has called "a gold mine waiting to be discovered." It is difficult to give an exact figure regarding the number of items in the library as in several cases a number of works are bound together and although the cataloguing system only goes up to 414, there are often multiple items under one catalogue number. So, for example, the first fifty catalogue numbers represent some 85 titles. If that is an average, we are talking about nearly 700 titles. Further, some few items are not titles that belonged to

Beddome but later additions.[73] Most works are in English but many are in Latin. Perhaps the oldest book in the collection is a Calvin commentary on 1 John and Jude from around 1580. The newest book that Beddome would have owned may be a 1790 copy of the Baptist Confession.

His Writings

Catechism

In Beddome's lifetime he published little. His association letter was published in 1765 and some individual sermons and hymns also appeared in his lifetime. On February 27, 1752, he published *A Scriptural Exposition of the Baptist Catechism by way of Question and Answer*. Lamenting the demise of catechizing in families and noting the success of a similar effort by Matthew Henry (1662–1714),[74] he wrote, "May the great God smile upon this faint attempt for his glory, and may that church especially, to which I stand related, accept it as a small acknowledgement of their many favours and a token of the sincerest gratitude and affection from their willing though unworthy servant."[75]

Catechizing, the use of questions and answers to teach Christian doctrine, has a long and honourable history. The early church had a high view of it and appointed catechists whose main work was catechising men, women and children. Tom Nettles has spoken of the Reformation as "the Golden age of catechisms," the Heidelberg and Westminster Catechisms having had most impact.[76] In 1680 Hercules Collins (1647–1702)[77] adapted the Heidelberg document for Baptist use under the title *An orthodox catechism*. Henry Jessey (1603–1633),[78] another eminent early Baptist, produced a threefold catechism aimed at various levels called *A catechism for babes or*

73. An example would be an 1823 five-volume work by Timothy Dwight (1752–1817), *Theology, Explained and Defended*, once owned by a David Barclay.

74. This is Henry's *Scripture Catechism* of 1702. He also wrote a *Plain Catechism for Children*. See Holmes, "Early Years (1655–1740)," 62.

75. Beddome, *Scriptural Exposition of the Baptist Catechism*, iv.

76. Nettles, *Teaching Truth, Training Hearts*, 17.

77. Hercules Collins (d. 1702) was the respected minister from 1677 of a Baptist church at Wapping, London, that moved to Stepney ten years later. He had few educational opportunities but authored several books. He suffered imprisonment for Baptist beliefs in 1684 and is buried in Bunhill Fields.

78. Highly regarded as a scholar, author and humanitarian, Yorkshire-born Henry Jessey (1603–1663), a Cambridge graduate, left parish ministry for London, 1635, and pastored the persecuted church gathered by Jacob and Lathrop from 1637.

little ones.[79] Several other Baptist catechisms, including one by John Bunyan (1628–1688), appeared down the years but the one that was to become most popular among Particular Baptists was that based on the Westminster Shorter Catechism and known as *Keach's Catechism.* Nettles says, "Perhaps more than all others combined, this catechism defined what it was to be a Baptist throughout the eighteenth century and for some years into the nineteenth." It was prepared around 1693, the year in which a general assembly of Particular Baptist churches took place in London and where it was agreed, "That a catechism be drawn up, containing the substance of the Christian religion, for the instruction of children and servants; and that Brother William Collins be desired to draw it up."[80]

William Collins (d. 1702) was co-pastor with pastor and author Nehemiah Coxe (d. 1688) of a church in Petty France, London, from 1673–1688. With Coxe, he had been responsible for publishing the 1677 Confession of faith, the confession ratified in 1689 and now known as the *Second London Confession.* No one knows why the name of "Famous Mr. Keach" is so firmly connected with the catechism. Benjamin Keach was certainly the leading Baptist of his day. A prolific author, in 1664 he published *The Child's instructor or A new and easy primer.* For this he was arrested, jailed, twice pilloried and, "saw his book burnt under his nose."[81]

What Beddome's version of *Keach* does is to give supplementary questions and Scripture texts for each of the original 114 questions. Beddome's catechism was widely used and was reprinted in 1776. In his 1754 letter to the Midland Association, reporting on the church, Beddome mentions the successful use of the catechism with all ages. Holmes suggests that it was part of the key to his earlier success and points out that later decline coincided with the fall off of its use. He highlights Wilkins's refusal to engage in catechising due to other engagements. He also notes that on at least two occasions, 1753 and 1786, the church purchased catechisms for distribution to the poor.[82]

The catechism reveals Beddome to be no Hyper-Calvinist or antinomian but a Strict and Particular Baptist and a Sabbatarian in the best sense.

79. The simplest of these contained only four questions: what man was, is, may be and must be!

80. Ivimey, *English Baptists,* 1:533.

81. Nettles, *Teaching Truth, Training Hearts,* 47, 49, 50.

82. Holmes, "Early Years (1655–1740)," 145. See also below, chapter 2, for a study of Beddome's Trinitarianism in his catechism: Haykin, "Glory to the Three Eternal."

Hymns

Beddome is best remembered today as a hymn writer.[83] Hymn singing had been something of a controversy among Baptists for much of the first half of the eighteenth century. Michael Haykin notes the significance of the fact that John Beddome came out strongly on the side of the singers.[84] Benjamin Beddome loved to write poetry and when he became a minister, he followed the practice of other ministers of the period, producing a weekly hymn for the congregation to sing following his morning sermon. This was as a supplement to the hymns in Watts's and John Rippon's *Selection*. There were no PowerPoint screens or printed sheets for everyone then, of course, so hymns were usually "lined out" two lines at a time by the precentor or clerk and sung *a capella*. Beddome wrote well over eight hundred hymns altogether as well as other poems.

The hymns circulated first in manuscript form. In 1769 *The Bristol Baptist Collection*, compiled by John Ash (1724–1779) of Pershore and Caleb Evans of Bristol, was published. It included some thirteen hymns by Beddome. In 1787, influential London pastor John Rippon produced his famous *Selection*. This contained some 42 hymns by Beddome. The *Selection* eventually went through many editions.

Some hymns could also be found appended to printed sermons but it was not until more than twenty years after Beddome's death that the hymns were collected together and published in one volume. This collection of 830 hymns was published in 1818 by an anonymous editor with an introduction by Robert Hall Jr. and bore the title *Hymns adapted to Public Worship or Family Devotion*. It would appear that this collection was assembled chiefly by use of a fascinating collection of notebooks containing a fair copy of each one with dates. A number of loose copies in Beddome's own hand and from his later years also appear to have been used.[85]

In the book, the editor has divided Beddome's hymns into 25 categories, from "Perfections of God" through "Scripture doctrines" and "Bible Societies" to "doxologies." He begins by listing the first lines of every hymn and at the back gives fairly extensive scriptural and general indices. All this betrays the fact that Beddome wrote on a range of subjects.

Hall wrote of his excellence as a religious poet having been long known and especially commends his variety and the "poetical beauty and elevation" in some hymns and the "piety and justness of thought" in

---

83. See also, below, chapter 5: Connell, "Such Wondrous Grace."
84. Haykin, "Benjamin Beddome," 169.
85. This material is in the Archives of the Angus Library.

them all. He also refers to "beautiful and original turns of thought" and the experiential depth and breadth. Later hymn writer James Montgomery (1771–1854) spoke most appreciatively of them and David Breed placed Beddome "among the great English hymn writers" and particularly liked the fresh evangelistic emphasis.[86] Robert Oliver says they are "noteworthy for their beautiful blend of doctrine and Christian experience."[87]

Since Beddome's time, the hymns have tended to be more popular in the United States than in the United Kingdom and no one hymn has ever become very widely known. Early in the twentieth century some forty were in current use. For popularity as a hymnwriter, Beddome exceeds every other Baptist writer, even including Anne Steele, the next most popular. The most thorough appraisal of Beddome as a hymn writer in recent years is the relatively brief one by J. R. Watson in his 1999 study of the English hymn. He says Beddome made use of both ancient and modern writers and his hymns were "more than usually dialogic or intertextual," meaning that he was something of a plagiarist. Watson claims borrowings from Watts, George Herbert (1593–1633) and John Newton. He nevertheless praises his admirable and predictable clarity, quoting his baptismal hymn on "The signification of baptism."[88] He is critical of Beddome's clarity and balance but accepts that "a strong imagination" is at work more akin to Newton and William Cowper (1731–1800) and an advance on Philip Doddridge (1702–1751). Often predictable and homiletic, he rises above this elsewhere. Watson sees Beddome as transitional, between the grandeur of Watts and the sensitivity of Cowper.[89]

Preaching

It is clear that despite early deficiencies, Beddome was a greatly-used preacher and as he matured he was among the most acceptable Baptist preachers of his day. Robert Hall spoke of his sermons having "bone and sinew and marrow in them which shows a great mind."[90] Rippon says of him: "Though his voice was low, his delivery was forcible and demanded attention. He

---

86. Breed, *History and Use of Hymns*, 149–53.

87. Oliver, *Chapels of Wiltshire and the West*, 115.

88. Beddome, *Hymns*, #621.

89. Watson, *English Hymn*, 198–202.

90. This is a marginal comment in a book of Beddome sermons quoted in a life of Hall by J. W. Morris. See Holmes, "Early Years (1655–1740)," 68. In an appendix, Holmes quotes Hall saying, "I do not know any sermons of the kind equal to them in the English language."

addressed the hearts and consciences of his hearers. His inventive faculty was extraordinary and threw an endless variety into his public services. Nature, providence and grace had formed him for eminence in the church of Christ." And earlier, "The labours of this good man were unremitted and evangelical. He fed them [that is, his congregation] with the finest of the wheat. No man in all his connexions wrote more sermons, nor composed them with greater care—and this was true of him to the last weeks of his life. In most of his discourses the application of a student and the ability of a divine were visible."[91] He also remarks on Beddome's wide knowledge of Scripture and his gift for apt quotation of texts to bolster his arguments. As for his theology, he was, it says, "opposed to Arminianism and to Antinomianism." He held that believers are delivered from the Law as a covenant of works but subject to it as a rule of life.[92]

In his preface to the hymn collection of 1817, Robert Hall agreed. He favourably notes Beddome's wide reading, deep learning, originality and his, "chaste, terse and nervous diction." He also observes how, "As a preacher, he was universally admired for the piety and unction of his sentiments, the felicity of his arrangement, and the purity, force and simplicity of his language, all of which were recommended by a delivery perfectly natural and graceful."[93] He often took unusual texts but made them familiar and clear. In his mature years he had great facility as an extempore preacher. A.C. Underwood, quoting Rippon, speaks of his ability to "sketch his picture at the foot of the pulpit, to colour it as he was ascending, and, without turning his eyes from the canvas, in the same hour, to give it all the finish of a master."[94]

A classic example occurred at a meeting in Fairford, Gloucestershire.[95] Beddome did not always use notes and for some reason as he came to preach he forgot what the sermon text was to be. On the way from pew to pulpit he leaned over and asked the church's pastor, Thomas Davis, "Brother Davis, what must I preach from?" Thinking it an odd remark, Davis replied, in rebuke, "Ask no foolish questions." Not understanding correctly, Beddome went on to deliver a "remarkably methodical, correct, and useful" sermon on Titus 3:9 "Avoid foolish questions"![96]

There are some 223 extant sermons by Beddome in print. Between 1807 and 1820 a number of his sermons were printed in a series of eight

91. Rippon, "Benjamin Beddome," 320.

92. See, for example, Beddome, "Right Use of the Law," 134.

93. Hall, "Recommendatory Preface."

94. Underwood, *History of the English Baptists*, 140.

95. This would have been at the double lecture in 1777 or 1781.

96. This sermon appears to be Sermon X in Volume V of the Beddome's sermons.

slim volumes. They contain twenty sermons each (except for the last volume, which is two short) under the title *Short Discourses adapted to Village Worship or the Devotion of the Family*. By 1824, one volume was in its sixth edition and by 1831 another was in its fifth. These volumes were also issued in larger combined form and in 1835 another set of sixty-five sermons was also published. The sermons were undoubtedly popular. C. H. Spurgeon (1834–1892) is one eminent nineteenth-century preacher who positively refers to them.

They are all textual sermons, although there is a run of eight sermons on 1 Thessalonians 5:16–22 in volume four, and occasional pairs of sermons, such as a pair on self-examination, another pair on Hebrews 12:14, and a third pair on Revelation 3:20. They cover a fairly broad range of Scripture, from Exodus 13:21 to Revelation 17:14. There are awakening sermons, such as that on "Views of death" (Rev 6:7–8) or "The Sin and Danger of Delay in Matters of Religion"; evangelistic ones such as that on "Seeking the Lord" (Matt 28:5) or "Free Forgiveness" (Luke 7:42); searching ones such as that on "The Distinguishing Character of Christians" (John 17:16) or "On the Folly of Profession without Forethought" (Luke 14:28) and sanctifying sermons such as that on "The Christian's Pursuit" (Ps 63:10) or "The Duty of Imitating God" (Eph 5:1).

Brooks says of the written sermons, "Admired for their evangelical sentiments and practical tendency, they are scarcely less pleasing in the simplicity and clearness of their style."[97] The sermons are based on notes so cannot properly represent the actual preaching. However, in more recent years Peter Naylor has commended them as "models of the art of preaching, displaying as they do a lively understanding both of Scripture and of the soul of man." He cites Beddome as a living embodiment of his own dictum, "All that ministers can do is to persuade; God must do the rest. Without his efficacious influence, all the force of reasoning, and all the charms of eloquence will be lost. Paul may plant, and Apollos water; but it is God that giveth the increase."[98]

Conclusion

A moss-covered grave stone erected by his great-grandchildren can be found in the old burial ground in Bourton. It says he was "interred near this spot where the chapel formerly stood." Inside the present church building is a plaque that reads:

97. Brooks, *Pictures of the Past*, 61.
98. Naylor, *Picking Up a Pin*, 59–60.

Sacred to the Memory of
The Revd Benjn Beddome
Fifty two years
Pastor of the congregation
meeting in this place
He died Sep 3rd 1795
Aged 79

It then mentions his wife Elizabeth and says, "The memory of the just is blessed."

In a review article of the two-volume *The Blackwell Dictionary of Evangelical Biography* (1995), Alan Sell suggests that giving only 14 lines to Benjamin Beddome seems "niggardly."[99] There can be little doubt that Beddome has been unjustly neglected. While never a giant of Particular Baptist history, he was certainly a shining light and the fact that hardly any of his writings are currently easy to get hold of in print is an anomaly. In an age when so much material from previous centuries is being reprinted, it is a great shame that more Beddome material is not easily available. He is of interest not only to Reformed Baptists but to all Bible-believing Christians.

99. Sell, "Potted Evangelicals," 152.

2

"Glory to the Three Eternal"

Benjamin Beddome and the Teaching
of Trinitarian Theology[1]

MICHAEL A. G. HAYKIN

ONE OF THE HYMNIC treasures to come out of the eighteenth century is that by the East Anglian Calvinistic Baptist Robert Robinson (1730–1790), "Come, Thou Fount of every blessing." Robinson had been converted under the powerful ministry of George Whitefield (1714–1770) and, after a short career as a Methodist preacher, he was used by God to build a thriving work at St. Andrew's Street Baptist Church, Cambridge, where he became known as one of the finest colloquial preachers in England.[2] About two and a half years after his profession of faith in 1756, Robinson wrote the above-mentioned hymn to commemorate what God had done for him when he

---

1. For assistance with various aspects of this chapter, I would like to acknowledge the help of Mr. Derrick Holmes of Abbeymead, Gloucestershire, England; Mr. Stephen Pickles of Oxford, England; Pastor Gary W. Long of Springfield, Missouri; Mr. Jason Fowler, Archivist at Southern Baptist Theological Seminary, Louisville, Kentucky; and Miss Ruth Labeth, Dean of Women at Toronto Baptist Seminary. The bulk of this chapter first appeared as Haykin, "Glory to the Three Eternal." Used by permission.

2. On the life and thought of Robert Robinson, see especially Hughes, *With Freedom Fired*; Champion, "Robert Robinson," 241–46; Addicott, "Introduction," viii–xviii; Smith, "Liberty," 15–170.

professed faith in Christ. "Thoroughly Scriptural in doctrine,"[3] the final stanza of this hymn runs thus:

> Oh! to grace how great a debtor
> Daily I'm constrained to be!
> Let Thy grace, like a fetter,
> Bind my wandering heart to Thee.
> Prone to wander, Lord, I feel it,
> Prone to leave the God I love;
> Take my heart, O take and seal it,
> Seal it from Thy courts above.[4]

Towards the end of his life, though, Robinson appears to have become increasingly critical of both this hymn's Calvinism and its implicit confession of the deity of Christ. In a letter written in 1788 he stated that he considered "a trinity of persons" in the Godhead "the most absurd of all absurdities," though in a letter written the following year he asserted that he was "neither a Socinian nor an Arian."[5] And the story is told of a certain occasion during these final years of Robinson's life when he was travelling in a stage-coach with one other passenger who happened to be a Christian woman. Robinson struck up a conversation with the lady that soon turned to the subject of hymns. The woman began to testify to the great spiritual blessing that the hymn "Come, Thou Fount of every blessing" had been to her. Suddenly Robinson burst out, "Madam, I am the unhappy man who composed that hymn many years ago, and I would give a thousand worlds, if I had them, to enjoy the feelings I had then!"[6]

Further evidence of this shift in theological sentiments comes from Robinson's two final sermons. They were preached at the request of Joseph

3. See Routley, *I'll Praise My Maker*, 261.

4. This is the original version of this stanza, which more modern versions alter slightly. See Routley, *I'll Praise My Maker*, 261.

5. Robinson, *Two Original Letters*, 5; Letter to S. Lucas, September 16, 1789 (Robinson, *Select Works*, 286).

According to the *Posthumous Works of Robert Robinson*, Robinson "publicly declared his disbelief of the commonly received doctrine of the Trinity—that he thought . . . the word Trinity was 'a barbarous, popish word,' which had produced much evil in the Christian church" (Robinson, *Posthumous Works*, vii). Another posthumously published selection of his literary works maintained that Robinson was convinced "that the opinion of Athanasius, or Arius, or Sabellius, or Socinus, or Augustine, or Pelagius, or Whitby, or Gill, on the subjects in dispute between them, ought to be considered of such importance as to divide Christians, by being made the standards to judge of the truth of any man's Christianity" (Robinson, *Seventeen Discourses*, iv–v).

6. Hughes, *With Freedom Fired*, 106; Routley, *I'll Praise My Maker*, 262.

Priestley (1733–1804), the leading apostle of eighteenth-century Socinianism, in two Socinian meeting-houses in Birmingham on June 6, 1790. According to Priestley, one of these sermons assailed Trinitarianism in a manner that "savoured rather of the burlesque, than serious reasoning."[7] Robinson was found dead the following Wednesday. It was thus widely believed that he had died a convinced Socinian. In his funeral sermon for Robinson, Priestley gave added fuel to this belief when he triumphantly declared that Robinson had become "one of the most zealous unitarians" prior to his death.[8]

On the other hand, one of his oldest friends, Coxe Feary (1759–1822), pastor of the Calvinistic Baptist work in Bluntisham, Huntingdonshire, recorded a conversation that he had with Robinson but a month before the latter's decease in 1790. Robinson affirmed that when it came to the doctrine of the Trinity he was neither a Unitarian nor an Arian. "My soul rests its whole hope of salvation," he solemnly told Feary, "on the atonement of Jesus Christ, my Lord and my God."[9]

Calvinistic Baptist Trinitarianism in the intellectual milieu of the eighteenth century

Whatever the truth regarding Robinson's final beliefs about the doctrine of Trinity, there can be no doubt about where the community with which he was long associated, the British Calvinistic Baptists, stood on this issue. Throughout the eighteenth century, this community unhesitatingly affirmed that this doctrine is, in the words of the London Baptist preacher Benjamin Wallin (1711–1782), the "first and grand principle of revealed truth and the gospel."[10] Or, as Joseph Stennett II (1692–1758) put it: "The doctrine of the ever blessed Trinity, is of the greatest importance to his glory."[11] When, for example, in something of a cause célèbre in the London Baptist community in the 1730s, two pastors who were brothers, John and Sayer Rudd (d. 1757), both came to the conviction that "Trinitarian doctrine" was "entirely

---

7. Cited in Oliver, "Emergence," 71n143.

8. Priestley, *Reflections on Death*, 21. One of the most prominent of Robinson's Baptist contemporaries, Andrew Fuller (1754–1815), was certainly convinced that Robinson died a Socinian. See Fuller, "Calvinistic and Socinian Systems," 168, 222–24.

9. Belcher, *Complete Works*, 223–24.

10. Wallin, *Eternal Existence of the Lord*, iv–v.

11. Stennett, *Christian Strife*, 78, cited in Hayden, "Contribution of Bernard Foskett," 197.

consisting of words and phrases of men's own inventing" and totally un-scriptural, they were expelled from the London Baptist Association.[12]

Well typifying this Baptist grip on this doctrine was the voluminous John Gill (1697–1771), who wrote what was probably the major Baptist defence of the doctrine of the Trinity in the first half of the eighteenth century. His *The Doctrine of the Trinity Stated and Vindicated*—first published in 1731 and then reissued in a second edition in 1752—proved to be an extremely effective defence of the fact that there is "but one God; that there is a plurality in the Godhead; that there are three divine Persons in it; that the Father is God, the Son God, and the Holy Spirit God; that these are distinct in Personality, the same in substance, equal in power and glory."[13] The heart of this treatise was incorporated into Gill's *Body of Doctrinal Divinity* (1769), which, for most Baptist pastors of that day, was their major theological reference work. As John Rippon (1751–1836), Gill's successor at Carter Lane, noted in a biographical sketch of his predecessor:

> The Doctor not only watched over his *people*, "with great affection, fidelity, and love;" but he also watched his *pulpit* also. He would not, if he knew it, admit any one to preach for him, who was either cold-hearted to the doctrine of the Trinity; or who *denied* the divine filiation of the Son of God; or who *objected* to conclude his prayers with the usual *doxology* to Father, Son, and Holy Spirit, as three equal Persons in the one Jehovah. Sabellians, Arians, and Socinians, he considered as real enemies of the cross of Christ. They *dared* not ask him to preach, nor *could* he in conscience, permit them to officiate for him. He conceived that, by this uniformity of conduct, he adorned the pastoral office.[14]

He did more than "adorn the pastoral office." Through his written works he played a key role in shepherding the British Calvinistic Baptist community along the pathway of biblical orthodoxy.

This tenacious affirmation of Trinitarianism by these Baptists was in the face of some of the stiffest intellectual winds of their day. By and large the Trinitarianism of the Ancient Church had remained unchallenged until the seventeenth and eighteenth centuries. Even during that most tumultuous of theological eras, the Reformation, this vital area of Christian belief did not come into general dispute, though there were a few, like Michael Servetus (1511–1553) and the Italians, Lelio Francesco Sozzini (1525–1562) and his

12. Roberts, *Continuity and Change*, 35–36.

13. Gill, *Doctrine of the Trinity*, 166–67.

14. Rippon, *Brief Memoir*, 127–28.

nephew Fausto Sozzini (1539–1604),[15] who rejected Trinitarianism for a Unitarian perspective on the Godhead. As William C. Placher and Philip Dixon have clearly demonstrated, it was the growing rationalism of the seventeenth and eighteenth centuries that led to a "fading of the trinitarian imagination" and to the doctrine coming under heavy attack.[16] Informed by the Enlightenment's confidence in the "omnicompetence" of human reason, the intellectual *mentalité* of this era either dismissed the doctrine of the Trinity as a philosophical and unbiblical construct of the post-Apostolic Church, and turned to classical Arianism as an alternate perspective, or simply ridiculed it as utterly illogical, and argued for Deism or Socinianism.[17]

What is amazing is that this critical battle over Trinitarianism in the seventeenth and eighteenth centuries—its outcome would help determine the shape of later thinking about Christianity's God—is passed over in utter silence by the vast majority of modern studies of the history of this doctrine. Typically these studies leap over the seventeenth and eighteenth centuries, moving directly from the Trinitarian reflections of a Reformer like John Calvin (1509–1564) to various twentieth-century theologians.[18] Robert Letham, for example, in an otherwise excellent study of this doctrine, can state in the "Preface" to his *The Holy Trinity: In Scripture, History, Theology, and Worship* that since John Calvin "little of significance has been contributed to the development of Trinitarian doctrine by conservative Reformed theologians" till the dawn of the twentieth century. He certainly knows of the writings of the English Puritan John Owen (1616–1683) and the New England theologian of revival Jonathan Edwards (1703–1758) on the Trinity, but strangely maintains that these works "did not contribute anything significant to the *advancement* of the doctrine."[19] This claim is highly questionable. In fact, Richard Muller has argued that John Gill, a lesser theologian than either Owen or Edwards when it comes to Trinitarian thought, made a distinctive contribution to this branch of Christian doctrine by his inclusion of the Spirit in the eternal *pactum salutis*.[20] If this is true of Gill, should we not expect that we might find areas of original contribution in both Owen and Edwards?

---

15. His surname is sometimes rendered Socinus, hence Socinianism.

16. Placher, *Domestication of Transcendence*, 164–78; Dixon, *"Nice and Hot Disputes."* The quote is from Dixon, *"Nice and Hot Disputes,"* 212.

17. Bray, "Trinity," 694.

18. Dixon, *"Nice and Hot Disputes,"* xi–xiin1.

19. Letham, *Holy Trinity*, ix–x.

20. Muller, "Spirit and the Covenant," 4–14.

This chapter, though, does not focus on original contributions to the doctrine of the Trinity. Rather, in an era when there was a "fading of the trinitarian imagination," to use Dixon's expression, it seeks to discern the way that one Baptist pastor sought to keep that imagination vital and robust through the use of the form of instruction known as a catechism. Or to put it another way: this chapter's goal is to see how this most important of Christian doctrines—one that has exercised the greatest intellects of the Christian faith—was conveyed to the Christian in the eighteenth-century pew. The pastor is the subject of this monograph, Benjamin Beddome, and the catechism his *A Scriptural Exposition of the Baptist Catechism by Way of Question and Answer* (1752).

Benjamin Beddome— an eighteenth-century Baptist divine

Benjamin Beddome, pastor of the Baptist work in Bourton-on-the-water, Gloucestershire, for fifty-five years, is remembered today primarily as a hymn writer.[21] Yet, in his day he was also widely admired as a preacher. The Evangelical Anglican John Newton (1725–1807) once observed of him in this regard that he was "an admirable preacher, simple, savoury, weighty."[22] And the Baptist Robert Hall Jr. (1764–1831), himself one of the great preachers of the Regency period and the decade immediately following, noted that Beddome was "on many accounts an extraordinary person," for even though "he spent the principal part of a long life in a village retirement, he was eminent for his colloquial powers" and "universally admired" as a preacher.[23] Beddome's younger Baptist contemporary John Rippon, in the earliest biographical sketch of Beddome, similarly remarked that

---

21. In his magisterial study of English hymnody, J. R. Watson notes that many of Beddome's hymns have an identifiable "clarity of line and simplicity of image" and that they played a distinct part in the "transition of eighteenth-century hymnody from the grandeur of [Isaac] Watts to the sensitivity of [William] Cowper." See Watson, *English Hymn*, 202.

Incidentally, a clue to the pronunciation of Beddome's name is provided by the Baptist historian Joseph Ivimey (1773–1834), who spells the name of his father John Beddome (1674–1757) as "Bedham." See Ivimey, *History of the English Baptists*, 4:283.

22. Newton, *Diary (1703–1805)*, entry for August 7, 1776.

23. Hall, "Recommendatory Preface," vi.

"sermonizing was . . . his forte."[24] At his death, though, Beddome's published literary remains consisted simply of a catechism that will be examined below and some hymns. A series of eight volumes of his sermons, which went through a good number of editions, appeared in the early nineteenth century, as well as a larger volume of some 67 sermons in 1835.[25] A collection of some 830 hymns was published in 1818.[26]

Beddome came to Bourton-on-the-Water in the spring of 1740. Over the next three years he laboured with great success in the Baptist cause in Bourton. Significant for the shape of his future ministry was a local revival that took place under his ministry in the early months of 1741. Around forty individuals were converted, including John Collett Ryland (1723–1791), a leading Baptist minister in the latter half of the eighteenth century.[27] It may well have been this taste of revival that made Beddome a cordial friend to those who were involved in the evangelical revivals of the mid-eighteenth century, men like George Whitefield and the Mohegan Indian preacher Samson Occom (1723–1792),[28] and gave him an ongoing hunger to read of revival throughout the English-speaking world.[29] Within a year of the Bourton awakening, for instance, Beddome had purchased a copy of Jonathan Edwards's *The Distinguishing Marks of a Work of the Spirit of God* (1741), which would have given him a marvellous foundation for thinking about and labouring for revival.[30]

The early years of Beddome's ministry saw great numerical growth in the membership of the church. Between 1740 and 1750 the church

---

24. Rippon, "Rev. Benjamin Beddome," 314–26. Vital for studying the life of Beddome is the lengthy account of his ministry in Brooks, *Pictures of the Past*, 21–66. In this century, there have been relatively few studies of Beddome. The most important is Holmes, "Early Years (1655–1740)." See also Dix, "Thy Will Be Done"; Hayden, "Evangelical Calvinism," 140–60, 287–93; Haykin, "Benjamin Beddome," 167–83. See also chapter 1 above for the biographical sketch by Gary Brady.

25. Beddome, *Twenty Short Discourses*.

26. Beddome, *Hymns*.

27. Newman, *Rylandiana*, 3. On Ryland, see also Culross, *Three Rylands*, 11–66.

28. For Beddome's association with Whitefield, see Nuttall, "George Whitefield's 'Curate,'" 382–84. Samson Occom seems to have been converted under the preaching of James Davenport around 1740, prior to Davenport's period of fanaticism (Love, *Samson Occom*, 34). Occom preached at Bourton in April, 1767, during an extensive trip that the Native American evangelist made to Britain (Hayden, "Evangelical Calvinism," 152).

29. Hayden, "Evangelical Calvinism," 152.

30. Beddome's own copy of this book may be seen in the "Beddome Collection." It was published in Boston in 1741. On the title page, Beddome has written two dates, 1742 and 1747, which probably would indicate the dates when he read it.

membership more than doubled and by 1751 it stood at 180.[31] Describing the state of the church in 1750, Beddome could declare: "my labours have been, and are still, in a measure, blest unto them, above a hundred having been added since my first coming amongst them."[32] Derrick Holmes notes that the success of Beddome's ministry during his first ten years at Bourton is probably due to a number of factors. A central factor was that a number of good men were active as deacons and in the leadership of the church during this period, including Beddome's father-in-law, Richard Boswell. Then there was Beddome's gifted preaching as well as his practice of catechizing, the latter to be discussed below.[33]

During the 1750s and the first half of the 1760s the numerical growth of the church began to slow. As noted above, in 1751 the total number of members stood at 180. The next forty years of Beddome's ministry actually saw decline in the church membership. Between 1765 and 1795, 53 new members were added by conversion and baptism. But in this same period 105 of the members died, 12 were dismissed to other Baptist works and 2 were excluded. Thus, by 1795, the year that Beddome died, the church had 123 on the membership roll, sixty less than in 1764.[34] It is quite clear from letters that Beddome wrote on behalf of the church to the Midland Baptist Association, to which the church belonged, that he lamented this lack of growth in church membership. The size of the congregation maintained its own, probably around five or six hundred, to the end of his life, but that vital step of believer's baptism leading to church membership was taken by far fewer in the final three decades of his ministry than in the first two and a half.[35] Thus, the poignant prayer of Beddome in the church's 1786 letter to the Association: "Come from the 4 winds O Breath & breathe upon these slain that they may live. Awake O Northwind & come thou South, blow upon our Garden that the Spices may flow out."[36]

31. Brooks, *Pictures of the Past*, 50.

32. Letter to Prescot Street Baptist Church, November 22, 1750 (Brooks, "Ministerial Changes," 427).

33. Holmes, "Early Years (1655–1740)," 60–61.

34. Brooks, *Pictures of the Past*, 50–55.

35. See these letters in the *Bourton-on-the-Water Church Book*, 232–317. For the fact that the size of the congregation listening to Beddome maintained its own during the final years of his life, see the letters for May 15, 1785, and June 4, 1786 (*Bourton-on-the-Water Church Book*).

36. *Bourton-on-the-Water Church Book*. The punctuation has been added.

"That excellent little body of divinity"

Beddome's Catechism[37]

True to the Reformed tradition of which the Calvinistic Baptists formed a part, Beddome was thoroughly convinced that vital Christianity was a matter of both heart and head. As he noted on one occasion with Puritan-like pithiness: "If the head be like the summer's sun, full of light, the heart will not be like the winter's earth, void of fruit."[38] And like others in this tradition, Beddome found the use of a catechism helpful in matching head knowledge to heart-felt faith.[39] When John Rippon came to write his obituary of Beddome, he observed that "one considerable instrument" of the latter's success in his ministry at Bourton had been his use of catechetical instruction.

Catechisms had been central to the Calvinistic Baptist movement from its origins in the 1630s.[40] For example, Hercules Collins (d. 1702), the pastor of Wapping Baptist Church, London, which later moved to Prescot Street, put into print *An Orthodox Catechism* (1680), a Baptist version of the *Heidelberg Catechism*. The most widely used catechism among the Baptists, though, was the one commissioned by a General Assembly of the denomination that met in London in June, 1693. Although William Collins (d. 1702), the pastor of the Petty France Church in the capital, was asked to draw it up,[41] many would later know it as *Keach's Catechism*, so named after the leading Baptist author of the late seventeenth century, Benjamin Keach (1640–1704).[42] This catechism, formally called *The Baptist Catechism*, was primarily a Baptist revision of the Presbyterian *Shorter Catechism* (1648) and was still being reprinted in the middle of the nineteenth century.[43]

---

37. The description of Beddome's *Catechism* is taken from *Circular Letter*, 7.

38. Beddome, "Importance of Scripture Knowledge," 6.

39. Hayden, "Evangelical Calvinism," 259. In another context, Hayden notes that the use of Baptist catechisms like that of Beddome was "a very formative influence among eighteenth century Baptists and provided a Baptist identity which was set securely within Reformed and Evangelical orthodoxy" (Hayden, "This Failure," 4). See also similar remarks in Hayden, "Particular Baptist Confession," 410.

For an excellent collection of Baptist catechisms, see Nettles, *Teaching Truth, Training Hearts*. Beddome's catechism is not included in this collection.

40. For further details of these catechisms, see Hayden, "Particular Baptist Confession," 408–9.

41. Ivimey, *History of the English Baptists*, 1:533; 2:397.

42. For differing opinions as to Keach's responsibility for this catechism, see Vaughn, "Benjamin Keach," 66; Walker, *Excellent Benjamin Keach*, 219.

43. For a modern printing of the catechism, see Jewett, *Baptist Catechism*.

During the early years of his ministry Beddome regularly used this catechism, but clearly felt that the questions and answers of the catechism needed to be supplemented by further material. So he composed what was printed in 1752 as *A Scriptural Exposition of the Baptist Catechism by Way of Question and Answer*, which basically reproduced the wording and substance of *Keach's Catechism*, but added various sub-questions and answers to each of the main questions. In composing these additional questions and answers Beddome utilized, though not slavishly so, *A Scripture-catechism* (1703) by the quintessential Puritan Matthew Henry (1662–1714).[44]

Beddome's *Scriptural Exposition* proved to be fairly popular. There were at least two editions during Beddome's lifetime, the second of which was widely used at the Bristol Baptist Academy, the sole British Baptist seminary for much of the eighteenth century.[45] Due to its use at this seminary one can expect that it would have had a significant influence on many of the congregations that graduates of this seminary went on to pastor. In the nineteenth century it was reprinted once in the British Isles and twice in the United States, the last printing being in 1849.

Keach's Catechism had replaced the well-known first question of the *Shorter Catechism*—"What is the chief end of man?"—with "Who is the first and chiefest being?" and put the *Shorter Catechism*'s first question in second place. In his *Scriptural Exposition* Beddome retained the first question of *Keach's Catechism*, but for some unknown reason omitted the *Shorter Catechism*'s first question altogether. Instead he placed the question "Ought every one to believe that there is a God?" in second place.[46] This is one of the rare occasions in the *Scriptural Exposition* when Beddome introduces a main question for which there is no counterpart in *Keach's Catechism*. The intellectual climate of the eighteenth century, in which the Christian view of God was in dispute and some had gone so far as to even advocate atheism, may be the reason why Beddome introduced such a question.

Teaching the doctrine of the Trinity

The section of Beddome's *Scriptural Exposition* dealing with the Trinity opens with the question "How many persons are there in the godhead?" The answer in *Keach's Catechism*, which Beddome faithfully reproduces, is

44. Henry, *Scripture-Catechism*. I have used this catechism as found in Henry, *Complete Works*, 2:174–258.

45. The second edition, which came out in 1776, seems to have been largely paid for by Beddome. See *Circular Letter*, 7.

46. Beddome, *Scriptural Exposition*, 5–6.

as follows: "There are three persons in the godhead, the Father, the Son, and the Holy Ghost, and these three are one, the same in essence, equal in power and glory."[47] Beddome then adds five paragraphs of questions and answers together with Scripture texts as a further delineation of this basic question and answer.[48]

In the first paragraph he focuses on the triunity of the Godhead. As evidence he cites such passages as Genesis 1:26, where we have the statement "Let *us* make man" and the *Comma Johanneum*, 1 John 5:7, "there are three that bear record in heaven." Henry had also cited both of these texts to make the same point.[49] Beddome then turns to refute one of the main bugbears of the theologians of the Ancient Church, namely Sabellianism, which denied the proper distinction of persons within the Godhead.[50] Beddome cites Psalm 110:1, where the Son is mentioned as a distinct person alongside the Father, and John 14:26, where all three persons of the Godhead are distinguished, as clear indication that both the Son and the Spirit are distinct persons. Yet, as Beddome stresses, one can never forget that these two, along with Father, are one: "Are these the same in essence, affection, and operation? Yes."[51] As biblical proof, Beddome again cites 1 John 5:7.

None of this response to Sabellianism appears in Henry's catechism, though Henry does have a paragraph that focuses on each of the divine persons' distinguishing mark, which he terms "personal property." The Father's "personal property" is to "beget the Son," while that of the Son is "to be begotten of the Father" and that of the Spirit "to proceed from the Father and the Son."[52] While Beddome is clear on the fact that there are indeed three persons within the Godhead, it is probably not surprising that he omits the use of the classical terms of distinguishing the persons. In contrast to the Presbyterians for whom Henry was writing, Beddome's Baptist audience

47. Beddome, *Scriptural Exposition*, 23.

48. Beddome, *Scriptural Exposition*, 23–25. Henry's *Scripture-Catechism* has only four paragraphs.

49. Henry, *Scripture-Catechism*, 2:180.

50. For possible evidence of the presence of Sabellianism among some Calvinistic Baptists in this period, see Dutton, *Letter against Sabellianism*. See also Brown, *English Baptists*, 75–76.

51. Beddome, *Scriptural Exposition*, 23–24. In a sermon on Acts 8:29, where the Spirit tells Philip to draw near to the chariot in which the Ethiopian eunuch was traveling, Beddome notes from this verse that "the Holy Spirit is a divine and a distinct person in the godhead, issuing his commands, and exercising supreme authority . . . the Father is not the Son, nor the Son the Father; and the Holy Spirit is considered as distinct from both. Yet though distinct, they are not separate; for they are one in nature, power, and glory" (Beddome, *Twenty Short Discourses*, 5:40).

52. Henry, *Scripture-Catechism*, 2:180.

was far less learned and more suspicious of theology. On occasion, though, Beddome can allude to this classical way of differentiating the persons. In a sermon on Galatians 1:16, for example, Beddome can remark that the term "Son" is "a title belonging to Christ as the second Person in the ever-blessed Trinity, and expressive both of equality of essence, and the peculiar relation in which he stands to the Divine Father."[53] Yet, it is clear that his preferred way of clarifying the difference between the Persons is to simply use the terms "Father," "Son," and "Spirit."

Beddome's second paragraph deals with explicit references to the deity of the Son and the Spirit. While Henry does have a paragraph that makes the same point, the material in this paragraph and its arrangement are unique to Beddome. The Baptist theologian cites texts where both the Son and the Spirit are referred to as God and Jehovah.

> Is the Son called God? Yes. *Who is over all God blessed for evermore* (Rom 9:5). Is the Spirit called God? Yes. *Why hath Satan filled thine heart to lye to the Holy Ghost, thou hast not lyed unto man but unto God* (Acts 5:3–4). Is the Son called Jehovah? Yes. He is *the Lord* (Heb. Jehovah) *our righteousness* (Jer 23:6). Is the Spirit called Jehovah? Yes. *They tempted the Lord* (Heb. Jehovah) (Exod 17:7; cf. Isa 63:10). *They vexed his Holy Spirit*—Is this name given to any but God. No. *The most high over all the earth, is he whose name alone is Jehovah* (Ps 83:18).[54]

In addition to Romans 9:5, there is a relative abundance of New Testament texts from which Beddome could have chosen that explicitly ascribe deity to the Lord Jesus.[55] On the other hand, there are no New Testament texts that are explicit in calling the Spirit "God." One of the closest to such an affirmation is Acts 5:3–4, where Peter tells Ananias that in lying to him and the Jerusalem Church he has lied to the Holy Spirit, whose indwelling of that community identified it as God's new covenant people. He has thus really lied to God.[56]

Beddome also believes that various Old Testament verses, seen now through the lens of the New Testament, contain adumbrations of the deity of the Son and the Spirit. Unique to the God of the Old Testament, for instance, is the covenant name of Jehovah, an English transliteration of the Hebrew tetragrammaton YHWH.[57] Beddome is convinced that this Old

---

53. Beddome, "Christ Manifested to the Soul," 119.

54. Beddome, *Scriptural Exposition*, 24.

55. For other unambiguous texts, see John 1:1; 20:28; Titus 2:13; 1 John 5:20.

56. Similarly Gill, *Doctrine of the Trinity*, 162.

57. The term "Jehovah" had first appeared in a 1516 Latin text. In 1530, William

Testament term of divine address can be also applied to the Son and the Spirit. When Jeremiah 23:6 speaks of "Jehovah our righteousness," this can be understood, from the vantage-point of the New Testament, as a description of Jesus as Jehovah, for—and Beddome appears to assume the reader will know this—the New Testament describes Jesus Christ on one occasion as our "righteousness" (1 Cor 1:30).

Beddome sees a similar intertextuality between Exodus 17:7 and Isaiah 63:10. Here, though, the link is not a specific word as that between Jeremiah 23:6 and 1 Corinthians 1:30, but a similar description of the same event, Israel's testing of the patience of God in the wilderness after the Exodus from Egypt. Beddome obviously regards the Isaiah verse as clarifying that it was the Holy Spirit whom Israel grieved during this period of her history. The name of Jehovah is thus applicable to the Spirit.[58] Here, Beddome's questions and answers reveal a hermeneutical practice that stretches back to the patristic era. It is a biblicistic hermeneutic that assumes the unity of the entire Scriptures—they are the product of a single author—and that Scripture is its own best interpreter. By means of cross-referencing and intertextual links the meaning of texts can be clarified and a biblical theology developed.

The next paragraph, also unique to Beddome and not dependent on Henry, continues to focus on the deity of the Son and Spirit. Beddome refers to divine attributes and activities that the Spirit and the Son share with the Father and are the sole prerogative of a divine being.

> Is the Son eternal as well as the Father? Yes. *Before* Abraham *was, I am* (John 8:58). Is the Spirit eternal? Yes. *He is called the eternal Spirit* (Heb 9:14). Is the Son omnipresent? Yes. *Where two or three are gathered together in my name there am I* (Matt 18:20). Is the Spirit so too? Yes. *Whither shall I go from thy Spirit* (Ps 139:7). Is the Son omniscient? Yes. *Thou knowest all things* (John 21:17). And is the Spirit so? Yes. *He searcheth all things* (1 Cor 2:10). Is the work of creation ascribed to the Son? Yes. *All things were made by him* (John 1:3). Is it also ascribed to the Spirit? Yes. *The Spirit of God hath made me* (Job 33:4). And is creation a work peculiar to God? Yes. *He that built all things is God* (Heb 3:4).[59]

Tyndale (c. 1494–1536) used it in his translation of Genesis, from whence it entered into the mainstream of English biblical thought and writing. See Daniell, *William Tyndale*, 284.

58. Beddome is following Gill here, who also deduced the same point from the two texts that Beddome uses here. See Gill, *Doctrine of the Trinity*, 161.

59. Beddome, *Scriptural Exposition*, 24–25.

If the Son and the Spirit are eternal—that is, have no beginning—and possess such incommunicable divine attributes as omnipresence and omniscience and if they do what only God can do—namely, creation—then they must be as divine as God the Father.

In the fourth paragraph the Baptist minister seeks to demonstrate the full deity of the Son and the Spirit from the fact that both of them are the object of prayer and worship in the Scriptures. He rightly notes that the Scriptures allow for only one who is fully divine to be the recipient of prayer and worship: "Is religious worship a prerogative of deity? Yes." To show this of the Son is relatively easy, and Beddome can refer to a passage like Acts 7:59, where Stephen, the first martyr, prays, "Lord Jesus, receive my spirit."[60] In a sermon on praying to Christ, Beddome describes this verse from Acts as "a strong and irrefragable proof of the supreme deity of Christ."[61]

To find a text where the Spirit is actually the object of prayer is far more difficult. Beddome cites Revelation 1:4, where the "seven spirits," which Beddome rightly notes to be a symbolic representation of the "one holy and eternal Spirit," are included along with God the Father and Jesus Christ in a salutation to seven churches in the Roman province of Asia.[62] It might be argued that while this passage clearly has significant Trinitarian import, it does not really serve Beddome's purpose, for a salutation is simply not equivalent to a prayer. And yet, essentially the revelator John is praying, for he is asking for the seven churches to be given "grace . . . and peace from him which is, and which was, and which is to come; and from the seven Spirits which are before his throne; and from Jesus Christ" (Rev 1:4–5, KJV).[63]

The fourth paragraph ends with a reference to the baptismal formula of Matthew 28, where command is given to baptize believers into "the name of the Father, and the Son, and of the Holy Ghost" (Matt 28:19). Matthew 28:19, is, of course, a classical proof-text for the Trinity, and one that Henry had included also in the section of his catechism on the Trinity.[64] However, it is noteworthy that while Henry prefaces his citation of the Matthean text with the question "ought we to believe it [i.e., the doctrine of the Trinity]?"

60. Beddome, *Scriptural Exposition*, 25. For other passages where prayer is offered to the Son, see 1 Cor 1:2; 2 Cor 12:8–9.

61. Beddome, "Christ the Subject of Prayer," 237.

62. Beddome, *Scriptural Exposition*, 25; For a contemporary discussion of the identification of the "seven Spirits" as a symbolic allusion to the Holy Spirit, see Bauckham, "Role of the Spirit," 75–77.

63. Gill also cites Revelation 1:4 to argue this point. Gill, *Doctrine of the Trinity*, 70–71, 166.

64. Henry, *Scripture-catechism*, 2:180.

thus employing the text as a simple proof-text, Beddome embeds his citation of Matthew 28:19 in a paragraph dealing with worship. By so doing,
Beddome is declaring his conviction that baptism is an act of worship in
which those being baptized dedicate themselves to the Father and to the Son
and to the Holy Spirit.[65] But only God can be worshipped.

In the fifth and final paragraph Beddome turns to the way in which
our blessings as Christians reflect the Trinitarian nature of God.[66] "Divine
blessings" come from all three persons of the Godhead as shown by the
benediction of 2 Corinthians 13:14. Then, a passage like Ephesians 2:18
("Thro' him we both have access by one spirit unto the Father") tells Beddome that each of the persons of the Godhead have "their distinct province
in the affair of man's salvation." Here, the reasoning is that if the Son and the
Spirit enable men and women to come to the Father, and so be saved, then
they must be fully divine for ultimately only God can save sinners. One of
Beddome's hymns succinctly celebrates this truth in a single stanza:

> Ye children of the Father's choice,
>
> And purchase of the purchase of the Saviour's blood,
>
> Sealed by the Spirit, now rejoice,
>
> And bless and praise the triune God.[67]

Then, reflecting a question from Henry's *Scripture-catechism*, Beddome asks,
"Is the unity in the godhead a motive to unity among the saints? Yes," and
he cites John 17:21 as proof. Beddome was clear in his Baptist convictions,[68]
but, as his relationship to George Whitefield noted above indicates, Beddome seems to have possessed a catholic spirit. But it was a catholicity of
orthodox Christianity that he affirmed, as the last question reveals: "Should
we hold fast this doctrine [of the Trinity]? Yes. *Hold fast the form of sound
words* (2 Tim 1:13)."[69]

---

65. Cf. "Is baptism an engagement to yield ourselves unto God? Yes" (Beddome,
Scriptural Exposition, 160). See also Gill, *Doctrine of the Trinity*, 145: "Baptism is a solemn act of divine worship."

66. *Scriptural Exposition*, 25.

67. Beddome, *Hymns*, #257, stanza 3. See also #255, stanzas 1–3, for a similar expression of worship of the members of the Godhead centred around their differing
spheres of activity in the divine work of salvation: the Father's "rich displays of grace"
and "special love," the Son for his incarnation so as "to prepare our way to heaven," and
the Spirit, "who the stubborn will subdues" and who "humbles and renews" sinners.

68. See, for instance, *Scriptural Exposition*, 158–66, where Beddome deals with the
subject of baptism.

69. *Scriptural Exposition*, 25.

Conclusion

Beddome's last appearance at the association to which his church belonged, the Midland Association, was in 1789.[70] Over the years Beddome had frequently preached at and acted as moderator of the summer Association gatherings.[71] From the mid-1770s on, though, Beddome had begun to suffer from gout and experience tremendous difficulty in walking,[72] and eventually the joy of the Association gatherings had to become a memory of the past. His influence lived on, though.

In the year after his last appearance, his fellow pastors issued a letter—it was usual for the Association to issue an annual circular letter—in which they detailed the core doctrines that held them together as Calvinistic Baptists. At the head of the list, "of very great importance," was the "doctrine of three equal persons in the ever-adorable Trinity." After citing a number of Scripture texts that supported this doctrine, the letter continued:

> Each person [of the Godhead] is truly and properly divine, according to the scriptures of truth; and yet we are informed that there is but one God. This, indeed, is a mystery, and it must remain so to us, at least in the present state.[73]

Beddome would undoubtedly have approved, not only with regard to the theological sentiments, but also of the medium in which these sentiments were expressed. For the Association letter was sent out to the churches and distributed among their members and so became a crucial means of theological instruction. Though a "mystery," as the above quote states, the doctrine of the Trinity was the heart and foundation of Christian living and thought and must be taught to God's people if they were going to mature in Christ. And this Beddome had sought to do in his catechism.

In the section of Beddome's catechism discussed above, Beddome did not explicitly mention this element of mystery with regard to the Trinity. Yet, it is something that does appear in one of the three hymns he wrote to celebrate the triunity of God.

> Glory to the Three eternal,
> Yet the great mysterious One,

70. Stokes, *History of the Midland Association*, 90.

71. For a list of the occasions when Beddome preached or acted as moderator, see Stokes, *History of the Midland Association*, 88–90.

72. Purdy, Letter to John Sutcliff, April 11, 1775.

73. Rippon, *Baptist Annual Register*, 1:37–38.

Author of all bliss supernal,
Be unceasing honours due.[74]

Here Beddome rightly recognizes that the doctrine of the Trinity, mystery though it be, is to find its ultimate expression in unceasing adoration and worship of the Triune God.

74. Beddome, *Hymns*, #255, stanza 4.

3

Benjamin Beddome's Christology

Jeongmo Yoo

Introduction

IN THE EIGHTEENTH CENTURY, England was going through profound intellectual changes which threatened many of the previous traditional religious thoughts and ideas, especially ideas which originated from English Calvinists of an earlier time.[1] Under the influence of the Enlightenment already dawning by 1685, the eighteenth century witnessed the development of a rationalistic theological approach which led ultimately to the rejection of classic orthodox Christology. The Christology espoused by the orthodox theologians of previous centuries faced many new challenges: the rise of Socinianism, Deism, Arminianism, Quakerism, the natural sciences, the flowering of the new philosophies such as those of John Locke (1632–1704), Isaac Newton (1642–1727), and Immanuel Kant (1724–1804), and the emergence of the Cambridge Platonists and the Latitudinarians. Fierce debates between the Protestant orthodox theologians and those adversaries were unavoidable throughout the century.[2]

1. Concerning the change of the intellectual world and the emergence of new religious and philosophical ideas in England during the Restoration and its aftermath, see Wallace Jr., *Shapers of English Calvinism*; Hazard, *European Mind*; Israel, *Radical Enlightenment*; Cragg, *From Puritanism*; *Church and the Age of Reason*; Stromberg, *Religious Liberalism*; Mulsow and Rohls, *Socinianism and Arminianism*; Redwood, *Reason, Ridicule and Religion*.

2. Daniels, *Christology of John Owen*, 22–48; Sell, *Christ and Controversy*, 22–88. Cf. Regarding the Christological controversy in the European continent in the eighteenth century, see Brown, *Jesus in European Protestant Thought*; McGrath, *Making of*

In this intellectual context Christology became a highly significant theological topic for the eighteenth-century British Particular Baptists as well. Seeing that Christological thought in eighteenth-century British Baptist churches was radically influenced by Socinianism,[3] they actively engaged in the Christological debate with their opponents and produced a number of significant theological works on the theme to defend orthodox Christology against the rising influence of the unorthodox ideas of Christ.[4]

Benjamin Beddome was one of the faithful defenders of the traditional orthodox Christology among the eighteenth-century Particular Baptists. Unlike other prominent Particular Baptists leaders such as John Gill (1697–1771) and Andrew Fuller (1754–1815), Beddome was neither explicitly involved in the controversies with the adversaries nor wrote any polemical work on the theme during his ministerial career. The doctrine of Christ, however, occupies a significant portion of his extant writings, and it provides an adequate source of information to analyze his understanding of Christology.[5]

This chapter will discuss Beddome's view of Christ as an illustration of the way the Christology of the Particular Baptists was established and developed in eighteenth-century England. The examination of his writings will especially permit us to observe three things in detail. First, following the Chalcedonian formula, Beddome affirms the full deity of Christ and the true and complete humanity of Christ. Second, in line with the classic Reformed tradition, Christ's threefold role of prophet, priest and king particularly serves to explain his mediatorial function in Beddome's thought. Third, even though the multi-faced nature of Christ's atoning work is found in Beddome's writings, vicarious satisfaction appears in Beddome's writings as the most central work of Christ for human salvation. In Beddome's view, Christ has come principally as a priest to render a perfect substitutionary satisfaction of divine law and justice which was offended by human sin.

Modern German Christology.

3. Nettles, *By His Grace*, xxv; Bush and Nettles, *Baptists and the Bible*, 83. For more detailed information on this, see Timmons, "Cause of Christ and Truth," 13–18.

4. For example, Fuller, "Calvinistic and Socinian Systems," 2:108–233; "Deity of Christ," 3:693–704; Gill, "Answer to the Birmingham Dialogue"; *Trinity Stated and Vindicated*. In addition to these, many more works could be listed. Indeed, in spite of the importance of the theme in the life and thought of eighteenth-century British Baptists, so little secondary literature has been written on the eighteenth-century Baptist Christology.

5. Beddome's Christology is mainly found in his sermons and catechism. In addition to these works, it can be observed in his hymns as well.

Beddome's View of Christ as Mediator

Beddome's idea of Christ's mediatorship arises in connection with the doctrines of creation and the fall. He teaches that Adam and Eve were made after the image of God in righteousness and holiness.[6] They enjoyed an intimate and personal loving relationship with God in the Garden of Eden. Before the fall, there was no need for a mediator between God and humanity, though there was an infinite distance in nature between these parties. After the fall, the situation was altered. Adam and Eve sinned against God, and their sin brought a number of desperate consequences to humanity.[7] They were alienated from God through sin and lost every blessing of God. Excluded from all hope of salvation, they then became heirs of wrath, the slaves of Satan, captive under the yoke of sin. God was indeed dishonored and highly offended, and humans were subject to the curse of eternal death.[8]

How then can this broken relationship between God and human beings be reconciled? Beddome affirms that human beings cannot do this. In his understanding, a radical change takes place in them after the fall. This change is so radical that it entails the soul's total corruption in every part.[9] In the fall, human beings lost the ability to yield any acceptable obedience unto God.[10] Simply stated, they lost free choice. Human beings became unable to satisfy the claims of the divine law which they had violated.[11] Beddome argues that this restoration cannot be done by human beings themselves through a return to God in obedience, nor by rendering satisfaction for themselves through their own works.[12]

Beddome teaches that if human beings were to be restored to the favor of the offended Sovereign, the interposition of another person was requisite in order to expiate their guilt and to lay the foundation of peace.[13] They need a mediator who interposes between the two parties at variance and procures reconciliation between them. In Beddome's thought, this is the very context in which Christ mediated between God and human beings.[14] He maintains that in order to fulfill this mediatorship, Christ partook of

6. Beddome, *Scriptural Exposition*, 35; Beddome, *Catechism*, 29.

7. Beddome, *Sermons Printed from the Manuscripts*, 2, 35.

8. Beddome, *Twenty Short Discourses*, 1:93–94; 6:122, 124; *Sermons*, 14, 199–200.

9. Beddome, *Sermons*, 192.

10. Beddome, *Twenty Short Discourses*, 2:36–37.

11. Beddome, *Twenty Short Discourses*, 2:143; 6:112.

12. Beddome, *Catechism*, 41.

13. Beddome, *Twenty Short Discourses*, 3:73; *Sermons*, 203; *Catechism*, 42.

14. Beddome, *Sermons*, 83.

human flesh and suffered the punishment from God's righteous judgment.[15] More specifically, Christ died on the cross to take away our condemnation and made "satisfaction" duly to God, the Father, for our redemption.[16] As mediator Christ has appeased God's wrath, and the guilt that held us liable for punishment has been transferred to the head of the Son of God.[17] On this very foundation, God and human beings are reconciled, and they can now experience peace with God.[18]

In Beddome's mind, the main purpose of the coming of Christ into the world lies in the salvation of sinners.[19] This is the core of the office and work assigned to Jesus Christ as the one mediator between God and humanity. Since Christ was offered to the Father in death, as an expiatory sacrifice, and he discharged all satisfaction through this sacrifice, those who believe in Christ as their Lord and Savior will not perish but be saved.[20]

In his discussion of Christ's mediatorship, Beddome consistently emphasizes that Christ is the only way to the Father.[21] For example, interpreting Proverbs 15:24, "The way of life is above to the wise," Beddome argues as follows:

> By the "way" here spoken of we may understand the Lord Jesus Christ. "I am the way, the truth, and the life," says he; or, the true way to eternal life. No man cometh to the Father, either here or hereafter, but in and through him. He is the way to church-fellowship and the ordinances of the gospel, the way to the throne of grace and the throne of glory. From him we derive both our title to heaven and our meetness for it. In a word, this is a way

15. Beddome, *Twenty Short Discourses*, 6:123; *Catechism*, 43.

16. Beddome, *Sermons*, 203; *Twenty Short Discourses*, 6:124, 138–39. Cf. Beddome consistently uses the term "satisfaction" or its verbal form "satisfy" with reference to the death of Christ. It is his primary doctrinal descriptor for the work of Christ on the cross. Beddome does not use the older scholastic distinction of the sufficiency and efficiency of Christ's satisfaction. It is uncertain whether he accepted this traditional, scholastic idea, which is generally found in many Reformed thinkers' discussion of the limitation of Christ's work. Concerning the use of the traditional sufficiency/efficiency formula, see Muller, *Calvin and the Reformed Tradition*, 70–106; Muller, *Dictionary*, 271–73. It should be also here noted that "*Satisfactio* has been inappositely rendered into English as 'atonement.' The impression of the word 'atonement' is exacerbated when the Reformed view is characterized as 'limited atonement'" (Muller, *Dictionary*, 273). For the more detailed discussion of the issue of the term "atonement," see Muller, *Calvin and the Reformed Tradition*, 70–106.

17. Beddome, *Twenty Short Discourses*, 3:74; 6:19.

18. Beddome, *Twenty Short Discourses*, 1:124; 4:7.

19. Beddome, *Twenty Short Discourses*, 3:115.

20. Beddome, *Twenty Short Discourses*, 5:154.

21. Beddome, *Sermons*, 103.

calculated both for the honour of Him that appointed it, and the security and everlasting felicity of those who walk in it.[22]

For Beddome, "No relief is left for such; there is no other way of satisfying divine justice, of expiating human guilt, or of providing for the exercise of mercy in a way of righteousness."[23] He argues that unless one wholly relies on Christ's righteousness, no one can come to God and be restored to peace with God.[24]

Along with Christ's sole mediatorship between God and human beings, Beddome also affirms that faith is the only means to the forgiveness of sin and the salvation of the soul.[25] According to him, no other ways can save; even "The highest degree of morality, nay, of Christianity, which a man may attain to without real faith will not save him, so indissoluble is the connexion [sic] established between faith and a justifying righteousness."[26] Beddome also claims that faith is a free gift of God and is not consequent upon human choice at all. That is, the bestowing of faith has nothing to do with the meritorious works of human beings or the foresight of their believing.[27]

Beddome's view of Christ as mediator is an important aspect of his Christology. For him, in order to bridge the gap between God and human beings, mediation was requisite, and it was enacted by Jesus Christ as mediator.[28] Simply speaking, "Jesus Christ came into the world to save sinners, even the chief, that God hath given to us eternal life, and this life is in his Son."[29] This idea that Christ in his compassion condescended to human beings' level and assumed human flesh to save fallen humanity confers on Beddome's entire Christology an enormous soteriological orientation.

In this soteriological view of Christology, Beddome's position is essentially identical with that of the Reformation and the Post-Reformation. For example, John Calvin (1509–1564) begins his treatment of Christology by amply developing the idea that the purpose of the incarnation was to

---

22. Beddome, *Sermons*, 103.

23. Beddome, *Twenty Short Discourses*, 3:72. See also, Beddome, *Twenty Short Discourses*, 6:123, 125.

24. Beddome, *Twenty Short Discourses*, 7:145; *Sermons*, 97.

25. Beddome, *Sermon*, 163. Beddome persistently teaches that even though God predestined some to salvation, faith is required from the human side as the means of salvation in the process of conversion. Cf. Beddome, *Catechism*, 62, 71.

26. Beddome, *Sermons*, 165.

27. Beddome, *Twenty Short Discourses*, 5:111.

28. Beddome, *Twenty Short Discourses*, 3:74.

29. Beddome, *Twenty Short Discourses*, 6:27.

fulfill the office of mediator.[30] Far more than the limited scope of this chapter can fully address, numerous other Reformed theologians employed this soteriological framework in their discussions of Christology. This implies the intimate continuity between Beddome and the Reformed tradition in the doctrine of Christ.

Beddome's View of the Person of Christ

This part of the chapter will discuss Beddome's understanding of the constitution of the person of the Mediator. A brief account of the polemical situation in his time will lay a foundation for a better appreciation of Beddome's view of the person of Christ. During the Post-Reformation era, orthodox Christianity battled against heresies, especially those concerning the doctrine of the Trinity.[31] One of the main controversial topics was the constitution of the person of Christ because the right view of it is essential to resolve the issue of the Triunity of God.[32] Who was Jesus Christ? Was he fully divine? Did Christ assume true and complete humanity? How then can those two natures coexist in one person? Those questions were hotly debated issues in the churches in the eighteenth century, and the British Particular Baptists in Beddome's time were not an exception to this controversial situation.[33] They particularly engaged in the debate with the Socinians on the issues.[34] In this context though, Beddome was not polemical. He faithfully insisted on the orthodox understanding of the person of Christ in his writings. He stood in opposition to the Socinians and Unitarians, who maintained that Christ was merely a man and had no existence before he was born of Mary; and in opposition to the Arians, who, though they admit the pre-existence of Christ, maintained that he is a creature, and possesses only a subordinate divinity.[35] Beddome faithfully taught three things in detail regarding the

30. Calvin, *Institutes of the Christian Religion*, 464–68.

31. For a more detailed discussion of this, see Muller, *Triunity of God*.

32. Trueman, *Claims of Truth*, 151.

33. Cf. Sell, *Christ and Controversy*, 22–60.

34. Cf. Timmons, "Cause of Christ and Truth," 21–41, 61–86. Concerning the influence of the Socinianism on the General Baptists in eighteenth-century England, see also Timmons, "Cause of Christ and Truth," 42–50.

35. For more detailed information on the Christological thought of Arians, Socinians, and Unitarians, see Sell, *Christ and Controversy*, 5; Hanson, *Search for the Christian Doctrine*; Seeberg, *Text-Book*, 1:201–18; Williams, *Arius*; Timmons, "Cause of Christ and Truth," 1–20, 64–68; Pelikan, *Reformation of Church and Dogma*, 322–32; Mclachin, *Socinianism in Seventeenth-Century England*; Berkhof, *History of Christian Doctrines*, 189–91.

constitution of the person of Christ: (1) Christ not only existed before his incarnation, but was from all eternity the Son of God, of one substance, and equal with the Father; (2) in the fullness of time, he assumed a complete human nature into union with the divine; (3) Christ is both very God and very man, having two distinct natures, yet but one person. In order to grasp the more detailed picture of these teachings, the following three sections will examine the nature of divinity and humanity in Christ and the relation between them in turn.

The Deity of Christ

The divine nature of Christ, or more accurately, Christ according to his divine nature, receives considerable attention from Beddome.[36] In particular, the vindication of the deity of the Son occupies much of his Christological labors. Such emphasis on the deity of Christ in Beddome's writings is reasonable considering the fact that the core of the Christological controversies in his time lies in whether or not Christ is fully divine.[37]

In order to prove the deity of Christ, Beddome thoroughly appeals to the Holy Scriptures. The principal source for Beddome's whole Christology is the Bible itself. He consistently relies on it to support his ideas. He does not rely on any individual thinkers or church traditions. The authority that he cited was the voice of God speaking in the Scriptures alone. In his defense of the deity of Christ, he focuses on presenting positive scriptural evidence of the doctrine. His scriptural proof of the deity of the Son as delivered in his works uses the standard texts such as Hebrews 1:3 and Zechariah 13:7.[38]

Beddome does not deal with or answer the objections of those who were undermining the doctrinal foundation of the deity of Christ. His writings do not expose his opponents' faulty exegesis or the logical fallacies involved in their arguments. This characteristic might be best understood in the context of the genre of Beddome's writings. Beddome's works that provide information of his Christology are not polemical or systematic ones. Rather, they are sermons, hymns, and a catechism which are relatively less disputatious in nature. It seems that Beddome is satisfied with demonstrating that this orthodox doctrine is neither unscriptural nor dependent upon any human idea and instead that the doctrine of the deity of Christ

36. Michael Haykin deals with Beddome's view of the deity of Christ in his discussion of Beddome's Trinitarian theology in chapter 2 above.

37. Cf. Muller, *Post Reformation Reformed Dogmatics,* 4:275–332; Sell, *Christ and Controversy,* 22–88.

38. Cf. Beddome, *Catechism,* 42–43.

is required by the Scriptural evidence. In the face of such overwhelming evidence, the rejection of this doctrine was an assertion against divine revelation.

On the basis of the examination of Scriptural texts, Beddome presents four main types of evidence for the deity of Christ. First, according to Beddome, various divine names and titles are ascribed to Christ in the Scriptures, and they prove that Christ is God. For example, in his interpretation of Psalm 109:21, Beddome argues that Christ is expressly called God in this verse. He states as follows:

> The petition [of the verse] may be considered as addressed with equal propriety to each of the Persons in the Godhead, who are the joint objects of religious worship, possessed of the same adorable perfections, and equally concerned in carrying on the work, and conveying the blessings of salvation. The titles, Oh God, the Lord, are equally applicable, and are actually applied, to all the Divine Persons. The Father is God, the Son is God, and the Holy Spirit is God; not the first properly and supremely so, and the two latter in an inferior sense, by office or delegation; but they are one in nature and essence, one JEHOVAH, which is a name expressive of the incommunicable properties of Deity.[39]

In his *Catechism*, Beddome also states that the application of the title of Jehovah to Christ testifies to Christ's full deity:

> "Is the Son Called God? Yes. *Who is over all God blessed for evermore* (Rom 9:5). . . . Is the Son Called Jehovah? Yes. *He is the Lord* (Heb. Jehovah) *our righteousness* (Jer 23:6). . . . Is this name given to any but God? No. *The most high over all the earth, is he whose name alone is Jehovah* (Ps 83:18)."[40]

As shown in these statements, for Beddome, since the incommunicable names of God such as the Lord, Jehovah, and God are frequently applied to the Son, Jesus Christ is certainly very God.[41]

The second type of evidence of Christ's full deity is that divine attributes are ascribed to the Son no less than to the Father.[42] For instance, omniscience is attributed to Christ. Beddome maintains that Christ is all knowing; he possesses the exhaustive knowledge of past, present, and

---

39. Beddome, *Twenty Short Discourses*, 2:55.
40. Beddome, *Catechism*, 20.
41. Beddome, *Sermons*, 150.
42. Beddome, *Catechism*, 20–21.

future, and even fully comprehends the Father, a knowledge of which no creature is capable.[43] Interpreting Acts 4:4, Beddome states the following:

> He who knew not the day of judgment as man, or had no commission to reveal it as mediator, knows all things as God. He also views things in their proper light, and calls them by their proper names. What Saul called doing God service, he calls persecution. Omniscience and omnipresence are attributes peculiar to Deity, yet both belong to Christ: he is therefore truly and properly God.[44]

For Beddome, the eternity, or the eternal generation, of the Son is another significant example which vindicates his full deity.[45] On the basis of Scripture, such as Revelation 1:8, he argues that Jesus Christ not only existed prior to his incarnation but is the eternal Son of God, of one substance and equal with the Father.[46] Christ's Sonship is neither founded upon his mission, nor upon his miraculous conception, nor upon his resurrection, as is claimed by many heresies. Instead, Christ is the Son of God by an eternal, necessary, and ineffable generation. Beddome elaborates on this idea as follows:

> The pre-eminence that is here ascribed to Christ, implies his eternity and self-existence. He is not God by derivation, or by commission; but is really and properly so. He is before all things, and by him all things consist; he is therefore the beginning, and the fountain of all created existence. What he is as a divine person that he ever was, and will never cease to be. He who is the first beginning and last end of all things, must himself be without beginning or end; and is the same yesterday, today, and forever. The same in the perfections of his nature, and consequently in his claim to our regard. As man he had beginning of days, and end of life; but as God he has neither. His goings forth have been of old, from everlasting. He is in himself the mighty God, and towards his church the everlasting Father. He is self-originated, and underived, and was eternally All, when all things which ever were, now are, or ever shall be, were nothing.[47]

---

43. Beddome, *Sermons*, 79. Beddome also specifically claims that the fulfillment of Christ's prophecy testifies his full divinity. See Beddome, *Sermons*, 238.

44. Beddome, *Twenty Short Discourses*, 3:100.

45. Beddome, *Catechism*, 20. Christ's eternal Sonship was a hotly debated issue during the Reformation and the Post-Reformation eras. Concerning this, see Muller, *Post Reformation Reformed Dogmatics*, 4:283–88.

46. Beddome, *Twenty Short Discourses*, 7:114; *Sermons*, 119.

47. Beddome, *Twenty Short Discourses*, 4:5–6.

In Beddome's thought, Christ is not the Son of God by creation, as Adam was; nor by adoption, as is every believer; but in a manner peculiar to himself, a manner totally inapplicable to any other.[48] Since the eternal generation of the Son is to us an inconceivable mystery, Beddome does not pretend to explain the manner of the eternal generation of the Son in further detail. He is certain that the eternity of the Son or the eternal generation of the Son is confirmed by many passages of Scripture and that it necessarily implies the Son's equality with the Father.[49]

The third type of evidence for Christ's full deity is that divine activities ascribed to Christ prove his full deity. Beddome particularly mentions the work of creation. Upon the basis of John 1:3, he maintains that the creation of all things out of nothing is "a work peculiar to God," and therefore, Christ, who is the creator of heaven and earth, is God. Also, as an additional proof that the Son, no less than the Father, is the supreme God, Beddome briefly points out the preservation and government of all things by Christ.[50]

Fourth, the ascription of Christ as the object of prayer and worship in Scripture indicates the divinity of Christ.[51] In order to explain this, Beddome especially relies on Stephen's dying prayer:

> He [Christ], jointly with the Father and Spirit, is the proper object of prayer; and, indeed, Stephen's dying prayer has, with propriety, been adduced as a strong and irrefragable proof of the supreme deity of Christ, and that with the same force of argument as Christ's dying prayer, to which it bears a striking resemblance, may be brought as a proof of the divinity of the Father.[52]

Considering all this evidence, in Beddome's mind, there is no doubt that Christ is truly and fully God.[53] Thus, declaring Christ as "the second Person of the ever-blessed and adorable Trinity," he affirms Christ's unity of essence with the Father: "There are three coequal and coeternal persons, between

48. Beddome, *Twenty Short Discourses*, 4:5–6; 7:114.

49. Beddome, *Twenty Short Discourses*, 4:5–6; 7:114. Consequently, in Beddome's idea, the various descriptions of Christ as God's own Son also imply the divinity of Christ: "It is sufficient to say, that he is God's own Son—his dear and well-beloved Son—his only-begotten Son. And these titles are given to him in the scriptures, not on account of any peculiar qualifications bestowed but in reference to his divine preexistent nature, and his eternal relation to the Father; so that he is before all things, and by him all things consists" (Beddome, *Twenty Short Discourses*, 7:114). See also, Beddome, *Sermons*, 119.

50. Beddome, *Twenty Short Discourses*, 7:114.

51. Beddome, *Catechism*, 21.

52. Beddome, *Sermons*, 237.

53. Beddome, *Sermons*, 82.

whom there is no difference or inequality but what is made by the covenant of grace. Their names, Father, Son, and Holy Spirit, are not descriptive of their nature, but of their office. . . . Christ as the second Person in the ever-blessed Trinity, and expressive both of equality of essence, and the peculiar relation in which he stands to the Divine Father; this Son, this coessential, coeternal, Son of God."[54]

In a similar vein, Beddome elsewhere acknowledges Christ's full equality with God the Father as follows:

> As a Son he is not inferior, but equal to the Father; being the brightness of his glory, and the express image of his person. He is personally distinguished as the Son of God, and as Mediator he acts in a subordinate capacity; but in his divine nature, he possesses a full equality with God. The assumption of human nature cast a veil over his original dignity, but did not diminish it; for while he was of the seed of David, according to the flesh, he was at the same time over all, God blessed forever (Rom 9:5; Col 1:17; 2:9; Heb 1:3).[55]

For Beddome, the eternal Son of God is coequal with the Father "by an ineffable union, and a full participation in all the attributes of the divine nature."[56] Like the matter of the eternal generation of Christ, Beddome does not discuss in further detail the manner of this coequal relationship between God the Father and God the Son. Acknowledging the mystery of the Triunity of God, he comments, "On a subject surpassing all our comprehension, it is better to be silent, than to darken counsel by words without knowledge."[57] Thus, without delving into the sophisticated issues of the Trinity, Beddome is satisfied with presenting a general treatment of Christ's deity and his relation with God the Father in his writings.

---

54. Beddome, *Sermons*, 119.

55. Beddome, *Twenty Short Discourses*, 7:114.

56. Beddome, *Twenty Short Discourses*, 6:51. Beddome similarly states that Christ participates in "the same nature, and the same infinite and adorable perfections" (Beddome, *Sermons*, 150). See also, Beddome, *Twenty Short Discourses*, 3:68; *Sermons*, 187.

57. Beddome, *Twenty Short Discourses*, 7:114. Beddome also comments in his *Catechism*, "Is the Son of the same nature with the Father? Yes. *He is the express image of his Person* (Heb 1:3). And equal to him? Yes. *He is the man his fellow* (Zech 13:7). Is this a mystery which we cannot comprehend? Yes. *What is his name, and what is his Son's name, if though canst tell* (Prov 30:3)" (Beddome, *Catechism*, 42–43).

The Humanity of Christ

In comparison to the idea of the deity of Christ, Beddome's discussion of the humanity of Christ is relatively brief. Since it has been opposed by heretics of various kinds in the history of Christianity, the doctrine of Christ's humanity was still an important topic for Beddome's Christology. As with the case of the deity of Christ, Beddome's teaching and vindication of Christ's humanity is also thoroughly based on Scriptural proofs. Relying on the standard texts, such as John 1:14 and 1 John 1:1–2, Beddome argues that in the fullness of time, the Son of God assumed a complete human nature into union with his divine person.[58]

Beddome teaches that this human nature of Christ was conceived by the power of the Holy Spirit in the womb of the Virgin Mary, and was formed of her substance. That is, the body of Christ was not created out of nothing, neither did it descend from heaven, but was formed, by the agency of the Holy Spirit, of the substance of the Virgin.[59] Even though Christ assumed human nature, he did not inherit any of human sin and depravity:

> His miraculous conception. [sic] He was born, but not begotten; made of a woman, and made flesh, but not in the ordinary way. He partook of our nature, and became man, but did not **inherit any of our depravity. He was conceived, but not in sin;** and was fashioned according to a man, but not shapen [sic] in iniquity. He was in the likeness of sinful flesh, but that was all; for he himself knew no sin. His conduct was inoffensive, and his nature undefiled: he neither brought pollution into the world, nor contracted any during his stay in it. He was a Lamb without blemish, and without spot: he was manifested to take away sin, but in him was no sin. Hence when the tempter came, he could find nothing in him (1 John 3:5).[60]

Beddome affirms that the human nature which the Son of God took upon himself is a real and genuine humanity.[61] Since Christ partakes of a true human nature, Beddome argues that Christ was subject to the common infirmities of human nature such as hunger, weariness, and pain, but was altogether without sin. Beddome maintains that due to the true and genuine humanity of Christ, he was fully acquainted with the power of emotions and affections without sin. Beddome particularly mentions Christ's

58. Beddome, *Sermons*, 371.
59. Beddome, *Twenty Short Discourses*, 7:114.
60. Beddome, *Twenty Short Discourses*, 3:67.
61. Beddome, *Twenty Short Discourses*, 4:116.

friendship as such an example: "Christ as a man had all the sinless passions and affections of that nature which he assumed. He was capable of performing acts of friendship, and tasting its sweets, as well as other men."[62] For Beddome, Christ truly shared our human condition of dependence and creatureliness.[63]

Beddome specifically opposes the heretical idea that the heavenly Christ-spirit could not be flesh, but only appeared to be a man:[64]

> Luke 22:48 That he is really and properly man, as well as truly divine. In the assumption of our nature, he was found in fashion as a man; he took on him the seed of Abraham, and was made in the likeness of sinful flesh. There were some in the early ages of the church who supposed that the body of Christ was only an aerial substance, not flesh and blood, but having the form and appearance of it; imagining that it was incompatible with divinity to become really incarnate. Against this John 1:14; 1 John 1:1–2; 4:2–3 [sic].[65]

For Beddome, there is no doubt that Christ in the Gospels was not a mere phantom. He argues that Christ's humanity was really his own, as any human being's humanity is his or her own.[66]

Beddome strongly insists that Christ actually assumed human nature, and this nature was "the nature of a man subject to the same infirmities and anxieties as the rest of mankind."[67] This emphasis upon the true and genuine humanity of Christ does not mean that Jesus Christ ceased to be God. Beddome affirms that in spite of his condescension to the human level by partaking of human nature, with respect to his divine nature, Christ is "the essential with God."[68] Beddome maintains that the eternal Son of God, coequal with the Father "originally possessed of all the rights and prerogatives of deity, and . . . continued to possess them even in his state

62. Beddome, *Twenty Short Discourses*, 2:95.

63. Concerning the reality of Christ's human nature, however, Beddome does not further delve into the sophisticated issues such as whether Christ assumed a human nature in its perfection, as before the fall, or whether he assumed a human nature clothed with infirmities, as after the fall.

64. Even though he does not mention it, it is certain that Beddome particularly is addressing the Docetism from the primitive times of the Christian Church which held that Christ had not a real, but a mere shadowy body. Concerning Docetism, see Kelly, *Early Christian Doctrines*, 197–98; McGuckin, *Westminster Handbook*, 105–6.

65. Beddome, *Twenty Short Discourses*, 4:118.

66. Beddome, *Twenty Short Discourses*, 4:118.

67. Beddome, *Sermons*, 371; *Twenty Short Discourses*, 8:29.

68. Beddome, *Sermons*, 11.

of humiliation, though their ordinary exercise was for a time suspended."[69] Christ's actual assumption of human nature was "no robbery to be equal with God."[70] Rather, Beddome claims, "The glory of deity shone through the veil of humanity."[71] In his thought, in order to be "the physician, redeemer, and saviour of our souls," Jesus Christ, the second person of the ever-blessed and adorable Trinity, "assumed our nature, lived a despised life, and died an accursed death."[72] God the Son really became the man Jesus!

The Mystery of Two Natures in One Person

The critical question is how these two distinct natures, the Godhead and the human nature, can be joined together. Beddome believes that due to the incomprehensibility of God and the creaturely limitation of human knowledge, the complete grasp of the mystery of the incarnation is not possible. The conviction that the doctrine of the two natures of Christ is a heavenly mystery pervades Beddome's writings.

Upon the basis of several Scriptural evidences, Beddome teaches two significant principles concerning the doctrine of the two natures of Christ. First, in opposition to the Nestorians who held to the two persons of Christ, Beddome strongly maintains that the Son of God assumed the human nature into union with the divine, so that two distinct natures, the Godhead and the human nature, are inseparably joined together in one person.[73] Employing the traditional Chalcedonian view, he teaches that in the hypostatic union, while there are two natures, there is only one person (*hypostasis*) in Christ and that person is the eternal Son of God.[74] Even though Beddome does not give a detailed account of the way in which Christ's humanity is related to the person of the Son of God, the human nature of Christ, in Beddome's view, never had a separate subsistence or personality of its own.[75]

Second, unlike the heretical ideas such as those of the Eutychians who insisted on only one nature in Christ, Beddome teaches that the incarnation

---

69. Beddome, *Twenty Short Discourses*, 4:51.

70. Beddome, *Twenty Short Discourses*, 8:29–30.

71. Beddome, *Sermon*, 83.

72. Beddome, *Sermon*, 214. See also Beddome, *Twenty Short Discourses*, 6:51.

73. Beddome, *Catechism*, 43. For Nestorianism, see Kelly, *Early Christian Doctrines*, 310–30; Seeberg, *History of Doctrines*, 261–66; McGuckin, *Westminster Handbook*, 237–38; *St. Cyril of Alexandria*, 126–75.

74. Beddome, *Twenty Short Discourses*, 7:34; *Catechism*, 43.

75. This point was firmly asserted by all the Reformed orthodox thinkers as well. Cf. Beeke and Jones, *Puritan Theology*, 338.

did not result in either subtraction from Christ's deity or the absorption of his human nature.[76] Though this is an intimate union, the two natures are not confounded; each retains its own essential properties. For Beddome, this is confirmed by many passages of Scripture, such as Romans 9:5, and 1 Timothy 2:5, which speak of the two natures as belonging to the Savior.[77]

In his discussion of the two natures of Christ Beddome does not delve into the sophisticated theological issues of the Reformation and the Post-Reformation eras, such as the communication of properties (*communicatio idiomatum* or *communicatio proprietatum*).[78] For example, even though following the Western church tradition, Beddome distinguished between the two natures of Christ, who is both consubstantial (*homoousios*, "the same in substance") with humanity and consubstantial with the Father, it is not clear whether, opposite to Roman Catholic and Lutheran views, Beddome understood this twofold consubstantiality from the Reformed perspective or not.

In Beddome's mind the preservation of the integrity of Christ's full deity and true humanity is fundamental to the truth of the gospel and to every doctrine contained in it. In particular, having the Socinian claim in mind, Beddome firmly argues that the denial of the full deity of Christ is to divest his obedience and sufferings of their inherent value, and consequently, to subvert the grand doctrine of the redemption of the Church by his blood:

> It is the blood of Jesus Christ, as the Son of God, that cleanseth us from all sin. He by Himself purged our sins, who is the brightness of the Father's glory, and the express image of his person. If the blood of bulls and of goats sanctifieth to the purifying of the flesh, how much more shall the blood of Christ, who through the eternal Spirit offered himself without spot to God, purge your conscience from dead works to serve the living God (Heb 1:3; Isa 14; 1 John 1:7). Separate the divinity from the humanity, and the death of Jesus would have been of no more avail than that of Stephen or of Paul, or of any of the martyrs, who sealed the truth with their blood; but by means of this mysterious union a sacrifice of infinite worth has been offered up, and God now can be just while he is the justifier of all them that believe. . . . Now Christ is both the sacrifice, the altar, and the priest. His human nature was the sacrifice, for divinity could not suffer. His divine

---

76. Beddome, *Catechism*, 43. For Eutychianism, see Kelly, *Early Christian Doctrines*, 330–43; Seeberg, *History of Doctrines*, 131–32, 260–71; McGuckin, *Patristic Theology*, 132–33; *St. Cyril of Alexandria*, 229–32.

77. Beddome, *Sermons*, 83.

78. Concerning the issue of the communication of properties and operations during the Reformation and the Post-Reformation eras, see Muller, *Dictionary*, 72–74; Beeke and Jones, *Puritan Theology*, 337–40.

nature became the altar, which was holiness itself, sanctifying the gift, and rendering the sacrifice acceptable and efficacious; while in both natures he exercises the office of a priest. The man Christ Jesus was the bleeding victim, but without an intimate and a mysterious union with the deity, no adequate atonement for sin could have been made. Hence it is that the scriptures uniformly ascribe the efficacy of the Redeemer's death to the infinite dignity of his person, and not to the degree of his sufferings, though these were such as to surpass our comprehension.[79]

Beddome was confident that Christ was really human, and it was necessary that he should be so, in order that he might suffer. However, at the same time, Christ was really God, and it was equally necessary that he should be so, in order that he might satisfy divine justice and pay the penalty of sin.[80] Christ's satisfaction was meritorious before God because of the worth of his person. He is the God-man, and both natures were necessary in order for Christ to represent his people and make sufficient payment on their behalf.[81] If either of the two natures of Christ are ignored or denied, it would result in the conclusion that Christ could not properly have made atonement for fallen humanity.

In Beddome's thought, Jesus of Nazareth was beyond a doubt both God and man in one person. In Christ, deity and humanity are not contradictory, and testimony for one must not be rejected because of the other. Rather, in spite of the infinite gap and contrast between them, the divine

79. Beddome, *Twenty Short Discourses*, 7:34–35. Cf. In this paragraph, Beddome uses the term "atonement" and, in order to avoid a confusion, its meaning needs to be highlighted. As clearly shown in the works of many British Reformed thinkers such as Samuel Rutherford and James Ussher, the English verb "to atone" or its noun form "atonement," in English theological works of the early modern era, "typically refers to Christ's objective sacrifice for sin universally considered, namely, according to its sufficiency, or with reference to texts in the Epistle to the Hebrews, to the crucifixion understood as blood sacrifice or sin offering after the manner of the Old Testament Levitical priesthood" (Muller, *Calvin and the Reformed Tradition*, 75). Beddome uses the term "atonement" in this nuance. Cf. Beddome, *Sermons*, 201; *Twenty Short Discourses*, 2:130–131; *Hymns*, #95. The modern use of the terms, "limited" and "unlimited atonement" are not found in Beddome's writings at all. Regarding the problem of the modern concept of limited and unlimited atonement as it has been retrojected onto early modern theological debates concerning the sufficiency, efficiency, intention, and extent of Christ's satisfaction, see Muller, *Calvin and the Reformed Tradition*, 70–106.

80. Beddome, *Twenty Short Discourses*, 3:75.

81. Beddome, *Twenty Short Discourses*, 3:74. Consequently, in Beddome's view, there is a unity of the person and work of Christ, for Christ came to humanity in and through his saving work. Beddome particularly united the person and work by presenting Christ in the threefold office of prophet, priest, and king which the following section will examine.

and the human are united in the one person of Christ to human advantage. Consequently, the examination of Beddome's view of the two natures in one person indicates that Beddome is in strong continuity with the orthodox Patristic creeds, especially the Chalcedonian formula (451 AD).[82]

The Work of Christ: Christ's Threefold Offices

Along with the person of Christ, the other essential component of Beddome's Christology is the work of Christ. In order to explain Christ's work, he employs the traditional Reformed view of the threefold office of Christ.[83] For Beddome, this teaching of Christ's threefold office of prophet, priest, and king clearly explains which roles Christ assumes with regard to humanity and what transpires between God and humanity.

Christ's Prophetic Office

In Beddome's view, the first office of Christ is that of prophet.[84] How is the office of a prophet executed? Beddome teaches that Christ executes "the office of prophet in revealing to us, by his word and Spirit, the will of God for our salvation."[85] Christ can enact this prophetic activity because he himself is the living and life-giving Word of the triune God and, in his divine nature, Christ is omniscient.[86]

82. The Council of Chalcedon (451 AD) asserts that Christ is one person with two natures: "One and the same Christ, Son, Lord, Only-begotten, recognized in two natures, without confusion, without change, without division, without separation; the distinction of natures being in no way annulled by the union, but rather the characteristics [*idiomata*] of each nature being preserved and coming together to form one person and subsistence, not as parted or separated into two persons, but one and the same Son and Only-begotten God the Word, Lord Jesus Christ" (quoted in Beeke and Jones, *Puritan Theology*, 347–48). Arguably, the Chalcedonian definition of Christ's person provides Beddome with a basic understanding of what Christians are to affirm concerning the person of Jesus Christ.

83. Beddome, *Catechism*, 45; *Hymns*, #131. Concerning the use of the threefold office in the Reformed tradition, see Sherman, *King, Priest, and Prophet*, 63–76; Heppe, *Reformed Dogmatics*, 448–87; Muller, *Dictionary*, 197; Beeke and Jones, *Puritan Theology*, 347–58; Edmondson, *Calvin's Christology*.

84. In Beddome's *Catechism*, the order of Christ's offices follows the order of execution. There Christ is described first as Prophet of righteousness and the herald of salvation; then as Priest approaching the altar he offered himself as a sacrifice to God; and lastly as King he was seated at the right hand of the Father. Beddome, *Catechism*, 47–53.

85. Beddome, *Catechism*, 47. See also Beddome, *Hymns*, #128.

86. Beddome, *Catechism*, 47–48; *Twenty Short Discourses*, 7:117.

One may think of Christ's prophetic office principally in terms of his ministry on earth for roughly three years. Beddome does not confine Christ's prophetic office to such a limited period. In his thought, Christ already exercised this prophetic activity from eternity. As *logos incarnandus*, he is from eternity as prophet, high priest, and king.[87] In line with the Reformed view, Beddome teaches that Christ's office of prophet did not cease at his death and resurrection, but he still continues to perform this prophetic office in heaven.[88]

In Beddome's mind, Christ's public prophetic function on earth represents a significant part of the content of his role as prophet. This portion of Christ's prophetic office began with the full participation of his humanity in it, from the moment he was baptized by John the Baptist and anointed by the Father as the only-begotten Son and proclaimed to the world. During this time, Christ outwardly proclaimed divine truth and the gospel.[89] For Beddome, however, in the broader sense of the term, Christ's miraculous activity also belongs to his prophetic office, as does his holy and righteous life, by which Christ confirmed and guaranteed his proclamation.[90]

With regards to the contents of Christ's teaching, it is on the one hand a *prophetia legalis*.[91] For Beddome, Christ did not come as a new legislator at all.[92] Christ did not give believers a new moral law that would merely supersede and replace the law given by Moses.[93] This is particularly evident in that instead of abrogating the law, Christ as the author of the law reaffirmed it in his teaching and fulfilled it in his life and ministry.[94] Additionally, Christ's prophetic office is a *prophetia evangelia,* since Christ imparts and enables the most blessed knowledge of the gracious salvation extended to the world. Christ taught that being justified by faith, Christians are no longer under God's law but under his grace.[95] The law still stands, but it cannot condemn

---

87. Beddome, *Catechism*, 48.

88. Beddome, *Catechism*, 48.

89. Beddome, *Catechism*, 48.

90. Beddome, *Catechism*, 47.

91. Beddome does not use this scholastic term itself. Nevertheless, as with the case of *prophetia evangelia*, the idea of *prophetia legalis* is evident in his writings. For example, Beddome, *Twenty Short Discourses*, 2:146; 6:111, 124, 138.

92. Beddome, *Twenty Short Discourses*, 2:141–142.

93. Beddome, *Twenty Short Discourses*, 1:147; *Catechism*, 89–90; *Hymns*, #364, #367.

94. Beddome, *Twenty Short Discourses*, 1:147; *Twenty Short Discourses*, 2:141–42.

95. Beddome, *Twenty Short Discourses*, 2:157; *Catechism*, 89.

the saints because they are made free from the law in Christ Jesus, in whose righteousness they now stand.[96]

According to Beddome, the manner and mode in which Christ exercises his prophetic office is also twofold. First, it was directly enacted by Christ himself without aid of human instruments. Christ threw direct light upon particular patriarchs and prophets and spoke in the New Testament with his own lips.[97] In Beddome's view, Christ's direct role as prophet during his public ministry on earth is not limited to his verbal teachings. As prophet, Jesus taught his people through the example of his life as well.[98] As the perfect and archetypal man, Christ provided an example of what was due to God from all humans.[99] Second, it has been indirectly performed because Christ sends out his servants as his instruments to instruct and illuminate the world.[100] In both the Old and the New Testaments Christ employed and ordered the numerous prophets and apostles to reveal divine truth in their addresses and writings, truth which is necessary to be known for salvation. This indirect role of prophet is significant for the ongoing church because the church is now assigned the task of the proclamation of God's will and Word.

Christ's Priestly Office

Beddome never explicitly mentioned a priority among the three offices of Christ. Nevertheless, there is no doubt that since Christ's work as priest is the foundation to a proper understanding of his role as Mediator, the most important office is that of priest in Beddome's mind.[101] As already noted, Beddome teaches that Christ became incarnate to save the fallen world. The purpose of the incarnation of Christ is to reconcile us to God and Christ

96. Beddome, *Twenty Short Discourses*, 6:138–39; *Hymns*, #361–62, #365, #369.

97. Beddome, *Catechism*, 47–48.

98. In his discussion of Christ's life and ministry on earth, Beddome indicates that Christ's life is continually set before us as an example that we should follow. For instance, Beddome states that Christians are to follow his example in his condescension and humility: "He came not to be ministered to, but to minister, and hath set us an example of infinite condescension, and the deepest and most undissembled humility" (Beddome, *Sermons*, 371). Nevertheless, Beddome never brings up the Abelardian moral influence theory into his discussion of the effect of Christ's prophetic office. Cf. Concerning the Abelaridan moral influence theory, see van Asselt, "Christ's Atonement," 62.

99. Cf. Beddome, *Catechism* 56; *Sermons*, 11, 370.

100. Beddome, *Sermons*, 305–8.

101. Considering that the doctrine of Christ's priesthood is far more frequently and substantially found in Beddome's writings, it is also evident that for Beddome, the Christ's most important office is that of priest.

accomplishes this by offering himself as a pure and holy sacrifice. Here, a couple of key biblical motifs, substitution and suretyship, enter into Beddome's exposition of the priestly work of Christ. In order to articulate Beddome's doctrine of Christ's priesthood, each will be examined in detail.[102]

SUBSTITUTION

According to Beddome, all the sacrifices offered by divine appointment, under the legal dispensation, were typical of the death of Christ.[103] He teaches that the nature of all the legal sacrifices in the Old Testament were vicarious. The guilt of the offenders was transferred to the sacrificial offering, which was indicated by the offenders laying their hands on the head of the sacrifice. Beddome maintains that this type of sacrifice is realized in Christ's death in the place of his people.[104]

On the basis of this background idea, Beddome maintains that Christ's priestly work is presented as the substitutionary sacrifice for the full restoration of sinners to God. Concerning this, he comments as follows:

> The Lord Jesus Christ himself could not do this but by dying as a propitiatory sacrifice in the room and stead of his people; for it is by blood, as the Scripture informs us, that all things are purified and purged, "and without shedding of blood there is no remission." Our tears, services, or sufferings, can make no satisfaction to that justice which we have offended, no reparation to that law which we have broken. The blood of bulls and of goats effected a typical, the blood of Christ a real purgation; and the perfection of his sacrifice makes any other as unnecessary as it would have been inefficient.[105]

102. Following the traditional Reformed understanding, Beddome teaches that the priestly work of Christ was twofold: oblation and intercession. He maintains that in addition to the work of oblation, Christ carries out the second duty of the priestly office, intercession. Beddome's discussion of Christ's work of intercession is not substantially discussed in his writings. For example, he simply describes Christ as "able," "wise and skillful," "righteous," "kind and affectionate," "constant," "successful," "the only advocate who makes intercession for his people" (Beddome, *Catechism*, 50). Cf. Beddome, *Sermon*, 238. Beddome does not discuss the benefit of Christ's intercession such as the preservation of believers which the Reformed theologians generally considered as the major intent of Christ's intercession. Regarding the classic Reformed view of Christ's intercession, see Heppe, *Reformed Dogmatics*, 458, 479–81; Beeke and Jones, *Puritan Theology*, 371–85; Muller, *Dictionary*, 157.

103. Beddome, *Twenty Short Discourses*, 3:77.

104. Beddome, *Twenty Short Discourses*, 3:77.

105. Beddome, *Sermons*, 203.

Elsewhere, Beddome also states the following:

> It is also included in the nature of a sacrifice that it be vicarious,
> or offered in the room and stead of another, so that the punish-
> ment due to the offender should be borne by the substitute. And
> such was the sacrifice of Christ. Not like the high priest under
> the law, had he to offer first for himself, and then for the sins of
> the people; for he himself knew no sin, neither was guile found
> in his mouth: all he did and suffered was for our sakes, that he
> might bring us unto God.[106]

In these statements, Beddome's point is that Christ himself died in our stead
and became an expiatory sacrifice for the sake of the reconciliation between
God and human beings. This shows that Beddome understands Christ's
death as a vicarious sacrifice, and thus Christ's saving activity for fallen humanity is substitutionary in its nature.

Why, then, is Christ's substitutionary death required? Or to put it
another way, how does our forgiveness and salvation depend on Christ's
vicarious death? According to Beddome, since the holy and righteous God
cannot tolerate or overlook sin, it is absolutely necessary to satisfy God's
holy standards before human beings can be right with God.[107] Once cap-
tivated by sin, human beings lost the ability to satisfy the holy God, and
Christ's substitution became essential for human salvation. Christ took our
punishment by offering himself as a bloody sacrifice. Christ endured, in his
innocent person, the penalty our sins deserved, and thereby, his sacrifice
satisfied God's justice and law.[108] Regarding Christ's satisfaction of God's
justice, Beddome states as follows:

> By the vicarious sacrifice of his well-beloved Son, the honour
> of the divine government is maintained, and justice abundantly
> satisfied, while the richest mercy is exercised towards the un-
> worthy. The law is fulfilled, in all its precepts and sanctions, and
> yet the sinner is saved to the very uttermost. By a most myste-
> rious constitution, God hath made him to be sin for us, who
> knew no sin, that we might be made the righteousness of God in
> him. So that justice and grace are equally displayed, and equally
> combined, in the great plan of human redemption (Rom 3:25;
> 2 Cor 5:21).[109]

---

106. Beddome, *Twenty Short Discourses*, 3:73. See also Beddome, *Hymns*, #129.

107. Beddome, *Twenty Short Discourses*, 2:137.

108. Beddome, *Twenty Short Discourses*, 1:199. See also Beddome, *Twenty Short Discourses*, 4:7.

109. Beddome, *Twenty Short Discourses*, 6:122. See also Beddome, *Hymns*, #109.

He similarly emphasizes that Christ satisfied the demands of the law by his vicarious death:

> The curse of the law fell upon him, and crushed him under its weight. The law required the death of the sinner, and Christ satisfied its demands in the sinner's stead. He was made under the law, so as not only to fulfil [sic] its precepts, but also to endure the punishment it inflicted. Having voluntarily made himself a debtor to it, it took him as it were by the throat, and with a voice more terrifying than the loudest thunder, said, Pay me what thou owest. Nor did our most gracious Surety reject the claim, but immediately made full satisfaction. What the Jews and Pilate were openly, that the law was secretly, his accuser and condemner. He bore the same curse and the same death that was due to sin, and to us for sin; so that both law and gospel sweetly harmonise in our salvation. Christ legally suffered, and the sinner is legally saved.[110]

As shown in these statements, Christ's atoning work is characterized as vicarious satisfaction either of God's law or of God's justice throughout Beddome's writings.[111] Christ's work of propitiation and expiation is considered as payment for sin made for the sake of believers and in their place. In Beddome's view, the forgiveness of sin is made possible because the consequence of sin, the deserved penalty of the violation of divine law and justice, has been borne by Christ in our place.

From the perspective of God the Father, Christ's satisfaction of divine law and justice can also be understood as God's simultaneous expression of his holiness in judgment and his love in pardon. The work of satisfaction manifests the constancy of God's justice or righteousness while at the same time revealing God's mercy in the fact of forgiveness. One may think that divine love and justice cannot stand together. Beddome asserts that since God provided a divine substitute for the sinner so that the substitute would receive the judgment and the sinner the pardon, God's justice and mercy do not collide with each other in the matter of human salvation: "You may observe, it [love] is not said against justice, for we are not to suppose that one attribute in the Divine Being can militate against, or exult over, another. God is just, infinitely and inflexibly just, at the same time that he is a Saviour. Salvation by Christ is no impeachment, but a manifestation of Divine justice."[112]

---

110. Beddome, *Twenty Short Discourses*, 6:124.

111. Cf. Beddome, *Hymns*, #95.

112. Beddome, *Sermons*, 32.

Beddome argues that "Through the atoning blood of Christ he cannot only pardon sin consistently with the love of righteousness, but even declare his love of it in the very act of forgiveness."[113] According to him, the doctrine of vicarious satisfaction alone meets the requirements of the biblical view of God as both merciful and just, gracious and righteous. Justice and righteousness are satisfied, and in the vicarious nature of the work, mercy and grace are manifest.

Finally, Beddome's view of Christ's vicarious satisfaction indicates that his position stands firmly in continuity with that of the Reformed theologians during the Reformation and the Post-Reformation eras.[114] As with Beddome, the classic Reformed thinkers commonly relied on the doctrine of Christ's vicarious satisfaction to explain Christ's mediatorial work for human salvation. For example, John Calvin states that Christ did bear the punishment of human sin and that it truly satisfied God the Father:

> At this point Christ interceded as his [man's] advocate, took upon himself and suffered the punishment that, from God's righteous judgment, threatened all sinners; that purged with his blood those evils which had rendered sinners hateful to God; that by this expiation he made satisfaction and sacrifice duly to God the Father; that as intercessor he has appeased God's wrath; that on this foundation rests the peace of God with men; that by this bond his benevolence is maintained toward them.[115]

113. Beddome, *Twenty Short Discourses*, 2:137. Thus for Beddome, Christ's satisfaction can be understood in a twofold perspective: "it is an act of justice with respect to him [God], while it is an act of free mercy towards us" (Beddome, *Twenty Short Discourses*, 2:136).

114. Beddome also basically is in continuity with Anselm because the Anselmian idea of satisfaction is clearly present in Beddome's idea of Christ's substitutionary sacrifice. Interestingly enough, albeit only in a couple of passages, Beddome shows a certain commonality with Anselm in that he thinks not only of God's justice but also of his honor. In a similar vein to Anselm, Beddome's view of the nature of satisfaction also includes the restoration or maintenance of divine honor. Beddome, *Sermons*, 14; *Twenty Short Discourses*, 6:122. This is rarely found in the works of other Reformed thinkers. Concerning this, Muller states, "It is characteristic of the Reformers and of the orthodox that they depart from the medieval scholastic theory of a satisfaction made for the sake of the divine honor and rest their views of satisfaction on the justice or righteousness of God which is angry and wrathful against sin" (Muller, *Dictionary*, 272). The idea of vicarious satisfaction of divine justice and law still dominates Beddome's writings. Even though crucifixion is a form of retribution for both, for Anselm it is understood in a civil sense as a form of merit (*meritum*), while for Beddome the suffering of Christ is *satisfactio poenalis* in nature. Cf. van Asselt, "Christ's Atonement," 60–61. In spite of Beddome's recognition of divine honor in Christ's substitution, his doctrine of reconciliation cannot merely be identified with Anselm's.

115. Calvin, *Institutes of the Christian Religion*, 505.

In a similar vein to Calvin, Wilhelmus à Brakel (1635–1711) also maintains that Christ satisfied divine justice for human sins:

> First of all we state that Christ by His suffering has in essence and truth on behalf of God's children satisfied the justice of God relative to their sins. The Socinians deny this. We maintain that Christ is not only a Savior because He revealed the truth and the way of salvation, confirmed this by His miracles and His death, was an example for us in His holy life, etc. and thus suffered and died to the benefit of man. Instead, we maintain that Christ as Surety has taken the place of His elect, taking upon Himself all their sins; that is, original as well as actual sins committed both prior to baptism and conversion and to the very last moment of their lives. On their behalf He Himself has borne the punishments which they deserved, and thus has completely, essentially, and truly satisfied the justice of God without overlooking any sin or by accepting a part as being equivalent to the whole. On the basis of this satisfaction and His merits, He delivers them from all punishment, temporal eternal. This is the cardinal point and distinctive of Christianity. He who errs here and denies this truth cannot be saved.[116]

Francis Turretin (1623–1687) also elaborates on the nature of vicarious satisfaction for human sin as follows:

> Hence we infer that three things were required for our redemption—the payment of the debt contracted by sin, the appeasing of divine hatred and wrath, and the expiation of guilt. And hence secondly, the nature of the satisfaction to be made for sin may be easily perceived (viz., in which these three relations [scheseis] at the same time concur): the payment of the debt, the appeasing of the divine wrath (by reconciling us with him) and the expiation of guilt (by the endurance of punishment). But as the principal relation to be attended to in sin is its criminality, so satisfaction has relation [scheseis] to the punishment imposed by the supreme Judge.[117]

The idea of Christ's vicarious satisfaction is commonly manifested in other eighteenth-century British Particular Baptists' writings, as well. For instance, John Gill argues that Christ's sacrificial death fully satisfied God for human sin:

---

116. Brakel, *Christian's Reasonable Service*, 1:586.

117. Turretin, *Institutes of Elenctic Theology*, 418–19.

That it might appear, that by his death and sacrifice, he had made full satisfaction for sin, and a complete atonement for it; that as by his hanging on the tree, it was manifest that he bore the curse, and was made a curse for his people; so by his body being taken down from the cross, and laid in the grave, it was a token that the curse was at an end, and entirely abolished, agreeable to the law in Deuteronomy 21:23.[118]

The London Baptist Confession of Faith (1677/1689), which significantly influenced the formation of Particular Baptists' theology in eighteenth-century England, also declares that Christ's sacrifice fully satisfied divine justice: "The Lord Jesus, by his perfect obedience and sacrifice of himself, which he through the eternal Spirit once offered up unto God, hath fully satisfied the justice of God, procured reconciliation, and purchased an everlasting inheritance in the kingdom of heaven for all those whom the Father hath given unto him."[119]

In this way, as with Beddome, in the thoughts of Calvin, Brakel, Turretin, and Gill, Christ, as the representative of those whom the Father had given unto him, made a true and proper satisfaction to divine justice, by enduring in humans' stead the very punishment which their sins deserved. Further cases of the Reformed theologians' or the eighteenth-century British Particular Baptists' appeal to the doctrine of vicarious satisfaction are too numerous to mention them all. It is hardly an exaggeration to say that most Reformed thinkers, including eighteenth-century British Particular Baptists, distinctively emphasized the idea of substitutionary satisfaction in their discussion of Christ's priestly work.

SURETYSHIP

Along with the image of substitution, Beddome often uses the motif of surety in order to discuss the nature of Christ's priestly work. In that Christ represents fallen human beings and in that the usage of the term explicitly indicates the core of Christ's saving work as payment for human sin, the metaphor of suretyship basically overlaps with substitution. In his use of the suretyship motif, Beddome describes the state of the fallen human beings particularly as the insolvent debtors to God:

---

118. Gill, *Complete Body*, 837. See also Gill, *Body of Doctrinal and Practical Divinity*, 857, 878, 885.

119. *London Baptist Confession of Faith*, §8.5.

> But alas, we are debtors also as sinners, in having come short of
> the glory of God. We owe a debt of punishment, a debt which
> we can never discharge; and though in a future state it will ever
> be paying, yet will never be fully paid. Finite beings can never
> satisfy the demands of infinite justice, nor make atonement for
> infinite transgressions.[120]

According to Beddome, since Adam's fall, human beings became so infinitely indebted to God that they cannot repay him.[121] Thus, a surety who engages to pay a debt or to suffer a penalty incurred by them became absolutely necessary. In this desperate situation for human beings, Christ willingly, by his Father's appointment and his own voluntary engagement, undertook the office of a surety to be Mediator, and through his death on the cross, paid the debt of obedience which fallen human beings owed to the law, as a covenant of works, and the debt of punishment which they had contracted by sin.[122] Concerning Christ's gracious act as surety, Beddome elaborates as follows:

> It is the love of a debtor to his surety, or of a criminal to the per-
> son by whose means his pardon has been obtained. We are all
> indebted, infinitely indebted, to the law and justice of God, and
> have nothing to pay! Now Christ became a surety for insolvent
> sinners, saying to the Father, under the character of a creditor
> or judge, as Paul to Philemon concerning Onesimus, "If he hath
> wronged thee, or oweth thee aught, put it to my account, and I
> will repay it." Such suretyships are represented in Scripture as
> dangerous: "He that is surety for a stranger shall smart for it."
> Christ became such a surety, and he smarted for it. It cost him
> his life—his heart's blood! The original threatening, "The soul
> that sinneth, it shall die," in its full weight fell upon him; the
> debt contracted was demanded of him, and he paid it; the wrath
> deserved was inflicted upon him, and he bore it: thus restoring
> honour to God, and bringing peace, comfort, and happiness to
> man. The process against the criminal is now staid; and instead
> of being cast into the prison of hell, he is reinstated in the favour
> of his Sovereign, and raised to a state of the highest dignity and
> glory.[123]

As stated above, in Beddome's thought, Christ obeyed and suffered as the surety of fallen human beings, and upon this ground, what Christ did and

---

120. Beddome, *Twenty Short Discourses*, 2:130–31.
121. Beddome, *Twenty Short Discourses*, 2:130–31.
122. Beddome, *Sermons*, 14–15.
123. Beddome, *Sermons*, 14–15. See also, Beddome, *Hymns*, #125, #126.

suffered is placed to their account. Fallen humans became set free from the debt of law and justice. In that divine forgiveness must satisfy divine justice, God cannot simply forgive sin without the repayment of the human debt to the law and the justice of God, and in that Christ obeyed and suffered on their behalf in order to pay the debt of obedience and punishment which fallen humanity was bound to pay as the penalty for sin, the motif of Christ's suretyship strongly supports that in Beddome's view, that the nature of Christ's atoning work can be essentially categorized as vicarious or substitutionary satisfaction.

As with Beddome, the metaphor of suretyship is commonly employed by the Reformed thinkers during the Reformation and the Post-Reformation eras.[124] For example, Brakel states the following:

> It is a known fact that a surety takes the place of another, be it that he is *fidejussor*, one who is obligated to pay when a debtor cannot pay, (which in this case no sinner is capable of doing); or be it that he is *expromissor*, who first takes the debt upon himself, makes payment as if it were his own, and releases the debtor from all obligations. Paul made himself such a surety on behalf of Onesimus towards Philemon (Phlm 18–19). Jesus, being Surety, has taken their place, however, and paid the debt on their behalf.[125]

Like Brakel, a great deal of Reformed thinkers taught that Christ undertook, in the everlasting covenant, to be responsible to the law and justice of God for that boundless debt which his elect were bound to pay. The concept of Christ's suretyship is also generally found among other eighteenth-century British Particular Baptists. One example is found in Gill's writing:

> By this it is a clear case, that Christ has done his work as the Surety of his people; that he has paid all their debts, finished transgression, made an end of sin, made reconciliation for iniquity, and brought in everlasting righteousness; that he has fulfilled the law, satisfied justice, and obtained eternal redemption, having given a sufficient price for it; and, in short, has done everything he agreed to do, to the full satisfaction of his divine Father; and therefore he is raised from the dead, received into glory, and set down at the right hand of God, having answered all his suretyship engagements.[126]

---

124. Cf. Daniels, *Christology of John Owen*, 360–63.

125. Brakel, *Reasonable Services*, 586–87.

126. Gill, *Body of Doctrinal and Practical Divinity*, 846–47.

These examples show that Beddome is not alone in the use of the image of Christ's suretyship. There are many other examples in Reformed tradition that employ the suretyship metaphor in the discussion of Christ's priesthood. Consequently, like the case of the substitutionary image, Beddome's use of the suretyship motif also indicates that Beddome stands firmly in continuity with the classic Reformed tradition regarding the doctrine of Christ's priestly office.

THE EFFECTS OF CHRIST'S SACERDOTAL ACTIVITY

What are the effects or benefits of Christ's priestly work for human beings? Having discussed the nature of the atoning work in Christ's priesthood, we now turn to the ends gained, or the effects accomplished, by the obedience and sacrifice in Christ's office of priest. In Beddome's thought, the ultimate benefit of Christ's priestly office is to reconcile us to God.[127] Since Christ has fully satisfied the justice of God the Father, God and human beings, who were formerly in a state of enmity, might be reconciled.[128] Beddome never approves the Abelardian and Socinian claim that the proper act of Christ is the exertion of an exemplary influence upon unbelieving human beings and not his substitutionary death on their behalf. Instead, in line with the traditional Reformed understanding, he argues that the reconciliation of God to human beings necessarily involves that sin separates God and sinners, and yet Christ made reconciliation between them by satisfying divine justice for sin. The cause of the separation is actually removed, and humans are fully reconciled to God by the death of Christ in their stead.[129]

Thanks to Christ's vicarious satisfaction, those who believe in Christ as their Savior and Lord are no longer under condemnation, but freed from the curse of the law and its punishment.[130] He states the following:

127. Beddome, *Sermons*, 12.

128. Beddome, *Twenty Short Discourses*, 6:123.

129. Beddome, *Twenty Short Discourses*, 6:122, 124.

130. Beddome, *Sermons*, 431. In his writings, Beddome does not discuss whether or not Christ suffered and died only for a definite number of our race. In fact, Beddome shows little interest in speaking to the issue of the limitation of the efficacy of Christ's satisfaction. As already noted, Beddome does not clearly use the sufficiency-efficiency distinction that one finds in the writings of many Reformed theologians. For Beddome, although the sacrifice of Christ was propounded to all indifferently or indiscriminately, Christ's work is by divine intention effective for the elect only. Beddome claims that "the application of redemption" is "limited" by "the purpose of God," "the purchase of Christ," and "the operations of the Spirit" (Beddome, *Catechism*, 62). Arguably, in Beddome's view, believers are recipients of God's grace which is only bestowed to the elect. Cf. Beddome, *Catechism*, 22–23, 63–67. Even though Beddome did not speak directly

Christ is the end of the law for righteousness, to everyone that believeth. There is therefore now no condemnation to them that are in Christ Jesus, either for sins committed or duties neglected. Accusations there may be, and to innumerable charges the believer pleads guilty; but there is no condemnation. Christ's satisfaction being instead of all legal righteousness, is accepted by the law, and is well-pleasing in the sight of God.[131]

Now, believers are forgiven of all their sins and trespasses, and on the basis of Christ's imputed righteousness to them, they are declared righteous before God.[132]

Here Beddome's doctrine of the imputation of Christ's righteousness needs to receive particular attention because it is an important concept in determining and formulating the nature of the justification of sinners. Beddome did not write substantially on the doctrine of Christ's atonement as it relates to his imputed righteousness. Nevertheless, the idea of the imputation of Christ's righteousness is clearly manifested in his writings. Beddome argues that the imputation of Christ's righteousness is the sole ground of the justification of human beings, "Who are not interested in the merit, or clothed with the spotless and beautifying righteousness of Christ. That the imputation of Christ's righteousness is the sole ground upon which God approves of the persons or services of any, is everywhere affirmed in Scripture."[133] For Beddome, the righteousness of Christ credited to believers enables them to be justified before God. In his thought the imputation of Christ's righteousness plays a key role in the doctrine of the justification of the sinners.

What is Christ's righteousness founded upon? According to the classic Reformed view, Christ's righteousness results from his active and passive obedience as Mediator.[134] Beddome does not employ these scholastic termi-

---

to the issue, his writings clearly indicate the limited application of Christ's satisfaction to the elect only. Beddome does not say like the Reformed that Christ did not die for all. It is certain that the divine intention in the accomplishment of Christ's saving work was the salvation of the elect only and not the hypothetical universal extension of Christ's work or the universal salvation of mankind.

131. Beddome, *Twenty Short Discourses*, 6:138–39. See also Beddome, *Twenty Short Discourses*, 2:146; 3:77.

132. Beddome claims that justification "consists in the non-imputation of sin, and the imputation of a perfect righteousness. This is frequently expressed by purging" (Beddome, *Sermons*, 201). Cf. Beddome, *Twenty Short Discourses*, 1:98; *Sermons*, 319.

133. Beddome, *Sermons*, 319. See also Beddome, *Twenty Short Discourses*, 7:145.

134. For a more detailed discussion of the Reformed view of Christ's twofold obedience during the Reformation and the Post-Reformation eras, see Heppe, *Reformed Dogmatics*, 458–57; Muller, *Dictionary*, 205–6. Muller distinguishes between active and

nologies. In continuity with the Reformed tradition Beddome teaches the idea of Christ's twofold obedience in his *Catechism*:

> Are we justified only for the righteousness of Christ? Yes. *Not having my own righteousness, which is of the law, but that which is through the faith of Christ* (Phil 3:9). Did Christ perform what the law required? Yes. *There was no guile found in his mouth* (1 Pet 2:22). And is this a part of our justifying righteousness? Yes. *By the obedience of one many are made righteous* (Rom 5:19). Did he suffer what the law threatened? Yes. *For he was bruised for our iniquities* (Isa 53:5). And is this the other part of it? Yes. *Thou wast slain and hast redeemed us to God by thy blood* (Rev 5:9). Is this righteousness satisfactory to God? Yes. *The lord is well pleased for his righteousness sake* (Isa 42:21). And sufficient for man? Yes. *For grace reigns through righteousness unto eternal life by Jesus Christ our lord* (Rom 5:21). And shall it never be abrogated? No. *My righteousness shall not be abolished* (Isa 51:6).[135]

According to Beddome, Christ's obedience to the law is the ground of the sinner's right to eternal life.[136] In order to explain the foundation of Christ's righteousness, he distinguishes three different kinds of laws that Christ obeyed:

> Christ was under three laws: the law of works as a man, the law of ceremonies as a jew [sic], and a peculiar law as mediator. This commandment, says he, have I received of my Father; and by his voluntary subjection to, and exact fulfilment [sic] of all these laws, his obedience was both personal and perfect, and that everlasting righteousness introduced which is the foundation of our acceptance with God.[137]

In Beddome's view, Christ's righteousness entirely rests upon his perfect obedience to the law and God's will which ultimately leads him to voluntarily give himself up on the cross on behalf of sinners in order to make perfect satisfaction to God the Father.[138] Christ's complete blood-atonement

---

passive obedience in the classic Reformed thought as follows: "The *obedientia activa* describes the life of Christ from his birth to his passion, and particularly his ministry, during which Christ acted sinlessly and in perfect obedience to the will of God. The *obedientia passiva* refers to Christ's passion, during which he accepted passively, without any resistance, the suffering and cross to which he was subjected for the satisfaction of sin" (Muller, *Dictionary*, 205).

135. Beddome, *Catechism*, 70–71.

136. Beddome, *Twenty Short Discourses*, 1:98.

137. Beddome, *Twenty Short Discourses*, 1:98. Cf. Turretin, *Institutes*, 14.13.15.

138. Beddome, *Catechism*, 70.

(his passive obedience) and perfect law-obedience (his active obedience) fully satisfy God's offended justice. Consequently, even though he does not use the terms of active obedience and passive obedience, his understanding of Christ's obedient work as the Mediator indicates that Beddome generally follows the Reformed position on the foundational issue of imputed righteousness.[139]

Beddome's similarity with Reformed tradition is also seen in his view of the mode or manner of the imputation of Christ's righteousness. How can this righteousness be imputed to sinners? Beddome claims that it is made possible only through faith.[140] Christ's righteousness is imputed to sinners purely by God's grace through faith in Christ alone. According to Beddome, human beings' own merit and worthiness are of no use in availing themselves of Christ's merit and worthiness.[141] Instead, faith is the only "instrument" which makes this resource available to human beings.[142] Ultimately, faith is given only to the elect whom God chose by his pleasing will regardless of their merit.[143] Even though human beings are saved by faith in Jesus Christ alone, faith is a free gift of God.[144] Beddome's doctrine of imputed righteousness is faithfully based on the Reformed doctrine of justification by grace through faith alone.

Following the Reformed tradition, Beddome also teaches the imputation of believers' sin to Christ. For him, while Christ's righteousness is imputed to sinners, their guilt is legally transferred to Christ. In order to explain this idea, Beddome once again uses the metaphor of Christ's proper suretyship:

> Sin was indeed imputed to him, when he became our Surety; yet in him was no sin. He is a righteous Mediator, and a righteous Advocate; sustaining the rights of moral government, and laying all the blame upon the sinner. In his ministry he vindicated the righteousness of the law; and by his death he wrought out a perfect righteousness for all his people. He suffered, the just for

---

139. In a similar vein to the case of the relation between the law and the gospel, Beddome, however, does not discuss the doctrine of imputation in the context of a covenantal scheme. In the Reformed tradition, the doctrine of imputation is inseparably linked to the framework of covenant theology. Cf. Witsius, *Economy of the Covenants*.

140. Beddome, *Catechism*, 71.

141. Beddome, *Catechism*, 71.

142. Beddome, *Catechism*, 71.

143. Beddome, *Twenty Short Discourses*, 5:111; *Catechism*, 39–40.

144. Beddome, *Catechism*, 151. Cf. Beddome, *Sermons*, 216.

the unjust, that he might bring us to God. He is righteous in all
his offices and administrations.[145]

In Beddome's mind, Christ was condemned for us even though he himself
committed no sin, and did nothing to earn condemnation. Since Christ undertook to be humans' "surety and representative," "the punishment of their
sins might be transferred to him."[146]

To sum up, in human salvation Jesus Christ takes our place, assuming
our demerits and giving us all his merits. For believers, God reckons the
unrighteousness of the ungodly to Christ's account and the righteousness
of Christ to the ungodly sinner's account.[147] By embracing Christ's merits in
faith, the soul is declared righteous, passes from death to life, and receives
an everlasting inheritance in the kingdom of heaven.

Christ's Kingly Office

The third office that plays a prominent role for Beddome is Christ's kingship.[148] This office is founded upon Christ's humiliation and sacrificial
death.[149] Once people have been reconciled to God through the atoning
work of Christ, the way is opened to acknowledge Christ as king:

> Is Christ a King? Yes. *There is another King, one Jesus* (Acts 17:7).
> Doth Christ execute the kingly office? Yes. *The government shall
> be upon his shoulder* (Isa 9:6). And is he duly qualified so to do?
> Yes. *He is the Lamb with seven horns and seven eyes* (Rev 5:6). Is
> he King as Mediator? Yes. *He hath authority to execute judgment,
> because he is the Son of Man* (John 5:27). And is his Mediatorial
> government founded upon the performance of his Mediatorial
> engagements? Yes. *Because he humbled himself and became obe-
> dient unto death, even the death of the cross, therefore God hath
> highly exalted him* (Phil 2:8–9).[150]

In Beddome's mind, Christ's triumph and rule as king is never considered
apart from His office as priest. He is entitled to the authority.

145. Beddome, *Twenty Short Discourses*, 4:19. See also Beddome, *Twenty Short
Discourses*, 3:74.

146. Beddome, *Twenty Short Discourses*, 3:74.

147. Beddome, *Twenty Short Discourses*, 3:74.

148. In comparison to Christ's priestly office, this topic is less frequently found in
his writings indicating that he puts more stress on Christ's priesthood.

149. Beddome, *Catechism*, 51.

150. Beddome, *Catechism*, 51.

Christ did not become a king only by virtue of his death and resurrection. He already possessed the kingly dignity by the nature which belongs to him as God.[151] In his divine nature the Son possesses dominion and majesty as an essential attribute of his Godhead. In this respect, the Father, Son, and Holy Spirit are coequal in wisdom, power, and glory. Their authority may be manifested more or less clearly, but it cannot be increased or diminished. This innate kingly authority of Christ is particularly manifested in the creation of the world. For Beddome, the work of the creation of the heaven and the earth, which reflects the kingly authority and power, is ascribed not only to God the Father but also to Christ the Son.[152]

Even though in Beddome's thought the kingly dignity is inherent to Christ from eternity, in reference to Christ, Beddome discusses his office as king primarily in terms of his mediatorial role. In this mediatorial context, Christ is King and sovereign Head over his Church and over all things concerned with his Church.[153] And he executes his office of king in a twofold manner.[154] First, Christ rules and guides the church through his Word and Spirit. Regarding the way Christ governs, Beddome specifically states as follows:

> Is Christ King over the Church? Yes. *Is not the Lord in Zion, is not he King in her* (Jer 8:19). Doth he enact laws there? Yes. *Teaching them to observe all things whatsoever I have commanded you* (Matt 28:20). Doth he commission officers? Yes. *He gave some apostles and some prophets* (Eph 4:11). And does he resent the introduction of anything without his authority? Yes. *In their setting their threshold by my threshold, and their post by my post, they have defiled my holy name* (Ezek 43:8).[155]

Moreover, as King and head of the Church, Christ cares for his people, provides goods that enable them to live, and maintains justice and righteousness:[156]

> Doth Christ as a King preserve his subjects? Yes. *We are preserved in Christ Jesus* (Jude 1:1). And protect them? Yes. *As birds flying so he defends Jerusalem* (Isa 31:5). And punish their faults? Yes. *Whom he loveth he chaseteneth* [sic] (Heb 12:6). And

---

151. Beddome, *Twenty Short Discourses*, 6:51; 7:114; *Sermons*, 119.

152. Beddome, *Catechism*, 20.

153. Beddome, *Catechism*, 52; Beddome, *Sermons*, 260.

154. Beddome, *Catechism*, 52.

155. Beddome, *Catechism*, 52.

156. Beddome, *Catechism*, 51.

reward their faithful services? Yes. *His reward is with him* (Rev 22:12).[157]

Second, in Beddome's mind, Christ protects and guards the Church against her enemies. Allowing them to stand unconquerable against all enemy assaults, the Heavenly King makes them victorious over the devil and every king of the world.[158] Beddome states the following:

> Doth Christ exercise his Kingly power in restraining his enemies? Yes. *I will put my hook in thy nose, and my bridle in thy lips* (Isa 37:29). And in subduing them? Yes. *He hath spoiled principalities and powers* (Col 2:15). And in destroying them? Yes. *He will break them with a rod of iron, and dash them in pieces like a potter's vessel* (Ps 2:9). Will the conquest of the saints' enemies be gradual? Yes. *I will drive them out by little and little* (Exod 23:30). But will it be total? Yes. *For he must reign till he hath put all enemies under his feet* (1 Cor 15:25).[159]

As shown in the above statement, Christ's kingly office is often depicted in terms of warfare and victory against the enemies. Beddome particularly associates this kingly victory motif directly with Christ's passion and exaltation. This kingly victory is founded upon Christ's decisive victory over the powers of evil and death which occurred in his death and resurrection.[160] Human beings were taken captive to Satan and enslaved by him. By his death and resurrection, Christ conquered the forces of evil and delivered his people from the power of Satan or their subjugation to him.[161] One of Beddome's hymns succinctly presents this truth in a couple of stanzas:

> No more can he [Satan] obtain his will,
> No more his dark designs fulfil;
> How great soe'er his strength may be,
> Yet Christ is stronger far than he.

> He breaks in twain his iron bands,
> And rescues captives from his hands;
> Treads him beneath their feeble feet,
> And makes their victory complete.[162]

157. Beddome, *Catechism*, 52.

158. Beddome, *Hymns*, #89, #91, #101.

159. Beddome, *Catechism*, 52–53.

160. Beddome, *Catechism*, 56; *Sermons*, 460.

161. Beddome, *Hymns*, #130; *Twenty Short Discourses*, 3:62, 68; 5:142.

162. Beddome, *Hymns*, #130.

From Beddome's point of view, Christ's death is conceived not only in terms of substitutionary satisfaction but also in terms of representative victory over the forces of evil and of death.[163] With regard to Christ's office and work, the former is far more frequently and substantially discussed in Beddome's writings. There is no doubt that the doctrine of vicarious satisfaction more fundamentally occupies Beddome's thought on the nature of Christ's mediatorial work.

For Beddome, Christ's kingly office refers to the supreme power and authority of the mediator whereby Christ inaugurated his kingdom, protects his Church against her enemies, and governs all things in heaven and on earth with full rights and authority. The incarnate Son who saves human beings is now the one who governs the church and will at last crown it victor in heaven forever and will deliver the final judgment to the world. Christ's reign and judgment are no threat but a source of hope and relief for the children of God, who now serve Christ as their King and Lord.[164]

The Significance of Christ's Threefold Office in Beddome's Theology

The foregoing discussion of Christ's threefold office reveals two implications regarding Beddome's doctrine of the work of Christ. First, the doctrine of the threefold office of Christ is basic to what Beddome wants to say about the mediatorship of Christ. Christ the Prophet mediated the truth and the gospel of God to fallen humanity; Christ the Priest mediated the holiness and forgiveness of God by his vicarious sacrifice, and Christ the King mediated the sovereignty of God by conquering evil and death through his death and resurrection. Christ's threefold office of prophet, priest and king form the framework of the essential soteriological structure of Beddome's Christology, and for that reason, neither the prophetic nor the high-priestly nor the kingly office can be disregarded or ignored in the mediatorial work of Christ.[165]

The fundamental significance of Christ's atoning work through his threefold office, however, does not mean that Beddome stresses only the second person of the Trinity to the exclusion of the others. Beddome also understands the idea of Christ's mediatorial work in the context of the

163. In this regard, Beddome's view of the kingly office shows a close affinity with the "classic" Christus victor theory. Concerning the Christus victor model of atonement, see Aulén, *Christus Victor*; van Asselt, "Christ's Atonement," 55–57.

164. Beddome, *Twenty Short Discourses*, 7:163; *Sermons*, 40, 124. Cf. Beddome, *Twenty Short Discourses*, 5:142; 6:57.

165. Beddome, *Sermons*, 285.

Trinity. In several passages of his writings, while Christ the Son is depicted as the accomplisher of what should be done, God the Father is portrayed as the source and initiator of this atoning work and the Holy Spirit as the one who makes Christ's accomplishment available and effective in the faithful.[166] Even though Beddome does not amply discuss Christ's atoning work from a Trinitarian perspective in his writings, it is certain that for him, the work of human salvation is not just the work of Christ but also the work of the Father and the Spirit.[167]

Second, Beddome's use of threefold office in the mediatorship of Christ indicates that Beddome's Christology was formed under the influence of Reformed or Puritan theology. Traditionally, the Reformed thinkers discussed Christ's ministry primarily as that of the mediator, and when it comes to unfolding the content of mediation, they employed the idea of the threefold office in Christ's mediatorship.[168] For example, Calvin comments, "Therefore, in order that faith may find a firm basis for salvation in Christ, and thus rest in him, this principle must be laid down: the office enjoined upon Christ by the Father consists of three parts. For he was given to be prophet, king, and priest."[169] Turretin also argues, "This mediatorial office of Christ is distributed into three functions, which are so many parts of it: prophetic, priestly and kingly."[170] Other eighteenth-century British Particular Baptists also employed the threefold office of Christ in order to explain the

166. See, for example, Beddome, *Twenty Short Discourses*, 1:49; 2:2.

167. Cf. Even though it is briefly stated, the idea of Reformed federalism, *pactum salutis*, which "refers to the pretemporal, intratrinitarian agreement of the Father and the Son concerning the covenant of grace and its ratification in and through the work of the Son incarnate" is seen in his *Catechism*. Muller, *Dictionary*, 217. Beddome states, "Doth God execute all special grace through Christ? Yes. *We are blessed with all spiritual blessings in Christ* (Eph 1:3). Were there mutual engagements for this purpose between the Father and Son? Yes. *The counsel of peace shall be between them both* (Zech 6:13). Were all the promises of the covenant primarily made to Christ? Yes. *Hence they are called the sure mercies of David* (Isa 55:3). Were all the conditions of it exacted from him? Yes. *The Lord that laid on him the iniquity of us all* (Isa 53:6). Did Christ freely undertake the work of our redemption? Yes. *Lo I come to do thy will, O God* (Heb 10:7). And did the Father engage for the success of his undertaking? Yes. *He shall see the travail of his soul and be satisfied* (Isa 53:11)" (Beddome, *Catechism*, 41). For a good discussion of the idea of *pactum salutis* in Reformed tradition, see Loonstra, *Verkiezing-Verzoening-Verbond*; Muller, "Toward the *Pactum Salutis*," 11–65; "Spirit and the Covenant," 4–14.

168. Cf. Heppe, *Reformed Dogmatics*, 452–87; Muller, *Dictionary*, 197–98; Hodge, *Systematic Theology*, 2:459–609.

169. Calvin, *Institutes of the Christian Religion*, 494.

170. Turretin, *Institutes*, 392. According to Turretin, the three aspects are in structural unity. In the aspect of prophecy the aspects of both priesthood and kingship are also present. They are mutually reflected in one another. Turretin, *Institutes*, 392. Cf. Ott, *Die Antwort des Glaubens*, 274, 303–12.

work of Christ. For instance, in Gill's thought, the triple office gives structure to the doctrine of the work of Christ as mediator:

> His office in general is that of Mediator, which is but one; the branches of it are threefold, his prophetic, priestly, and kingly offices; all which are included in his name, Messiah, or Christ, the anointed; prophets, priests, and kings, being anointed, when invested with their several offices; as Elisha the prophet, by Elijah; Aaron the priest, and his sons, by Moses; Saul, David, and Solomon, kings of Israel.[171]

In this way, numerous Reformed theologians, including eighteenth-century British Particular Baptists, typically employed the concept of Christ's threefold office to expound the nature of Christ's mediatorship. Beddome's discussion of the threefold office of Christ also reflects this traditional category and theme developed by Calvin, his associates and the immediate successors of the Reformed tradition. In line with Reformed theology, Beddome's Christology distinguished itself from other theological traditions regarding the view of Christ's mediatorship.

Concluding Remarks

The examination of Beddome's discussion of Christ's person and work permits us to present a few conclusions regarding his Christology. First, following the Chalcedonian formula, Beddome affirms both the full deity of Christ and the true and complete humanity of Christ. Also, insisting on Christ's single personality, Beddome sides with Nicene and Chalcedonian orthodoxy regarding his person. Second, in line with the classic Reformed tradition, Christ's threefold role of king, priest, and prophet is central to Beddome's understanding of Christ's mediatorship, and in his explanation of Christ's mediatorship, vicarious satisfaction is the most prominent motif or image of Christ's atoning work. For Beddome, in order to satisfy divine justice and law, Christ suffered the penal consequences such as the death, punishment and curse which our sins deserved.

Considering all these conclusions, one can easily find that, evaluated in the broader context of intellectual history, Beddome's view of Christ's person and work is not unique or distinct at all. The analysis of Beddome's Christology indicates two significant implications. First, in spite of the theological turmoil in eighteenth-century England, Beddome faithfully defended classic orthodox Christology, especially classic Reformed Christology.

171. Gill, *Complete Body*, 866.

Considering the intellectually chaotic state of eighteenth-century England, this would not be a just minor contribution and would have especially impacted the stabilization and growth of the Particular Baptist churches in Beddome's time. Second, as with other subjects such as the law and the gospel, Beddome's doctrine of Christ's person and work clearly shows how the Particular Baptists maintained and developed their theological ideas and thoughts in eighteenth-century England. In particular, Beddome's doctrine of Christ serves as one evident example of how the eighteenth-century British Particular Baptists embraced and elaborated the confessionally formulated Christology of previous centuries.

4

The Pneumatology of Benjamin Beddome

Daniel S. Ramsey

Benjamin Beddome's insatiable hunger for the blessings and power of the Spirit can be traced to the outset of his ministry at Bourton-on-the-Water, a village not far from the city of Bristol, where revival fires had broken forth five years earlier under the ministry of George Whitefield (1714–1770). In early 1741, Beddome too experienced a powerful awakening in Bourton, in which forty people came to faith in Christ. This event greatly shaped his theology, as his sermons and hymns were ever after replete with references to the Holy Spirit and continuous appeals for his renewing power. The pneumatology of most seventeenth-century Reformed confessions consisted of two principal areas: the ontology of the Holy Spirit, as well as pneumatology proper, which dealt with specific ministries of the Spirit. With regard to the latter, Particular Baptist pneumatology in Benjamin Beddome's day discussed the work of the Spirit under four categories. First, there was the Spirit's role in creation. Second, there were the Spirit's works pertaining to Christ's ministries. These included the incarnation, Christ's earthly ministry and miracles, as well as his crucifixion and resurrection. This also embodied Christ's current heavenly ministry as prophet, priest, and king. Third, much attention was given to the soteriological works of the Spirit pertaining to redemption. This included regeneration, the effectual call, the union with Christ, adoption, justification, sanctification, and perseverance. Finally, there were the Spirit's intercessory ministries among believers, such as the various means of grace, prayer, and the Spirit's role in the inspiration and illumination of the Scriptures.

The Word and the Spirit

Fully embracing the principal emphases of other Reformed confessions of his day, Beddome followed in the footsteps of earlier Baptists, who framed the *Second London Confession of Faith* (1677), and who, like John Calvin, "were careful not to separate the Spirit from the Word."[1] In what follows, Beddome's understanding of the role of the Spirit in the inspiration, illumination, discernment, and preaching of revealed truth, along with a love for Christ, is delineated.

Inspiration

Beddome held to a form of verbal-plenary inspiration in which he argued that "the Holy Scripture [was] delivered by the Spirit."[2] He clearly articulated the dual nature of biblical inspiration, noting that the human writers of Scripture were first "moved to speak what they did by the Holy Spirit," so that their very words expressed divine truth. God was pleased, therefore, to "own what men have thus written as his."[3] Although Beddome believed that the Bible is the primary source for inspired truth, he did not limit inspiration to the writings of the Scripture alone. He conceded that on very rare occasions the Spirit may choose to directly reveal truth apart from Scripture, as he did with the Apostle Paul.[4]

Illumination

God's existence can be innately perceived through his creation and "works of providence," but man is unable to decipher that evidence without the direct intervention of the Spirit. Even the special revelation of Scripture would be insufficient without the spiritual regeneration and illumination that is exclusively and graciously provided by the Holy Spirit.[5] Indeed, his role of enlightenment and personal application of the knowledge of God is essential, as the Scriptures are read, meditated upon, or verbally taught.[6] Even a true believer will struggle to grasp and apply the most basic principles of

---

1. Nuttall, *Holy Spirit in Puritan Faith*, 24.
2. Lumpkin, "Second London Confession," 252.
3. Beddome, *Scriptural Exposition*, 10.
4. Beddome, *Twenty Short Discourses*, 6:133.
5. Beddome, *Scriptural Exposition*, 9.
6. Beddome, *Scriptural Exposition*, 9.

Scripture without his assistance. Beddome lamented this natural handicap of the believer, but he was persuaded that the Spirit will not forsake any believer who asks for his assistance.[7]

Discernment

Beddome's works provide few direct references to the doctrine of inspiration, yet his precision in those instances reveals not only a depth of conviction, but an apparent belief in its self-evident nature, which required little or no defense. It was the "wisdom which is from above" and a gift from "the father of lights, in whom there is no variablness, nor shadow of turning." Thus, far more attention was given to the role of the Spirit in illuminating revealed truth to the believer.[8] The natural man is able to recognize and even differentiate between spiritual concepts, but he can neither understand them in depth, nor practically apply them, without the direct aid of the Holy Spirit.[9]

The Spirit not only enlightens the believer's understanding as he or she reads the Scriptures, but also opens the mind to incomprehensible truths, provides necessary wisdom and discernment, enhances one's love for Christ, and offers protection against the mental warfare of the enemy. Due to the prevailing effects of the fall, many things pertaining to God cannot be grasped by the human mind.[10] Not surprisingly, the Spirit's ministry in providing discernment was prevalent in many of Beddome's sermons and hymns.[11]

Gaining spiritual wisdom, which Beddome described as being in "the school of Christ," represents a gradual process akin to progressive sanctification. As such, the Spirit leads the believer to discover, understand, and apply the blessed truths that are hidden to the natural mind.[12] Human wisdom is primarily gained through learning or life experience, whereas spiritual wisdom must necessarily be "infused" by the Spirit. Such wisdom, as Beddome described it, is the "offspring of deity,"[13] and is both inward and experiential.[14] In God's economy, the comprehension of divine truth leads to

7. Beddome, *Scriptural Exposition*, 9.

8. Beddome, *Sermons*, 105.

9. Beddome, *Sermons*, 121.

10. Beddome, *Scriptural Exposition*, 8.

11. Beddome, *Hymns*, #715. See also *Hymns*, #135–36.

12. Beddome, *Sermons*, 3–4.

13. Beddome, *Sermons*, 92.

14. Beddome, *Scriptural Exposition*, 66.

action, worship, and transformation of character. Thus, the ministry of the Holy Spirit is absolutely essential, not only for spiritual enlightenment, but to stimulate the child of God to effectual action, which, in turn, produces godly fruit.[15]

The cooperative relationship between the Scriptures and the Holy Spirit is indispensable, as each plays a complementary role in the believer's spiritual growth. Although the Word of God leads mankind to salvation, its divine truth cannot be grasped by the natural man and remains clouded to the believer, without divine intervention. Beddome likened the Word of God to a rod that can be used as a tool. A rod was useless without a hand to employ it. Similarly, the Word had little efficacy without the assistance of the Holy Spirit.[16]

Preaching

Beddome defended the practice of preaching, which the Spirit uses to communicate the truth of Scripture.[17] He believed it to be the responsibility of the clergy, as well as people of all ages to make reading a priority, which he understood to include both the private and public reading of the Scriptures.[18]

The "divine testimony" or preaching was "the means of producing faith." It was "the incorruptible seed, which being sown in the heart, is quickened by the Holy Spirit and brings forth fruit unto eternal life."[19] Preaching is far more than a religious exercise. Beddome believed that the word, read aloud or preached, unleashed a divine power that was both active and effectual, enlivening the soul. It was "not the word without the Spirit, but the Spirit by the word; the one as the instrument, the other as the agent. Hence they are joined together."[20] This accounted for the life-giving nature of certain sermons, due to the obvious influence of the Spirit. In such cases, the Spirit works simultaneously in the preacher and in the hearer.[21] Conversely, well-crafted and skillfully-delivered messages may be able to stir the external senses, but without the Spirit, they will have little or no effect on the soul.

15. Beddome, *Twenty Short Discourses*, 4:62.

16. Beddome, *Scriptural Exposition*, 9.

17. Beddome, *Scriptural Exposition*, 32.

18. Beddome, *Scriptural Exposition*, 32.

19. Beddome, *Twenty Short Discourses*, 5:109.

20. Beddome, *Twenty Short Discourses*, 2:4–5.

21. Beddome, *Sermons*, 308.

By virtue of the unique character of God's truth revealed through the Scriptures, the essence of preaching is to communicate the word with power and authority.[22] This is the substance of being a good steward of the Gospel.[23] Due to the authority and divine character of the message itself, the one called to communicate it must necessarily exhibit a godly character commensurate with his message. For this reason, it is not man, but the Holy Spirit, who ultimately commissions the messenger. Beddome reiterated that a commission apart from the leading of the Spirit is "good for nothing."[24] He believed "it is a great mercy for any, especially ministers of the gospel, to act under the influence and direction of the Spirit of God."[25]

Love for Christ

The special teaching of the Spirit is instrumental in kindling the believer's love for Christ, which is foundational to the spiritual well-being of the child of God. Sadly, the natural man is inclined to self-love and is unable to fully appreciate the depth and the intricate nature of God's sovereign intervention and providential care. Such knowledge alone, when finally grasped, stimulates love for the Creator. Such love, generated by the Holy Spirit, becomes the driving force that propels the believer to accomplish great things for the Savior.[26] At the same time, the Spirit stimulates his or her longing to live eternally in the presence of the one who first loved and epitomized this love on the cross.

The Holy Spirit in Creation

Little is mentioned in Beddome's writings concerning the role of the Holy Spirit in creation, but it is apparent from *A Scriptural Exposition* that he credited the Holy Spirit with a pivotal role in both the first or old creation, as well as in the new creation, which occurs through regeneration. Adam, and subsequently all mankind, were created in the image of God in the first creation, but many would later become a new creation "in righteousness and true holiness" through the Holy Spirit (Eph 4:24).[27]

22. Beddome, *Twenty Short Discourses*, 1:124.

23. Beddome, *Sermons*, 360.

24. Beddome, *Sermons*, 307.

25. Beddome, *Sermons*, 116.

26. Beddome, *Sermons*, 20.

27. Beddome, *Scriptural Exposition*, 29.

The Holy Spirit in the Old Testament

Beddome made two explicit references to the work of the Spirit in the Old Testament in his writings. One concerned Moses's tragic confrontation in Numbers 20 with the people of Israel at Meribah. Highlighting Moses's offense, Beddome applied the words of Psalm 106:33, which explicitly states that the people of Israel "provoked his Spirit."[28] In Beddome's Trinitarian understanding, Moses's sin against the Lord, as referenced in Psalm 106, was grievous and offensive to the Spirit of Jehovah God.

A second Old Testament reference to the Spirit's work appears in Beddome's sermon "The Aged Sinner." In explaining the long lives of men on the antediluvian earth as compared to the much shorter life spans since the Genesis flood, Beddome referenced the Spirit in Genesis 6:3 as "the wisdom of God," who was responsible for prolonging the days of man."[29] Thus, the striving of God to preserve a semblance of godliness and longevity of life in man sheds great light on the unfathomable loving kindness, patience, and sanctifying work of the Holy Spirit.

The Holy Spirit and Christ's Ministry

Like Puritan divines before him, Beddome dedicated a significant portion of his writings to the role of the Holy Spirit in the ministry of Christ. Consequently, he was careful to include a thorough and insightful presentation of the three offices of Christ as Prophet, Priest, and King, in which, even today, the Holy Spirit continues to play a pivotal and vital role.

The Holy Spirit in the Virgin Birth

Beddome affirmed that Christ did not "come into the world in an ordinary way." Instead, he believed it to be a miraculous conception brought about by the direct intervention of the Holy Spirit, without the aid of Joseph or any other human father.[30] Looming large in this and in other expositions by Beddome on the Virgin Birth was the unmitigated influence and overshadowing of the Holy Spirit. While this miraculous event primarily concerns the incarnation of Christ and his means of entry into the world as the

28. Beddome, *Scriptural Exposition*, 141.
29. Beddome, *Twenty Short Discourses*, 2:102.
30. Beddome, *Scriptural Exposition*, 46.

Saviour, the Holy Spirit is no mere ancillary force, but the very source and origin of the God-Man, who was conceived and born to the Virgin Mary.[31]

The Holy Spirit and the Baptism of Christ

Christ's ability to carry out his earthly ministry and offices, as well as the Father's approval of him as a choice servant, was inseparably related to the empowerment accorded to him when the Spirit descended at his baptism. This is evident in Matthew 3:17, where the heavenly voice unequivocally states, "This is my beloved Son in whom I am well pleased." This, according to Beddome, was the very moment when the Father "put the finishing hand" to Christ's "appointed work" as High Priest, which Jesus confidently referenced in his High Priestly Prayer, declaring, "I have finished the work that thou gavest me to do" (John 17:4).[32]

The Holy Spirit in Christ's Earthly Ministry

The wellspring of the strength and holiness displayed by Christ throughout his earthly ministry was none other than the Holy Spirit.[33] His resolve and staying power to resist temptation and to perseveringly accomplish his redemptive mission was also the direct result of the Spirit's ministry in his life.[34] This profound truth has practical implications for believers, since they also receive an anointing of the Holy Spirit to empower and equip them for service. Beddome held that the believer's anointing resembled Christ's anointing, for "the Spirit of God and of glory rests upon them, as it did upon him."[35]

Since the Spirit's anointing is common to both, Beddome saws a direct correlation between Christ's earthy life and the way believers are to live theirs. A prescribed pattern of living by the power of the Holy Spirit emerges, which is intended to lead God's children to a holy and abundant life. The necessary source of all true spirituality in the believer is the anointing and subsequent enablement afforded by the Holy Spirit. It is through him alone, not through human effort, that the child of God is capable of living a godly

---

31. Beddome, *Twenty Short Discourses*, 4:18.
32. Beddome, *Scriptural Exposition*, 47.
33. Beddome, *Sermons*, 70.
34. Beddome, *Twenty Short Discourses*, 3:67.
35. Beddome, *Sermons*, 84.

and fruitful life. This power, modeled by Christ, is most efficacious when coupled with the believer's love and submission to the Father.[36]

The Spirit in the Crucifixion and Resurrection

Without the mediation of the Holy Spirit, Christ's offering on the cross would "otherwise have been ineffectual."[37] Beddome praised the Spirit's ministry in the crucifixion, whose power enabled Jesus's human nature to obey and persevere.[38] The Holy Spirit was also the quickening agent in Christ's resurrection. Beddome affirmed that Christ truly rose "by his own power,"[39] yet, he believed that it was "the same Spirit that revived and quickened him [Christ]" and became "the pattern and the pledge of the resurrection of all the saints, manifesting both its nature and its certainty."[40]

In what may at first seem contradictory, Beddome distinguished between the Holy Spirit's work of quickening, or bringing Christ back to life, and the physical act of the resurrection itself, which Christ performed as promised. This same dynamic prevails in Beddome's understanding of the effectual call to salvation, where the Holy Spirit first quickens the natural man, who was once dead in his trespasses and sins, and then enables him to believe by imparting the gift of faith, after which he himself desires and personally chooses to follow Christ.

The Holy Spirit and Christ's Prophetic Office

While Christ, as the Prophet, "reveals the will of God objectively by his word," Beddome saw the Holy Spirit working in conjunction with him, revealing and applying the subjective aspects of the Scriptures to the human heart which are essential for salvation.[41] The prophetic office, exercised by Christ during his earthly ministry, continues to this very day, and is fully dependent upon the cooperative work of the Spirit.[42]

36. Beddome, *Sermons*, 85.
37. Beddome, *Scriptural Exposition*, 47.
38. Beddome, *Twenty Short Discourses*, 8:125.
39. Beddome, *Scriptural Exposition*, 59.
40. Beddome, *Twenty Short Discourses*, 4:9.
41. Beddome, *Scriptural Exposition*, 50.
42. Beddome, *Sermons*, 11–12.

The Holy Spirit and Redemption

The vast number of references to the ministry of the Holy Spirit in Beddome's writings center on soteriology, and, in particular, the interrelated doctrines associated with redemption and sanctification. Beddome's emphases naturally aligned with those of John Owen, Matthew Henry, and other earlier divines of the Reformed tradition, yet taken together, they also reflect the specific theology of an eighteenth-century evangelical, with great attention being given to manifestations that were particularly evident in his day, such as "revival, widespread individual conversions, and the outpouring of the Holy Spirit."[43]

The Effectual Call

Beddome was careful to differentiate between the effectual call, which always results in salvation, and the "outward" or general call, which will tragically but inevitably fall on deaf ears unless the Spirit intervenes. The outward call is "given to all men" through God's "works of creation, works of providence, and by his word," which Beddome referred to as the "common motions of the Spirit."[44] However, due to the hardness of men's hearts, this call will ultimately be rejected unless the Spirit effectually intervenes. It is a graphic picture of the desperate spiritual condition of mankind.[45] Even though it will inevitably be rejected by those who remain spiritually dead, the general call of the Spirit is never altogether without effect, as it most certainly accomplishes other purposes of God apart from salvation, which often result in various convictions and impressions on the minds.[46]

According to Beddome, "the motions of the Spirit" in the effectual call are twofold. First, the Spirit brings about spiritual life so that he who was once spiritually dead is able to hear and respond to the gracious call.[47] This happens without overpowering the will of an individual and it takes place in such a manner that the person will readily and happily respond. The Spirit forces no one to respond, but makes the gospel so attractive in the now spiritually awakened person that he or she unquestionably responds to the call.[48]

43. Kidd, *Great Awakening*, xix.

44. Beddome, *Scriptural Exposition*, 64.

45. Beddome, *Sermons*, 106–7.

46. Beddome, *Twenty Short Discourses*, 2:43.

47. Beddome, *Twenty Short Discourses*, 2:49–50.

48. Beddome, *Twenty Short Discourses*, 1:12.

Not only does the Spirit awaken and spiritually renew the sinner in the context of the effectual call, but also imparts the ability to produce lasting spiritual fruit unto salvation.[49] Through the Spirit's indwelling, the believer becomes the actual dwelling place or temple of the Holy Spirit. Thus, the effectual call is intimately connected to the doctrine of election, in which God, being "no respecter of persons," chooses "a certain number of the fallen race of mankind to grace here and glory hereafter, to holiness in this world, and happiness in the next."[50]

Quickening or Spiritual Regeneration

One of the doctrines most frequently mentioned in Beddome's writings was the quickening of the Spirit. It not only accounts for the initial miracle of re-generation, but includes the on-going spiritual refreshment of the redeemed as well. The latter applies to the Spirit's work of progressive sanctification, which begins after the moment of salvation, while the former is directly related to the salvation experience itself. Since regenerative quickening was intimately tied to other works of the Spirit that occur near the outset of the redemptive process, Beddome defined regeneration as "an instantaneous change" which differs from the Spirit's progressive work of sanctification.[51]

The "great and effectual work" of redemption is "wrought only upon the elect" by the Holy Spirit, who "quickens" the elect (John 6:63), and ef-fectually makes them to be partakers of the redemption through belief in the Son of God (John 3:36).[52] He differentiated between the first birth into this natural world and the second or new birth generated by the Holy Spirit at the moment of regeneration.[53] Although Scripture explicitly states that it is the Spirit who "quickeneth," Beddome rightly gave each person in the Trinity his due. However, he was also not demure in highlighting the pre-dominant role of the Spirit as he moves sovereignly among men and works in whomever He desires.[54]

For Beddome, regeneration was to "be born of God, and changed by his grace into a child-like disposition, before we can be followers of Christ." The internal operation of the Spirit is "absolutely necessary to qualify us

49. Beddome, *Sermons*, 115.
50. Beddome, *Sermons*, 24.
51. Beddome, *Twenty Short Discourses*, 3:35.
52. Beddome, *Scriptural Exposition*, 62.
53. Beddome, *Twenty Short Discourses*, 4:20.
54. Beddome, *Twenty Short Discourses*, 2:2.

for, and excite us to, this and every other good work."[55] Spiritual quickening always brings a pronounced change of values. Interests and impressions change as well. Holiness becomes desirable, while sin grows increasingly abhorrent.[56]

The Gift of Faith

The act of faith at salvation represents a person's grateful response to God's antecedent gift of the Spirit, who not only renews and quickens, but also acts as the ultimate source of a person's faith. Beddome considered faith to be a benefit of the Spirit, which set the elect of God apart from all others.[57] The Christian faith is inherently different from other religions, for it goes beyond mere "show and appearance," and "lies inward and deep, and is that circumcision, not of the flesh, but of the Spirit."[58] The "ornament of true religion" is the "fear of the Lord," which is wrought in the soul by the Holy Spirit, and consists in a reverential regard for divine authority and glory.[59]

According to Beddome, this faith was bestowed as a gift and is not something that can be earned or merited.[60] He also had much to say about the true essence of faith and, in particular, the role of the Holy Spirit in its application. Left to their own devices, natural men experience distress, but by the teachings of the Spirit, they are brought to Christ, where they find "pardon, peace, righteousness, strength, joy, comfort, grace, and glory."[61]

The nature of the gift is immediately evident, as the benefits and the inner peace that accompany it are overwhelmingly attractive and irresistible so that they are heartily embraced and received. Beddome believed that faith is the result of having new spiritual eyes, a new awareness, and a radically different mindset.[62] Confronted with one's emptiness and utter sinfulness, the need of a Savior becomes overwhelming and the response is inexorable. Since faith is the gift and the work of the Holy Spirit, it will naturally lead to the believer's perseverance and assurance. This is not because of one's own efforts or tenacity, but because of an irreversible work within the heart and a divine transformation of the mind. Beddome distinguishes between pseudo

55. Beddome, *Sermons*, 144.

56. Beddome, *Sermons*, 75.

57. Beddome, *Scriptural Exposition*, 147–48.

58. Beddome, *Sermons*, 248.

59. Beddome, *Twenty Short Discourses*, 8:63.

60. Beddome, *Twenty Short Discourses*, 5:103.

61. Beddome, *Sermons*, 277–78.

62. Beddome, *Sermons*, 112.

and genuine disciples. The former "leave Christ, for they have received the gospel only in letter of it," but the latter remain firmly in the faith because "they have received the truth in love, and felt its efficacy upon their hearts," impressed upon them by the Holy Spirit.[63]

Conviction of Sin

Coupled with the effectual calling is a new sense and conviction of one's own sinfulness. Beddome believed this awareness was directly attributable to the Holy Spirit, which occurs in close conjunction with the effectual call and initial regeneration, but he did not delineate the order in which these acts of the Spirit occur. Those who are effectually called become convicted of gross sins, as well as the secret sins of the heart, and gratefully receive God's grace.[64] This conviction, according to Beddome, is the result of the Spirit's work on the human conscience.[65] No longer clouded by sin, the awakened sinner sees sin from God's perspective, sees the gravity and depth of his or her transgressions, and realizes the overwhelming need of a Savior. The reaction leads to self-loathing and remorse, which not only causes people to hate sin itself, but to hate most the sin they see in themselves.[66]

Overwhelmed by his or her own wretchedness, the awakened sinner sees that God's wrath and judgment is deserved, and consequently seeks God's mercy and compassion. According to Beddome, the Spirit begins his work by revealing sin, which in turn, leads to self-loathing. However, the Spirit's purpose at this point is not to bring the believer to despair, but to lead him or her to repentance and to begin the gradual process of sanctification.[67]

Repentance

Beddome considered "true repentance unto life" to be "a grace," with "the word as an instrument" and the Holy Spirit as "an agent," both working together to lead the sinner to salvation.[68] The essence of true repentance in the new believer is twofold. First, the sinner turns away from his or her

63. Beddome, *Twenty Short Discourses*, 2:94.

64. Beddome, *Scriptural Exposition*, 65.

65. Beddome, *Twenty Short Discourses*, 1:34.

66. Beddome, *Twenty Short Discourses*, 1:107.

67. Beddome, *Twenty Short Discourses*, 1:107.

68. Beddome, *Scriptural Exposition*, 149–50.

sin, which has suddenly become both abhorrent and unbearable. This is followed by the firm resolve to abandon its practice for good. Just as it is important to turn away from one's past sins, it is also imperative for the sinner to consciously turn back to God, yet, not out of coercion, but out of a love for Christ.[69]

While repentance is most often viewed as a purely human response to the gracious working of the Holy Spirit, Beddome suggested that the act of turning to God is completely impossible in one's own power, since the desire, as well as the subsequent enablement, is the work of the same Spirit. He cited Jeremiah 31:19, where the prophet was first moved by the hand of God, but then enabled by the Spirit to both repent and receive further instruction unto righteousness.[70] This, according to Beddome, was the general pattern of the Spirit's work in the believer today.

Union with Christ

Beddome believed that the effectual calling and the gift of faith were intimately related to the believer's union with Christ through the Holy Spirit. While the union officially begins at the moment of the effectual call and the gift of faith, he believed it had been a fact in God's eternal plan, long before the Spirit's call.[71] This theological view was made popular by seventeenth-century Puritan theologians, who suggested that the salvation of the elect, and in this case their union with Christ, was first "rooted in the eternal unchangeable decree of God," and then gradually unfolded in three stages, or the "imminent, transient, and applicatory works of God."[72]

Peter Bulkeley sheds greater light on the exact nature of these stages in Puritan theology in the work of justification, noting that it was first "purposed and determined in the mind and will of God," then "impetrated and obtained for us by the obedience of Christ," and finally "applyed [*sic*] unto us."[73] While Bulkeley tacitly accepted a threefold implementation of justification, he appears to reject any notion that anyone can actually be justified prior to the act of faith. This was Beddome's perspective as well. He referred to the "imminent" stage of the believer's eventual union with Christ, while at the same time accepting the notion that it had already been

69. Beddome, *Scriptural Exposition*, 152.

70. Beddome, *Scriptural Exposition*, 152.

71. Beddome, *Scriptural Exposition*, 63.

72. Beeke and Jones, "Puritans on Union with Christ," 482.

73. Bulkeley, *Gospel-Covenant*, 358.

firmly established in the mind of God long before its actual application in redemptive history.

Justification

Since justification is considered a benefit of the Spirit's effectual working, Beddome also understood it to be a work of the Spirit. While it is Christological in nature, being directly accomplished by Christ on the cross, its application is only possible through the agency of the Holy Spirit. While it was Christ's blood that actually washed away the stain of sin and made possible the sanctifying transformation of the believer into His image, his atoning work would be unavailing without the Holy Spirit.[74]

Reconciliation

Few references exist in Beddome's writings concerning the Holy Spirit in reconciliation, but he did provide an excellent summary of his views in a sermon entitled "Reconciliation with God." Drawing again upon the Puritan concept of the imminent, transient, and applicatory stages in God's salvific enterprise, he asserted that "the ground-work of our reconciliation was laid in the eternal counsels of God," yet was first "brought about in time by the effectual operation of the divine Spirit."[75] The Holy Spirit acts as the agent, applying the benefits of the cross of Christ to the pardoned sinner, which, in turn, leads to reconciliation and divine satisfaction.[76] Thus, the Spirit both initiates this divine work of grace and then works to transform the believer's thinking and behavior to be more and more like Christ.

Adoption

For Beddome, adoption represented a two-fold ministry of the Spirit.[77] While Christ is the mediator of the believer's adoption, it is the Spirit who actually applies it, causing the believer to receive the "Spirit of sons" (Galatians 4:6) and partake of the divine nature. It is also the Spirit's indwelling presence that lends credence to the believer's adopted status and future inheritance. Beddome believes that the indwelling of the Spirit is the first step

74. Beddome, *Hymns*, #825.
75. Beddome, *Twenty Short Discourses*, 1:119.
76. Beddome, "Reconciliation with God," 119.
77. Beddome, *Scriptural Exposition*, 71.

of an adoption that had already been established from eternity, yet, after much hardship and anticipation, will someday be reality and the source of the believer's joy at the resurrection and the final redemption of God's creation.[78]

Perseverance

The perseverance of the saints is yet another benefit that is directly related to justification, adoption, and sanctification. The "Spirit of sons," imparted to the believer in the work of adoption, is at the same time the "earnest" or down payment that guarantees that the redemptive transaction will surely be paid in full. The Spirit's presence is sufficient to keep true believers "from fundamental errors" and "retain the vital principle of grace implanted in their souls."[79] He also offers comfort and assurance as he bears "witness with our spirits that we are the children of God" (Rom 8:16).[80]

Sanctification

Similar to the regenerative quickening of the Spirit, which gives life to the spiritually dead, his ministry of sanctification is initially necessitated by the raw condition of the natural man at the moment of faith and his need for spiritual transformation, both at the moment of faith and throughout his entire life.[81] Living without the Spirit leaves the natural man in a desperate condition. Hence, the gift of the Holy Spirit is bestowed in order to make sinful and desperate men holy and restore the lost image of God to them.[82] The Holy Spirit, as the agent of sanctification, first sets apart the believer positionally, then continues the on-going process incrementally, and finally completes the life-long work of transforming the believer into the very image of Christ.[83]

Like other Reformed theologians of his day, Beddome believed that the transformation wrought by the Holy Spirit was best accomplished in conjunction with the word of God. While the Scriptures are to function as "a mirror in which we behold our own deformity and the glory of the

78. Beddome, *Twenty Short Discourses*, 7:31.

79. Beddome, *Scriptural Exposition*, 77.

80. Beddome, *Sermons*, 133.

81. Beddome, *Twenty Short Discourses*, 4:65–66.

82. Beddome, *Twenty Short Discourses*, 3:83.

83. Beddome, *Scriptural Exposition*, 66.

Saviour," it is "by the Spirit of the Lord that we are changed into his image and likeness."[84] Out of this grows a Christ-likeness or holiness, produced by the effectual grace and agency of the Spirit.[85] This divine work is not instantaneous, like justification or adoption, but is gradual in nature.[86] For Beddome, it represented a type of cleansing that enabled the believer to walk with God. It is with a new heart, with transformed motives, and a growing desire to please God, that the believer is enabled to work along with the Spirit to grow in godliness and bring glory to God.

Beddome expected the believer's growth in holiness to be directly proportional to the depth of his or her knowledge of Christ.[87] Conversely, the Christian's growth in godliness would incrementally heighten his or her abhorrence of sin, in preparation for eternal life in God's holy presence.[88] The soul of the believer is humbled by the remembrance of the wicked ways of the past, and is resolved to turn away from them, thereby gradually growing day-by-day in holiness. This twofold work of sanctification, once begun, will be "carried on to perfection, so that those who have begun in the Spirit, shall not end in the flesh, but will hold their way, waxing stronger and stronger."[89] Beddome expressed both the conviction and the expectation, that sanctification is not only significant, but is absolutely indispensable for the Christian's growth, development, and relationships, as well as his or her **ultimate transformation into the image of Christ.**[90]

The Holy Spirit and the Believer

The Baptism/Indwelling of the Spirit

Benjamin Beddome's *A Scriptural Exposition*, along with his many sermons and hymns, were replete with references to the work of the Spirit in the believer, a grace made possible by Spirit baptism and his indwelling at the moment of belief. Beddome did not differentiate between Spirit baptism and his indwelling, although it is clear that he at least recognized both. In fact, he appeared to see Spirit baptism, the Spirit's indwelling, and the filling of the Spirit as separate motions of the same work of grace. Spirit baptism is

84. Beddome, *Twenty Short Discourses*, 5:109.

85. Beddome, *Twenty Short Discourses*, 4:152.

86. Beddome, *Sermons*, 130.

87. Beddome, *Twenty Short Discourses*, 4:154.

88. Beddome, *Sermons*, 27.

89. Beddome, *Twenty Short Discourses*, 4:155.

90. Beddome, *Twenty Short Discourses*, 4:62

the initiatory act, introducing the Spirit into the believer's life and establishing his or her union with Christ, being henceforth "in Christ." The Spirit's indwelling remains a constant throughout life, while the Spirit's filling can vary quantitatively according to the spiritual condition of the believer at any given time.

That the Holy Spirit has taken up permanent spiritual residence in the believer is evidenced by the biblical metaphor of the believer's body being his temple.[91] The Spirit's indwelling in this life is also indicative of a permanent future condition. Beddome was convinced that "the saints who in this world partake of the Spirit of Christ, shall also partake of his glory in the next."[92]

The Graces of the Spirit

When speaking of the Spirit's work of grace, Beddome divided the graces of the Spirit into two categories: the gifts of the Spirit, "which are from him, and those fruits of righteousness which are by him."[93] Once imparted, the Spirit's work of grace in the believer was "a permanent and abiding principle and subject to many ebbings and flowings."[94]

The Gifts of the Spirit

Spiritual gifts are divinely bestowed and not earned by any merit or effort of our own. Beddome warns that we bring dishonor to the Holy Spirit, if we become "puffed up with knowledge, elated with our gifts, and filled with a high opinion of our own sanctity and holiness." Clearly, the gifts of the Spirit are meant for the benefit of others, but above all for the glory of Christ.[95]

The Fruits of the Spirit

In his sermon, "On Christian Fruitfulness," Beddome expounded on the graces of the Spirit and lists, in particular, some of their fruits or dispositions, such as "faith, hope, love, meekness, humility, sincerity, and the

---

91. Beddome, *Sermons*, 79.
92. Beddome, *Twenty Short Discourses*, 8:37.
93. Beddome, *Twenty Short Discourses*, 2:53.
94. Beddome, *Sermons*, 158.
95. Beddome, *Twenty Short Discourses*, 4:67.

like."[96] Such qualities or dispositions are not merely decorative or superficial, but absolutely essential to the spiritual and emotional well-being of the believer.[97]

The Comforts of the Spirit

Joy, peace, and hope are referred to in Beddome's writings as "the comforts of the Holy Ghost."[98] In fact, all three, and in particular the calm that is derived from them, were frequently on his lips, perhaps in response to the hardships of life that were typical in the eighteenth century. Inner tranquility leads to praise, which, in turn, has a wholesome effect on the believer's sense of well-being. As a result, believers are "better capacitated for this heavenly employment," since "they have the Spirit to teach them, grace to assist them, and the most enlarged expectations to excite unceasing praise."[99] Beddome assured his hearers that the love, the purpose, and the promises of God behind this comfort are never in a state of flux and can never pass away.[100]

The believer's ever-present need for the "comforts of the Holy Ghost" stems from his chronic unbelief. Even after experiencing God's faithfulness, it invariably returns and robs the believer of his or her emotional security and confidence in God.[101] Beddome noted that it is the Spirit who helps the Christian to focus on the hope set before him or her and keeps the same from being presumptuous or falling into despair.[102]

Joy

The Christian's joy is based upon God's "precious promises," an accomplished redemption, and the "hope of glory."[103] Beddome defined this joy as "a calm and inward delight."[104] To accomplish this, God speaks to believers by his Spirit through the Scriptures.[105] This can be acquired through the

96. Beddome, *Sermons*, 250.

97. Beddome, *Twenty Short Discourses*, 4:41.

98. Beddome, *Sermons*, 210.

99. Beddome, *Twenty Short Discourses*, 4:54–55.

100. Beddome, *Twenty Short Discourses*, 4:42.

101. Beddome, *Twenty Short Discourses*, 7:57.

102. Beddome, *Twenty Short Discourses*, 4:41.

103. Beddome, *Scriptural Exposition*, 77.

104. Beddome, *Twenty Short Discourses*, 7:70.

105. Beddome, *Twenty Short Discourses*, 4:111.

personal reading of the Scriptures or through the exposition of the Scriptures by the clergy.

Peace

The comforting ministry of the Holy Spirit is built upon the knowledge of truth, such as the surety of redemption or the believer's eternal hope. As amazing and inspiring as those truths can be, they can also become theoretical unless they are vitally energized and reemphasized through the agency of the Spirit. Peace is a by-product of the gospel, and the gospel "derives all its influence and all its energy from the grace of the Holy Spirit," who "restores to us divine comfort forfeited by sin."[106] Similarly, the believer's hope of glory through Christ is made real by the Spirit in the heart through the continual reminder of its foundational truths. The Spirit's ministry of comfort, bestowing inner peace, is disparate and inexplicably diverse and the consequences are both effectual and convicting.[107]

Hope

Inseparably coupled with joy and peace is the believer's hope. Throughout Beddome's writings, the source of this comforting hope was threefold. First, it was "grounded on the promises of God." Second, the more the believer understood and embraced the richness and depth of his salvation, a work initiated and wrought by God, the greater his or her hope would be. "By enlightening the understanding in the great mysteries of redemption, and applying them with power to the heart, we are made to abound in hope, through the power of the Holy Ghost."[108] God's far-reaching plan of redemption becomes evident, which transcends the forgiveness of sins on the cross and extends to the future, when God's ultimate objective in the redemptive process is finally completed and the believer is fully transformed into the very image of Christ.

The third source of hope was the believer's future resurrection and the prospect of spending eternity in the glorious presence of God. Beddome carefully emphasized that it is actually God, not the splendors of heaven, which was the focus of the believer's hope.[109]

106. Beddome, *Scriptural Exposition*, 186.

107. Beddome, *Twenty Short Discourses*, 2:96.

108. Beddome, *Twenty Short Discourses*, 7:59–60.

109. Beddome, *Twenty Short Discourses*, 3:59.

Empowerment

The means and strength to live the victorious Christian life flow directly from the Holy Spirit. True fruitfulness is only possible when there is total dependence upon God. This flies in the face of the selfish, independent spirit that epitomizes the human heart. According to Beddome, the strength by which believers are to walk in the Spirit and persevere in godliness is "not natural, but moral strength . . . not bodily or mental, but that which is communicated by the holy Spirit."[110] Failure and unfruitfulness result when the believer attempts to live the Christian life or fight spiritual battles in his or her own strength. Thus, in Christian warfare, believers "overcome not by their own strength, but by the strength of another."[111]

Guidance

The work of the believer, simply stated although often difficult in practice, is his or her response in obedience to the promptings of the Spirit, in which "the soul is brought to an absolute resignation of itself to him" in full dependence upon him for the path or the task ahead.[112] The guidance of the believer by the Holy Spirit is carried out in a multifaceted manner. In some cases, it can present itself through a "powerful impression," and is "scarcely distinguishable from the workings of our mind."[113] In special cases, however, the Spirit will choose to influence the believer by immediate inspiration, whereby he or she receives an absolute certainty from the Spirit about a particular truth or path ahead.[114]

The Conviction of Sin

The Spirit's work of convicting the believer of sin takes on an even greater dimension as his or her spiritual transformation unfolds. What began through an initial conviction of sin, leading to repentance and eventual salvation, will subsequently continue in an ongoing process of sanctification, as residual sins and imperfections are illuminated and subsequently eliminated, and the believer is gradually conformed to the image of Christ. Simply stated, it is the "office" of the Holy Spirit "to convince the world of sin, both as to its

110. Beddome, *Twenty Short Discourses*, 6:5.
111. Beddome, *Twenty Short Discourses*, 3:132.
112. Beddome, *Twenty Short Discourses*, 3:39.
113. Beddome, *Twenty Short Discourses*, 3:149.
114. Beddome, *Twenty Short Discourses*, 3:44.

direful effects and evil nature."[115] For the believer, the Spirit's role is first that of a prosecutor, but later as a Comforter, first revealing and then refining the defects that would otherwise go undetected.[116]

Beddome would concede that even the unregenerate have certain natural convictions concerning sin, but they pale in comparison to spiritual convictions or those specifically revealed through the sanctifying work of the Holy Spirit. "Natural convictions extend only to some sins, and those generally of a more gross and heinous nature."[117] However, the Spirit-engendered convictions that are experienced by believers are of a much more sensitive nature. Furthermore, natural and spiritual convictions are different in nature with dissimilar incentives. With "natural convictions, the soul is actuated by slavish fear—fear of temporal judgments, and eternal punishment; of God's justice, and the flames of hell." In contrast, "those convictions which proceed from the divine Spirit have more or less a respect of the honour of God, and the love of God."[118]

Walking in the Spirit

The normal Christian life is to be lived in obedience to the promptings of the Spirit, who points to areas of temptation and fleshly desires that lead to sin. Since it is the work of the Spirit to guide the believer in the way of righteousness, careful examination of one's life and motives is essential in determining whether he or she is truly following the Spirit's leading or not.[119] The reason for such close attention to thought, motive, and conduct is the danger of fulfilling the lusts of the flesh and disobeying the Spirit's clear direction and conviction. Such actions grieve the Spirit, which stifles or quenches His power and influence, leading to even greater temptation and increasing fruitlessness.

Grieving and Quenching the Spirit

When the believer no longer walks in the Spirit, ignoring His leading or rebelling against His admonitions, he or she not only grieves the Spirit through neglect and disobedience, but "impedes" or quenches "his

115. Beddome, *Twenty Short Discourses*, 2:152.

116. Beddome, *Twenty Short Discourses*, 6:87.

117. Beddome, *Twenty Short Discourses*, 1:141.

118. Beddome, *Twenty Short Discourses*, 1:140.

119. Beddome, *Twenty Short Discourses*, 4:83–84.

sanctifying operations."[120] Even though the Holy Spirit is "in his own nature unchangeable and his designs and purposes cannot be frustrated," it is still possible for the believer to hamper or stand in the way of the work of the Spirit, in his own life and within the body of Christ.[121]

Although grieving the Spirit is a serious offense, Beddome did not believe it can ever result in the loss of salvation or the Spirit's complete withdrawal from the offending believer. Since the Spirit already dwells permanently in all saints, "he will not leave nor forsake them, yet the enjoyment of his presence may be greatly interrupted" or quenched.[122] This differs from the experience of Israel's King Saul, from whom the Spirit entirely departed. Since the believer's sanctification is the will of God (1 Thess 4:3), Beddome warned that impeding the sanctifying work of the Spirit, and thus quenching him, was a great sin against God, but one which could be forgiven.

Individually and corporately, believers can grieve the Spirit through various forms of rebellion.[123] Most often it is expressed by an independent spirit when believers attempt to live life in their own strength, with little or no dependency upon the Holy Spirit. Equally grievous are sins that quench the work of the Spirit among believers, in which the "gifts and graces" of the Spirit "be damped by neglect, and by a contempt of their ministrations."[124] Similarly, "the heat of passion extinguishes the fire of love; and it is not likely that the Spirit of God should dwell with those who cannot dwell together in unity, but who are perpetually disagreeing among themselves."[125]

Renewal

After the Holy Spirit's initial work of regeneration, a residual sin nature remains, necessitating an ongoing work of renewal. Beddome believed that this operation is absolutely imperative due to lingering spiritual maladies. First and foremost is the believer's natural tendency toward apathy.[126] He or she is also predisposed to "wander."[127] Because of the enemy's ever present cunning and the Christian's ongoing struggle with discernment, the Holy Spirit "leads thus to distinguish between good and evil, truth and falsehood,

120. Beddome, *Twenty Short Discourses*, 4:62.

121. Beddome, *Twenty Short Discourses*, 4:62.

122. Beddome, *Twenty Short Discourses*, 4:63.

123. Beddome, *Sermons*, 311–12.

124. Beddome, *Twenty Short Discourses*, 4:64.

125. Beddome, *Twenty Short Discourses*, 4:64.

126. Beddome, *Twenty Short Discourses*, 2:3.

127. Beddome, *Hymns*, #823.

removing the natural darkness of the mind, and suitably affecting it with its own concerns," and he may choose various means to do so.[128] Sometimes the Spirit "makes use of alarming providences." At other times, he may "use the conversation and edifying discourse of Christian friends," or even the "recollection of past experiences," in order to "rekindle the dying coals of divine love," but "the principle means," according to Beddome, was "the word of truth."[129] To this Beddome would also add the avenue of prayer as a way of attaining guidance, discernment and wisdom.[130] Yet, regardless of the means, providence, Christian friends, recollection, the Scriptures, or prayer, God may choose to use any or all of them to "form the Christian character."[131]

The unrelenting and ongoing renewal of the believer occurs at the time of God's own choosing. As is also true of the special outpourings of the Spirit, it often does not come "when we look for and most passionately desire it." Beddome averred that "in dispensing his gifts and performing his operations" the Holy Spirit "acts as a Sovereign; and whilst he fulfils his own gracious purposes, frustrates our sanguine expectations."[132] Yet, in his perfect sense of time, he does graciously intervene in order to quicken our attention, judgment, will, conscience, memory, and the gifts of the Spirit.[133]

The Holy Spirit "stirs" the conscience to "instruct, reprove, applaud, and condemn as the case requires," and where "good things in the heart lie as embers under the ashes," he stirs them up and revives the dulled memory to "put liveliness and vigour into our affections."[134] This, Beddome reflected, is but one of many ways that God "mercifully" cares for the soul of a child of God by "sending his Holy Spirit to renew and sanctify; to rescue it out of the hands of its enemies, and prepare it for his heavenly kingdom."[135]

The Sin against the Holy Spirit

Beddome's understanding of the sin against the Holy Spirit began with the "outward call" or the "common motions" of the Spirit that are "given to all

128. Beddome, *Twenty Short Discourses*, 2:5.

129. Beddome, *Twenty Short Discourses*, 2:4.

130. Beddome, *Twenty Short Discourses*, 2:10.

131. Beddome, *Twenty Short Discourses*, 3:171.

132. Beddome, *Twenty Short Discourses*, 2:1.

133. Beddome, *Twenty Short Discourses*, 2:5–8.

134. Beddome, *Twenty Short Discourses*, 2:6–8.

135. Beddome, *Twenty Short Discourses*, 1:78.

men."[136] Thus, the general call is also heard by those who will eventually hear the effectual call of the Spirit, experience regeneration, and willingly receive the gift of faith as a result. Once the Spirit has begun his effectual work of salvation in the heart of the believer, it is not possible for him or her to fall away; neither will he or she ever desire to leave the arms of the Savior. However, the question of a sin against the Holy Spirit first becomes relevant when professed believers willfully turn their backs on the truth and leave the faith, or when hardened sinners refuse to accept the general call, and are subsequently left by God to persist in and ultimately die in their sins.

For Beddome, the general call was never without effect. Even a basic understanding of the holiness of God among the unregenerate, or their elementary sense of moral failure, can elicit strong feelings of conviction or troubled thoughts.[137] Those who choose to ignore this outward call and follow their sinful ways will also incur divine reprobation. In Beddome's view, this was not the sin against the Holy Spirit, even though the end and final judgment for both is similar. Those who persist in their indifference are left alone to continue in their path without further intervention.[138] The end result is judgment, both in this life and the next, as God allows the sinner to remain on his sinful course, and the gracious offer is rescinded.

For Beddome, the sin against the Holy Spirit, or the unpardonable sin, was the sin of apostasy. It can only be committed by a pseudo-believer, who has at some point in time professed faith in Christ and may have even submitted to baptism. Yet, despite the outward piety or pretense, this person remains "a perfect stranger to the cleansing influences of the Holy Ghost, remaining in the gall of bitterness and the bonds of iniquity."[139] The sin of apostasy goes beyond a willful rejection of the gospel. Turning away from the only truth that can save is an expression of contempt.[140] Thus, "doing despite unto the Spirit of grace: and under this load of aggravated guilt, the sinner is left without any hope of mercy and consigned to eternal punishment."[141]

The Holy Spirit and the Sacraments

In his discussion of baptism and the Eucharist in *A Scriptural Exposition*, Beddome dealt with basic sacramental teachings, as well as some of the

136. Beddome, *Scriptural Exposition*, 64.
137. Beddome, *Twenty Short Discourses*, 2:43.
138. Beddome, *Twenty Short Discourses*, 3:78.
139. Beddome, *Sermons*, 230.
140. Beddome, *Twenty Short Discourses*, 3:71.
141. Beddome, *Twenty Short Discourses*, 4:68.

common misunderstandings that are often associated with them. His primary objective was to eliminate all vestiges of Roman sacramentalism or any misguided notions concerning the efficacy of the ordinances, and he summarily dismissed any lingering conceptions of *ex opere operato* and *ex opere operantis* properties in their administration. Any efficacy inherent in the sacraments "depends upon the blessing and presence of Christ," as well as "the cooperating influences of the Spirit," which are common to every believer through his or her union with Christ.[142] While Beddome held that the sacraments were primarily outward signs of spiritual and invisible blessings, he also understood Christ to be present through the ubiety of the Holy Spirit.

Whereas baptism and the Lord's Supper are not efficacious in themselves, Beddome suggests that they were "useful to stir up inward affections," which, in turn, lead to deeper commitment in the believer and the subsequent blessings of God.[143] Consequently, he insisted, "We must be born of the Spirit, and circumcised in heart, before we can participate in the benefits," for any efficacy derived from the sacraments is dependent upon the presence of the Holy Spirit, both in the local church and within the individual believer.[144]

The Holy Spirit and Baptism

Beddome contended that baptismal candidates should have a "credible profession of faith" and "appear to be partakers of the Holy Ghost."[145] He also referenced Acts 10:47, where water baptism was first permissible after it was clear that the Gentile believers had received the Holy Spirit like the Jewish Christians before them. The work of the entire Trinity in the believer's salvation is to be celebrated in water baptism, "rightly administered by immersion or dipping in the whole body of the party in water, in the name of the Father, and of the Son, and of the Holy Ghost."[146] Thus, the physical act of water baptism is not only "a sign of our fellowship with [Christ] in his death," but is to depict the rich benefits derived from the believer's union with Christ through the Holy Spirit.[147]

142. Beddome, *Scriptural Exposition*, 158.

143. Beddome, *Scriptural Exposition*, 158.

144. Beddome, *Twenty Short Discourses*, 6:107.

145. Beddome, *Scriptural Exposition*, 161.

146. Beddome, *Scriptural Exposition*, 164.

147. Beddome, *Scriptural Exposition*, 159.

The Holy Spirit and the Eucharist

Beddome made relatively few references in his writings to the relationship of the Holy Spirit to the Lord's Supper. However, like baptism, any spiritual benefits derived from it are dependent upon the presence of the Holy Spirit, both in the believer and in the ceremonial observance itself. Beddome limited participation in this celebration to those who were baptized believers,[148] for he was convinced that "without a holy temper and disposition, Christ, with respect to us, died in vain, and his sacrifice can profit us nothing."[149]

Beddome further reminded his hearers of the sacred nature of the Lord's Supper. He observes, "This Passover was so desirable to Christ, and ought to be gratefully remembered by us, because in it he instituted that solemn feast which is to be considered as a standing memorial of his dying love."[150] Beddome urged "a proper attendance," for through a conscientious observance of Christ's ordinance "the benefits of his death are applied to us, and the gift and graces of his Spirit encreased [sic] in us, in order to our complete blessedness in the world to come."[151]

The Holy Spirit and Prayer

As already established, Beddome firmly believed in the permanent indwelling of the Spirit since Pentecost. His appeals for the Spirit to come or to descend are prayers for an additional moving of the Spirit, specifically to awaken apathetic believers.[152] The special ministry of the Holy Spirit in prayer is to both assist in "the acceptable performance of this and every other duty" and to "make intercession in us, as Christ should make intercession for us."[153]

Beddome's view of prayer follows closely in the footsteps of John Owen, who suggested that the Holy Spirit not only stirred the believer's soul to pray, but also assisted him or her in the avenue of prayer.[154] Formed by his Puritan heritage, Beddome naturally yearned for the same assistance of the Spirit to energize his prayers, but he also pleads for a special outpouring of

---

148. Beddome maintained this strict view for most of his life, but he changed in his later years. See Naylor, *Picking Up a Pin*, 60.

149. Beddome, *Twenty Short Discourses*, 6:107.

150. Beddome, *Twenty Short Discourses*, 1:100.

151. Beddome, *Twenty Short Discourses*, 1:100.

152. Beddome, *Hymns*, #145.

153. Beddome, *Sermons*, 364.

154. Beeke and Jones, "Puritans on Union," 426.

the Spirit to awaken the hearts of fellow believers in a great renewal, as well as stir the unregenerate en masse to seek Christ.

Beddome's pneumatology of prayer fell under two categories: first, the assistance of the Holy Spirit in the believer's prayer life, and second, the outpouring of the Spirit on a particular person or within a local body of believers.

The Assistance of the Holy Spirit

The Holy Spirit's assistance is necessary in two distinct ways. First, it is necessary to enable the believer to pray.[155] In fact, Beddome insinuated that the state of prayerlessness is actually the default behavior of the natural man, and remains a recurring habit against which the believer must constantly do battle and prevail. Prayer is a sign of true spiritual life, for it is the indwelling Holy Spirit who generates it before further assisting the believer in its practice. It is through the work of the Spirit that the believer's eyes are opened and first made aware of new opportunities, along with his or her own shortcomings and needs.[156]

The Holy Spirit also lends assistance through his ministry of intercession. This gracious mercy is God's answer to the believer's inability to pray, particularly in situations of great despair or emotional turmoil. During trying times, the believer finds it hard to formulate requests and to pray according to the will of God. It is then when the Holy Spirit prays in the believer's stead.[157] Thankfully, although the believer may at times find it nearly impossible to pray, "it is easy to pray when the Spirit helps our infirmities."[158]

The Outpouring of the Holy Spirit

References to the Holy Spirit being poured down from heaven are frequently found in Beddome's sermons and hymnody. In essence, it is a figurative expression, since Beddome recognizes that the Spirit has already come and indwells every believer, being also present in every local assembly of believers that gathers together in Christ's name. Despite the Spirit's presence, Beddome recognizes how quickly these same churches can become spiritual deserts in desperate need of the rains of heaven. Much human energy can

155. Beddome, *Twenty Short Discourses*, 6:80.

156. Beddome, *Twenty Short Discourses*, 3:13.

157. Beddome, *Twenty Short Discourses*, 4:52.

158. Beddome, *Twenty Short Discourses*, 5:55.

be expended for supposed godly purposes, but often with very little spiritual fruit.[159]

One can well understand Beddome's passion and compulsive desire for new outpourings and revivals in the church. Even with healthy theology and sound preaching, which was certainly true in Bourton-on-the-Water, there is always the bothersome human tendency toward dullness and apathy. Similar to the Spirit's periodic and necessary renewal to bring the believer back on course, the outpouring or special renewal is also needed from time to time in the local church. As a result, that particular body of believers is able to maintain its effectiveness and its God-given mission, as it welcomes, baptizes, teaches, and catechizes all new believers who enter the church as a result.

The Holy Spirit and the Sabbath

The Holy Spirit is mentioned twice in Beddome's writings concerning the Sabbath and he highlights what he sees as the Spirit's approbation of Sunday as the Christian Sabbath. The Holy Spirit not only showed his approval of that day by "bestowing his extraordinary gifts" on Pentecost (Acts 2:1), a day which always fell "on the morrow after the sabbath" (Lev 23:16), but likewise "conferred his special grace" on the Lord's day, when John the Apostle was "in the Spirit" and penned the Book of Revelation.[160]

Like his contemporary John Gill,[161] Beddome held that no specific ordinance was given by God at creation that specifies on which weekday the Sabbath was to be observed. This did not happen until the time of the Israelites, although a Sabbath observance of sorts, for worship, rest, and personal reflection, has always been intended by God. Beddome believed that the first day of the week was especially chosen and blessed by God. Noteworthy was his invocation of the Holy Spirit, who "conferred his special grace" on Sunday.[162] Christ's resurrection, his appearance to Thomas and the disciples, and the "gifts" at Pentecost all occurred on the first day of the week. Beddome notes that the Spirit also inspired the Apostle John on "the Lord's day," which he understands to be Sunday as well. He concluded that God's choice of Sunday for significant events in the ancient Church, along with the

159. Beddome, *Twenty Short Discourses*, 5:168.
160. Beddome, *Scriptural Exposition*, 113.
161. Gill, *Body of Practical Divinity*, 3:421.
162. Beddome, *Scriptural Exposition*, 113.

Spirit's clear direction, provide overwhelming evidence of the Holy Spirit's special blessing on that day as the Christian Sabbath.[163]

Beddome's doctrine of the Holy Spirit bears the unmistakable imprints of classic Reformed theology. It also shows amazing continuity with the Puritan pneumatology that lived on among Dissenters in the early eighteenth century. Like his Puritan forefathers, Beddome emphasized the work of the Holy Spirit in salvation, his indispensable agency in sanctification, and his ongoing renewal of the church, but, as an early evangelical, he also expected a great latter-day outpouring of the Spirit with millennial implications. For the historical theologian, Beddome's writings provide a clear and verifiable continuum between the Reformed theology of the Puritans and the pneumatological emphases of the early eighteenth-century evangelicals, which eventually set the stage for the Evangelical Revival in Great Britain and would later define a future evangelical movement.

163. Beddome, *Scriptural Exposition*, 113.

5

"Such wondrous grace demands a song"

The Hymns of Benjamin Beddome[1]

R. Scott Connell

John Newton (1725–1807), pastor at Olney, Buckinghamshire and author of the venerable hymn text "Amazing Grace," is one of the finest examples in the history of the church of a pastor-hymn writer. The notorious convert from slave-ship captain to Anglican pastor practiced the habit at Olney of writing a hymn for his congregation to sing each Sunday (or midweek service) after the sermon that related the truths of his message. This provided a mnemonic vehicle by which his people could recall his message during the week in musical form. While Newton is somewhat famous for this practice, he was not the first to do so. His pastorate at Olney began in 1764. William Cowper (1731–1800) joined him in 1767. The two collaborated for the *Olney Hymns* which were published in 1779. The bulk of Newton's hymn writing was accomplished largely during this time at Olney. However, he had a noteworthy Baptist predecessor who also excelled as a pastor-hymnwriter while writing almost twice as many hymns as Newton and doing so several decades earlier.

---

1. The title for this article has been taken from the last line of Benjamin Beddome's hymn entitled, "In God the Holy and the Just" under the heading, "God Hearing Prayer" (Beddome, *Hymns*, #408).

Benjamin Beddome (1717–1795) became the teaching elder of the Baptist church at Bourton-on-the-Water, Gloucestershire in 1743. It is unclear when he first began the practice of writing a hymn to accompany his sermon, but it likely began immediately for reasons discussed below. Unlike most Baptists of his day, he grew up singing hymns in church. His father John Beddome (1674–1767) was also a Baptist pastor and Benjamin was born during his father's pastorate at Alcester Baptist Church, Warwickshire. John had come there from the Baptist congregation that met in Horselydown, Southwark, London, where the pastor was the renowned pioneer for hymn singing among Baptist churches—Benjamin Keach (1640–1704).[2] It is generally agreed that Keach's church was one of the first to include hymn singing among Baptist churches—a practice that was introduced by Keach in the mid-1670's but formally affirmed by church vote on March 1, 1691. John Beddome's church at Alcester introduced hymn singing in 1713, four years before Benjamin was born.[3] It is certain that Benjamin Beddome came to Bourton-on-the-Water not only as an advocate for singing hymns in congregational worship (a still somewhat new practice in the first half of the eighteenth century), but also writing hymns for his people to sing in corporate worship—a practice that he appears to have been trying his hand at even before his arrival at Bourton.

Beddome's Hymn Writing Influences

Benjamin Beddome is at times cited as the Baptists "second" most famous hymn writer of the eighteenth century. Anne Steele (1717–1778) being their oft-cited frontrunner. It is not that she was more prolific than Beddome.

2. Tom Nettles notes that Benjamin Keach "was in the forefront of arguing for the use of hymns in worship as a part of the ordained worship of God. On that issue he wrote and published a number of early Baptist hymns and hymnals." See Nettles, "Benjamin Keach," 99n8. On Keach and hymns see also Martin, *Benjamin Keach*; Walker, *Excellent Benjamin Keach*. As early as 1663, Hanserd Knollys (c. 1598–1691) is also reported to have commended "the singing of hymns and spiritual songs along with the psalter as an ordinance of God's worship." See Howson, "Hanserd Knollys," 1:50–51. This note is cited in the excellent dissertation by Van Carmichael, "Hymns of Anne Steele," 3n11. For Keach's famous defense of hymn singing see Keach, *Breach Repair'd in God's Worship*.

3. Haykin, "Benjamin Beddome," 96. According to Alan Betheridge, the church book at Alcester states in an entry dated 20 August 1713: "Began by consent of all concern'd to sing praises to God in the publick worship at the weekly meeting on Wednesday." Betheridge continues, "Their church meeting on Christmas Day that year . . . extended this to 'every Lord's Day at Aulcester [sic]" (Betheridge, *Deep Roots, Living Branches*, 60).

She only has 144 hymns to her name, in addition to metered Psalms and other devotional poetry. But her hymns were at times more widely disseminated in some of the hymnals of the day and her skill in the craft is generally regarded as unprecedented among Baptists, including Beddome. Hoxie Fairchild (1894–1973) references Steele, a pastor's daughter, as "the all-time champion Baptist hymn-writer of either sex."[4] The impetus for Steele's hymn writing was to supplement the collections of Isaac Watts's (1674–1748) hymns being sung in her father's church in Broughton, where he preached for sixty years. Her hymns were eventually published in 1760 under the pseudonym, *Theodosia*.[5] Benjamin Beddome would essentially seek to do the same at Bourton-on-the-Water. Watts's psalms and hymns had demonstrated, persuasively to many, that the art form (i.e., hymns of "human composure") could be accomplished at a very high level of theological precision *and* poetical beauty. His hymns were firmly in place in hymn-singing churches and any effort to write additional hymns was generally intended to supplement them, not replace them. There was a simultaneous effort to write at the level set by Watts. Louis F. Benson, writer of *The English Hymn: Its Development and Use in Worship,* considers this time period beginning in 1750 as a new period in Baptist hymn writing "in the school of Watts."[6]

As the "Father of English Hymnody," Watts laid the foundation for non-conformist hymn singing that Baptists such as Steele and Beddome built upon. No one would surpass Watts's skill or excellence as a hymn writer. Just as Steele's hymns were intended as a supplement to Watts's hymns for her father's congregation, Beddome was supplementing his own church's hymnbook at Bourton-on-the Water (composed largely of the hymns of Watts no doubt), with a specific hymn he composed to be sung on the Lord's

---

4. Fairchild quoted in Arnold, *English Hymns,* 137:318. J. R. Broome adds, "No one has excelled Anne Steele in her tender, memorable, sensitive expression of the heart feelings of a tempted, exercised tried Christian" (Broome, *Bruised Reed,* 175). In Julian's *Dictionary of Hymnology,* W. R. Stevenson regards Steele as "by the far the most gifted Baptist Hymn-writer of this period" (Julian, *Dictionary of Hymnology,* 1:111–12). It should be pointed out that of the two, Beddome's hymns outranked those of Steele in terms of the number of hymns in "Common Use" in John Julian's *Dictionary of Hymnology.* "Beddome is thus seen to be in C.U. [Common Use] to the extent of about 100 hymns by 1907 (the publication date of Julian's dictionary). In this respect he exceeds every other Baptist hymn-writer; Miss Steele ranking second" (Julian, "Beddome, Benjamin," 1:124). Louis Benson contends that "in merit and in actual use Beddome stands beside Miss Steele" (Benson, *English Hymn,* 215).

5. Theodosia, *Poems on Subjects Chiefly Devotional.*

6. Benson, *English Hymn,* 213.

Day morning.[7] "It was his practice to prepare a hymn every week to be sung after his Sunday morning sermon."[8] J. R. Watson explains that it had been the practice of Benjamin Keach to use "hymn-singing as an aid to worship and for the exposition of scripture."[9] Coming out of Keach's church, John Beddome must have been *one* of the prominent influences upon Benjamin for this practice to continue so prevalently with his son. However, the influence of Bernard Foskett (1685–1758) may have been the most influential.

Foskett joined John Beddome as co-pastor of the church at Alcester in 1711, six years before Benjamin was born. He was an equally significant influence on the church's decision to affirm the appropriateness of hymn singing there just two years later in 1713, as he too had come from a hymn-singing congregation.[10] While Benjamin Beddome was born into that church and spent his youngest days there, the younger Beddome would be at a much better age to learn from Foskett when their paths crossed more significantly later at the Bristol Academy. As ministry callings tend to go, Foskett would depart Alcester in 1720 (when Benjamin was only three) to become the first principal of the academy. John Beddome subsequently moved his family to his new ministry calling at the much larger Pithay Church in Bristol in the summer of 1724, reuniting the family with Foskett and potentially at Foskett's urging to do so. The Bristol Academy would become highly influential in Calvinistic Baptist life in the eighteenth century and this included a remarkable influence upon hymn writing including most notably the compilation of the first Baptist hymnal in 1769 known as the "Bristol Collection."

Beddome would finally become interested in the things of Christ in 1737 and was quickly led to study under the mentorship of Foskett at the academy for two years before moving to London in 1739 to continue his studies at the Fund Academy in Tenter Alley, Moorfields. While it was in London that Beddome would be baptized and affirmed for ministry by the Prescot Street church and eventually sent out to Bourton-on-the-Water, the influence of Foskett and the Bristol Academy during those two most

7. Cramp, *Baptist History*, 449.

8. Stevenson, "Beddome, Benjamin," 1:121. Beddome has other types of hymns that served other purposes, but his main effort seems to be those used as sermon exposition or response.

9. Watson, *English Hymn*, 111.

10. Foskett had belonged to the congregation at Little Wild Street, London, during the pastorate of John Piggott (d. 1713) who according to David Music and Paul Richardson, "had sided with those supporting hymn singing in the 1690s" (Music and Richardson, *"I Will Sing the Wondrous Story,"* 31).

formative years (in Beddome's early 20s) should not be underestimated. David Music and Paul Richardson write,

> Bernard Foskett . . . promoted hymn singing among his stu-
> dents. Many of them such as Benjamin Beddome, Benjamin
> Francis, and Daniel Turner, incorporated hymn writing in
> their pastoral duties. The practice of ministry shaped at Bristol
> integrated moderate Calvinism with an evangelical welcome,
> infused these with devotional intensity, and placed them in the
> context of corporate worship where preaching and hymn sing-
> ing were intentionally and intimately related.[11]

For Beddome, hymn singing had been an integral part of the worship practice and doctrinal instruction of the Sunday morning service before he had
the opportunity to lead a worship service himself. It seems to have been a
forgone conclusion to him when he arrived at Bourton-on-the-Water, that
he would be responsible each week for writing both a sermon and a hymn
for the worship gathering. Preaching and hymn singing were "intentionally
and intimately related" in corporate worship.

One other noteworthy influence upon Beddome was none other than
that of his contemporary, Anne Steele. Just before assuming the permanent
position at Bourton-on-the-Water, a young, single Benjamin had become
quite intrigued by Miss Steele. It is unclear how they may have met. J. R.
Broome assumes it must have been through Beddome's traveling to preach
at various churches, either at Devizes, Broughton (Steele's home church), or
Ringwood.[12] Beddome offered a marriage proposal to Anne in December of
1742.[13] In a volume of sermons published after his death, a brief memoir is
included in which the following verses are attributed to the same year—1742:

> Lord, in my soul implant thy fear,

11. Music and Richardson, "I Will Sing," 30–31. Foskett and the Bristol Academy
would also train the likes of John Ash (1737–1791) and Caleb Evans (1737–1791) who
published the "Bristol Collection" of hymns and the illustrious John Rippon (1751–
1836) who produced the most significant Baptist hymn collection of the eighteenth
century—Rippon's Selection. Many of the students at Bristol not only were influenced
by Foskett's teaching, but would have attended either his (Foskett was pastor of the
Broadmead church in Bristol) or John Beddome's church (Pithay) where hymn singing
also was a regular practice. For more information about the influence of the Bristol
Academy, see Hayden, Continuity and Change. Foskett is also credited with writing
some of his own hymns for use in his church (see Hayden, "Contribution of Bernard
Foskett," 189). According to Cynthia Y. Aalders, the Steele Collection at the Angus Library contains a booklet of verses in Benjamin Beddome's hand, including five hymns
by Bernard Foskett (see Aalders, To Express the Ineffable, 17, n.35).

12. Broome, Bruised Reed, 111.

13. The written proposal letter is dated December 23, 1742. See Beddome, "Letter."

Let faith, and hope, and love be there;
Preserve me from prevailing vice,
When Satan tempts. Or lusts entice.
Of friendship's sweets may I partake,
Nor be forsaken, or forsake.
Let moderate plenty crown my board;
And God for all be still adored.

Let the companion of my youth
Be one of innocence and truth;
Let modest charms adorn her face,
And give her thy superior grace.
By heavenly art first make her thine,
Then make her willing to be mine;
My dwelling-place let Bourton be,
There let me live and live to Thee.[14]

It certainly appears that these verses were penned with Anne in mind given the date. However, her response, though not recorded, was clearly to decline Benjamin's proposal (though she obviously felt compelled to keep his letter). Beddome's poetic prayer was finally answered in 1749 when he married Elizabeth Boswell, whom he met in his ministry at Bourton. Beddome and Steele would remain friends for the duration of their lives and Steele would never marry, in spite of other proposals. Clearly the interaction between the two, that began at least by 1742 and possibly as early as 1740 when Beddome began travelling to preach, consisted of noteworthy influence upon each other. This influence would have likely centered, at least in part, upon the art of hymn writing. Steele's personal belongings after her death included hymns written in Beddome's hand, evidence of the nature of at least a portion of their correspondence.

---

14. Beddome, *Sermons*, 22. These verses are also cited by J. R. Broome (Broome, *Bruised Reed*, 112). Broome also cites a letter from Anne to her sister Molly many years later in which Molly seems to be pointing out the blessings of marriage, presumably attempting to persuade Anne to reconsider her commitment to singleness. Anne replies, "No indeed my sister, I have no mind to climb the stile you point to. It is true a gentle swain offered his hand to help me over, but I made a curtsie and declined his officious civility, for I looked over and saw no flowers but observed a great many thorns. Besides I think the path is much smoother on this side of the hedge than the other, and I am too staid to ramble for the sake of novelty." Broome confesses that it is unclear that she is referencing Beddome in this response but it does reveal her attitude toward marriage.

For Beddome, the hymn-singing ancestry of Benjamin Keach[15] chan-
neled through his father John Beddome, the practical tutelage and example
of Bernard Foskett at the Bristol Academy, and an influential friendship
with another prominent and active hymn writer in Anne Steele, converged
to ignite a new age in hymn writing for Baptists such as he. The "golden age"
of Baptist hymn writing began about mid-century as Benjamin Beddome
and his contemporaries stood upon the shoulders of the "Father of English
Hymnody," Isaac Watts. Their adaptation of Watts's style was in a new—
somewhat more experiential—ethos reflective of the burgeoning emphases
of eighteenth-century Calvinistic evangelicalism.[16] In Beddome's case it
would include a genre of sermonic hymn writing that hearkened back to
Keach and Foster, while laying the foundation for an Anglican slave ship
captain still to come.

Beddome's Hymns as Evangelical

The two primary collections of Watts, *Hymns and Spiritual Songs* (1707)
and *Psalms of David* (1719) had become the main source for hymn singing
among Baptists of the early eighteenth century.[17] The two collections were
eventually printed in one volume as the core repertory for congregational

15. This is not to imply that the "other" earliest Baptist hymn writer Joseph Stennett (1663–1713) had no potential influence on Beddome. His hymns were regarded
as being the first hymns exhibiting "artistic merit" in comparison to those of Keach,
which are generally regarded as relatively poor in comparison to the Baptist hymnody
to follow. Both Stennett and Keach were, however, exemplary in providing hymns to be
sung after communion and for baptism—two categories especially important to Baptists and generally not being employed by others. They also propagated the category of
the "homiletical" hymn, regarded by Music and Richardson as the "second principal
genre" of Baptist hymn writing (Music and Richardson, "*I Will Sing*," 22).

16. Andrew Fuller (1754–1815) theologically codified this emerging brand of Calvinism among the Baptists. "Fullerism" was a moderation of "High Calvinism" that
made Baptists think differently about the unsaved. Rather than seeing it as a disservice
and even condemnation to preach the gospel to those who may not be part of the elect,
"Fullerism" created a passion and burden to reach those who had not yet heard the
gospel. This led to the forming of the Baptist Missionary Society in 1792 and William
Carey's commission to India in 1793. The main tenets of Fuller's theology were outlined
in Fuller, *Gospel Worthy of all Acceptation*.

17. Some English Particular Baptist churches did not sing at all due to concerns
regarding "conjoined" or "promiscuous" singing—believers with unbelievers. Others
sang "Psalms only" in the tradition of Calvin. Watts's and Keach's movement was a
particular effort to sing "songs of human composure" in addition to the Psalms in some
places and in place of silence in others. Louis Benson writes that Baptists had a "pre-
dilection" for the "Spiritual Songs" over Watts's Psalms and Hymns (Benson, *English
Hymn*, 364).

worship among Baptists, Congregationalists, and others for nearly two centuries. Roger Hayden observes that the Watts's hymns

> made possible a direct and corporate response to God from the congregation, the response of the redeemed community who wished to converse with God. It is difficult to over emphasize the significance of these hymns for sustaining the evangelical Calvinism of Baptists. In these hymns were the doctrinal strength and personal warmth which sustained Baptist spirituality in an age of reason and increasing Unitarian tendencies.[18]

The Watts's repertory provided a welcome warmth and resonance in worship for these churches that had left the "Psalms-only" camp fostered by John Calvin (1509–1564), the English Puritans, and the earliest Baptists. Watts's *Psalms of David* provided a new way to sing the Psalms.[19] The hymns of Baptist hymn writers Keach and Joseph Stennett (1663–1713) were largely left in the past and the gap of almost half a century that was left between them and a new generation of Baptist hymn writers that arose mid-century was filled by the deluge of Watts's hymnody. It seemed that the entire evangelical world (that was singing at all) was singing Watts and any hymnal that wanted sales need only list it containing "the hymns of Dr. Watts" and a market share would almost certainly be earned. But there was room for something more—especially among the Baptists headed toward a missions' movement by the end of the century.

Richard Arnold explains that eighteenth-century "hymns were expected to educate, arouse, or spiritually benefit or satisfy a congregation, to propagate and support certain religious and theological principles and specific orientations toward Christian experience, and to provide hope or assurance for one's beliefs and aspirations."[20] There was a new desire in worship in the eighteenth century to reflect the gradually warming and intensifying spirituality of evangelical piety. The comparatively cooler corporate spirituality of Puritanism was giving way to a more experiential religion that concerned itself more with pietism; sought a more conversational exchange with God in corporate worship (the Puritans generally did not sing at all); and was beginning to intentionally emphasize evangelism and missions.

18. Hayden cited in Music and Richardson, "*I Will Sing*," 23.

19. *The Psalms of David Imitated in the Language of the New Testament, and apply'd to the Christian state and worship* (1719) were psalms that were "Christianized" for use in Christian worship. "By this process the content of a psalm was interpreted in light of the life, death, resurrection, and teachings of Jesus." For example, Psalm 72 begins "Jesus shall reign where'er the sun/Does his successive journeys run" (Music and Price, *Survey of Christian Hymnody*, 55).

20. Arnold, "Veil of Interposing Night," 374.

Beddome's hymns reflected this warming evangelical ethos with precise and focused theological truths, honest human emotions in the face of those truths, simple yet moving imagery, and a seeming prophetic voice for what was to come in distant lands. All of this was done simply and pastorally, as a shepherd caring for his Bourton flock. This gave his writing a biblical clarity and accessibility.

Beddome's hymns were not published in their entirety until after his death. *Hymns Adapted to Public Worship, or Family Devotion* was published in 1818. Robert Hall, Jr. (1764–1831) reflects the evangelical tenor of Beddome's hymns in his summation found in the Recommendatory Preface to Beddome's hymns when he writes:[21]

> The variety of the subjects treated of, the poetical beauty and elevation of some, the simple pathos of others, and the piety and justness of thought, which pervade all the compositions in the succeeding volume, will we trust be deemed a valuable accession to the treasures of sacred poetry, equally adapted to the closet and to the sanctuary. The man of taste will be gratified with the beautiful and original thoughts which many of them exhibit, while the experimental Christian will often perceive the most secret movements of his soul strikingly delineated, and **sentiments pourtrayed [sic] which will find their echo in every heart.**

These hymns were intended to move the soul deep within. They were not simple mental ascents to doctrine, though they included that. They reflected the pathos begun by Watts but now further developed and expanded by subsequent hymn writers such as Beddome. If Watts represented grandeur, Beddome and his contemporaries intended to bring that grandeur nearer. This created natural contrasts between the transcendent and at times mysterious doctrinal absolutes of God with the stark and simplistic experience of man in this life, fraught as it was with confusion and honest emotion. All of this was done from the heart of a pastor seeking to shepherd real people with real lives. Consider one of his most widely circulated hymns entitled, "Wait, Oh My Soul, Thy Maker's Will."[22]

Wait, oh my soul, thy Maker's will,

21. Hall, "Recommendatory Preface," vii–viii. Hall concludes, "Considerable pains have been taken to arrange the Hymns in such a manner as is best adapted to selection, from a persuasion, which we trust the event will justify, that they will be found the properest Supplement to Dr. Watts that has yet appeared."

22. Beddome, *Hymns*, #18. Hymnary.org lists this hymn as Beddome's fourth most published hymn with appearances in 184 hymnals (see "Benjamin Beddome").

Tumultuous passions, all be still;
Nor let a murmuring thought arise;
His ways are just, his counsels wise.

He in the thickest darkness dwells,
Performs his work, the cause conceals;
And though his footsteps are unknown,
Judgment and trust support his throne.

In heaven and earth, in air and seas,
He executes his wise decrees;
And by his saints it stands confest,
That what he does is ever best.

Then, oh my soul, submissive wait,
With reverence bow before his seat;
And midst the terrors of his rod,
Trust in a wise and gracious God.

The divine mystery of God's sovereignty is confronted here ("He in the thickest darkness dwells," etc.) with a surrender to God's supremacy but also the honest recognition of human weakness which is beset by "tumultuous passions" and the temptation to "let a murmuring thought arise." There must have been hundreds of situations in his decades of ministry that precipitated such thoughts. The exhortation he gives his people here is to command their souls to wait on the will of God. It is the heart of a pastor that begs his flock in spite of their circumstances to "trust in a wise and gracious God" for what they cannot yet see "with mortal eyes."

Worship in the eighteenth century was taking on a resonance in the heart for which only hymns could provide an adequate voice. The human condition was being allowed a voice for itself in the conversation with God in corporate worship. Honest emotions were being acknowledged while at the same time, doctrinal truth was being administered to the heart's condition. This is one of the things that sets Beddome as a pastor-hymn writer apart. He is not just writing hymns for people to sing in worship anywhere. He is writing hymns for *his* people to sing in the worship services *he* is leading. There is no objective detachment here. He had specific faces and circumstances in his mind when he wrote these words. Furthermore, triteness would never do. He had to own the words he put in their mouths because he would walk with them in life between the Sunday services.

Another aspect of Beddome's hymnody that would have been striking to his eighteenth-century congregation is represented by the theological
development of the perspective toward the unsaved in the hymns "Can sinners hope for heaven?", "Did Christ o'er sinners weep?", and "Oh may the
gospel swiftly spread." The first of these, "Can Sinners Hope for Heaven,"[23]
represents the hopeless state of the unconverted and the decided dichotomy,
with its eternal implications, between the saved and the unsaved.

Can sinners hope for heaven,
Who love this world so well;
Or dream of future happiness,
While in the road to hell?

Shall they hosannas sing,
With an unhallowed tongue;
Shall palms adorn the guilty hand,
Which does its neighbour wrong?

Can sin's deceitful way
Conduct to Zion's hill?
Or those expect with God to reign
Who disregard his will?

Thy grace, O God, alone,
Good hope can ne'er afford!
The pardoned and the pure shall see
The glory of the Lord

While there is absolute biblical truth in this hymn, the inherent message
here appears to be a warning that only the saved will see the glory of God.
The subheading for this hymn in *Hymns Adapted* is "Unrighteous Excluded
from Heaven." This is one of several hymns that Beddome wrote warning the
saved of the final end of the unsaved (while indirectly warning the unsaved
who may be attending his worship services of the same). Other hymns however, reflect a growing concern for the unsaved, including one in particular
that highlighted the example of Christ's concern for sinners. "Did Christ o'er
Sinners Weep?" became one of Beddome's most popular hymns, reflecting a
growing pathos among Baptists in the emerging evangelical age.[24]

23. Beddome, *Hymns*, #400.

24. Beddome, *Hymns*, #587. This hymn has appeared in over 300 hymnals and is
one of the few Beddome hymns to receive a renewed interest in singing today.

Did Christ o'er sinners weep?
And shall our cheeks be dry?
Let floods of penitential grief
Burst forth from every eye.

The son of God in tears
Angels with wonder see!
Be thou astonished, O my soul,
He shed those tears for thee.

He wept, that we might weep;
Each sin demands a tear;
In heaven alone no sin is found,
And there's no weeping there.

Joy beams in every eye,
And fills each holy heart;
All join to sound the triumph high
In praise to bear their part.

Beddome seems to be laying a foundation for an evangelistic concern by first drawing the worshipers' attention to Christ's attitude toward a sinner—that sinner being the singer! Simple extrapolation of this concern could lead quite naturally to the concern for others who were not yet converted, as demonstrated by "Oh May the Gospel Swiftly Spread."[25]

Oh may the gospel swiftly spread,
Revive the living raise the dead;
A glorious work be now begun,
And millions tell what God has done.

Let those who never felt before,
Now feel the gospel's vital power,
And languid souls who own thy love,
Receive fresh visits from above.

Arise, thou sun of righteousness,
With light and life the nations bless;
In Zion, long the sinner's scorn,
Be numerous sons and daughters born.

25. Beddome, *Hymns*, #697.

These hymn texts seem to indicate that the evangelical fervor that marked the modern missions' movement by the end of the eighteenth century was already beginning to be felt decades before in places like Bourton-on-the-Water.

Beddome is also somewhat novel in his hymns addressing the Holy Spirit, and this can be viewed in connection with evangelism as well, though the impetus is for illumination, empowerment, and guidance. "Come, Holy Spirit, come with energy divine;" "Come Spirit source of light;" Come blessed Spirit source of light;" and "'Tis God the Spirit leads" are four such examples. These invocations for the Spirit's energizing work upon the believer should be seen largely in the effort toward sanctification, but include evangelism (and later missions). "'Tis God the Spirit leads" is the most compelling of these examples.[26]

'Tis God the Spirit leads
In paths before unknown;
The work to be performed is ours,
The strength is all his own.

Supported by his grace,
We still pursue our way;
Assured that we shall reach
The prize, secure in endless day.

"Prayer is the breath of God in man" is a noteworthy demonstration of Beddome's view of prayer, reflecting his concern for his people's proper theological perspective behind their vigorous efforts to pray and be aware of its benefits.[27]

---

26. Montgomery, *Christian Psalmist*, 120. This hymn is unattributed in James Montgomery's collection even though Montgomery utilized a number of Beddome's hymns and attributed them to him. It is falsely attributed to Montgomery in some later hymnals due to its appearance in his *Christian Psalmist*. Other hymnals attribute this hymn to Beddome (see Colonial Church, *Psalms and Hymns*, 202). Although it does not appear in Beddome, *Hymns Adapted,* Hymnary.org lists Beddome as its author (see Beddome, "'Tis God the Spirit Leads").

27. Beddome, *Hymns*, #405. Beddome wrote no fewer than fifty hymns regarding the subject of prayer. J. R. Watson believes that he may have borrowed from the writing of George Herbert and John Newton for this hymn though there is no way to prove this since the date of this hymn is unknown (see Watson, *English Hymn*, 199). Hall does attribute Beddome's skill at least in part to having "an acquaintance with the best writers of antiquity, to which he was much indebted for the chaste, terse, and nervous diction, which distinguished his composition both in prose and verse" (Hall, "Recommendatory Preface," vi).

Prayer is the breath of God in man,
Returning whence it came;
Love is the sacred fire within,
And prayer the rising flame.

It gives the burdened spirit ease,
And soothes the troubled breast;
Yields comfort to the mourners here,
And to the weary rest.

When God inclines the heart to pray,
He hath an ear to hear;
To him there's music in a groan,
And beauty in a tear.

Perhaps the most remarkable example of his hymn writing is "God, in the gospel of his Son." In this hymn, the gospel is celebrated as the rich reservoir for knowing God. It is in the gospel that his "eternal councils" are known and his "richest mercy shines." More poignantly, it is in the gospel that Jesus "in ten thousand ways" displays his "soul-attracting charms" and "tells his love in melting strains." Note in particular the sharp contrast of gospel truth in the last two lines of the second verse. Of this hymn J. R. Watson explains that "the counterpoint is precise and obvious." Watson continues, "Beddome's clarity and balance, however, conceal a strong imagination which is closer to the Evangelical Revival of Newton and Cowper than to the sweet tones of [Philip] Doddridge."[28] This is Beddome's most popular hymn, appearing in no fewer than 310 hymnals.[29]

God, in the gospel of his Son,
Makes his eternal counsels known;
'Tis here his richest mercy shines,
And truth is drawn in fairest lines.

Here sinners of an humble frame
May taste his grace, and learn his name;
'Tis writ in characters of blood,
Severely just, immensely good.

Here Jesus, in ten thousand ways,

28. Watson, *English Hymn*, 201.
29. Beddome, *Hymns*, #371. For appearances in hymnals, see "Benjamin Beddome."

His soul-attracting charms displays
Recounts his poverty and pains,
And tells his love in melting strains.

Wisdom its dictates here imparts,
To form our minds, to cheer our hearts;
Its influence makes the sinner live,
It bids the drooping saints revive.

Our raging passion it controls,
And comfort yields to contrite souls'
It brings a better world in view,
And guides us all our journey through.

May this blest volume ever lie
Close to my heart, and near my eye,
'Till life's last hour my soul engage,
And be my chosen heritage!

The power of the gospel is on full display in this hymn. God reveals himself through it and sinners as a result learn of Him because of it. Jesus' love is revealed in "ten thousand ways" and wisdom is unveiled in such effect as to "form our minds," and "cheer our hearts." It can control our passions and bring "a better world" in view while guiding us through this one. It will guide us all the way home "till life's last hour."

Two pertinent examples of Beddome's warming ethos for the worship event may be seen in the remarkable language he chooses to describe what takes place in corporate worship. This hymn appears under the heading, "Pleasures of Public Worship" and demonstrates the delight in worship that stems from the dynamic encounter with and revelation of Christ Himself in corporate worship.[30]

My soul, how charming is the place,
Where Jesus makes his glories known;
There he unveils his lovely face,
And tells the wonders he has done.

How he unfolds with heavenly skill,
The mysteries of his dying love;
Bows stubborn sinners to his will,

---

30. Beddome, *Hymns*, #578.

And bids their guilt and fears remove.

And under the heading, "Delighting in Public Worship," he points to the appearance of God in Worship:[31]

> Blessed is the place where God appears,
> And all his charms displays;
> His gracious smiles forbid our fears,
> And gladden all our days.
>
> Here humble saints a transport feel,
> Beyond the joys of sense;
> Nor could they while on Zion's hill,
> E'er wish to move from thence.

Never has more exhilarating language been used to describe the worship service among Particular Baptists. What anticipation he places before his people as they gather each week. He expects that they will anticipate an encounter with the living God as they gather to worship.

In equally compelling language, Beddome wanted his people to think beyond this life. A somewhat morbid example of his style, and perhaps an extreme example of his intention to stir the heart with provocative imagery, is found in "Reflections on Death."[32] The images here seem to serve one purpose—produce uneasiness and inspire resolution regarding the thought of death while provoking concern for eternity.

> Learn, oh my soul, what 'tis to die!
> Th' event how solemn, and how nigh;
> When every tongue shall silent be,
> These eyes no pleasing object see.
>
> The active limbs, the comely face,
> Turned to mass of rottenness;
> The name forgot, the substance gone,
> No more admired, no longer known.

31. Beddome, *Hymns*, #579.

32. Beddome, *Hymns*, #777. Watson misrepresents Beddome's theology by excerpting only the first two verses in his work. He writes, "Such a graphic description of bodily decay is unusual in concentrating on the physical body in the grave rather than on the terrors of hell; it suggests that Beddome was thinking of life as ending in an existential pointlessness, for which the only remedy is gospel grace" (Watson, *English Hymn*, 201). If he had included the third verse he could have more accurately represented Beddome's theology of life after death.

But thou, my soul, must then remain,

In everlasting joy or pain;

The bliss of heaven with angels share,

Or else be plunged in black despair.

Then be these solemn thoughts impressed,

With power divine on every breast;

And ere another moment pass,

Oh let us seek renewing grace.

Quickly to Jesus may we fly,

And on his righteousness rely

Lo, our eternal all's at stake,

Awake our slumbering souls awake.

Beddome wants his people to see this life in light of the one that is certain to come. This day should be lived in light of the eternal day rather than for its own merits alone.

In each of these examples above it should be evident that Beddome is representing the heritage of Watts (i.e., "in the style of Watts") but in the context of a new era of evangelicalism. But he is doing so in a unique way that could not be duplicated by one who was not a Baptist pastor.[33] Beddome is writing for his people and as such, he is concerned that they think well so that they can live well. Watson rightly ascribes to Beddome, "A style which is usually recognizable, a clarity of line and simplicity of image. It gives him a certain individual voice in the transition of eighteenth-century hymnody from the grandeur of Watts to the sensitivity of Cowper."[34] Beddome seemed to know that something wonderful was coming, or needed to come, and he was preparing his people for it. Breed concludes, "What we call greatness is not all of one kind. . . . Beddome is great in that prophetic foresight, by reason of which he was the first to catch the spirit of the dawning era and give it voice in so large a variety of ways."[35]

---

33. Watts, Newton, Cowper, Doddridge, and Wesley were all remarkable hymn writers of the same century, but they were not Baptist. There is something to be said about singing Baptist hymns in a Baptist church. Anne Steele was Baptist but she was not a pastor. She could not represent the theological precision that Beddome could due to his thousands of hours of biblical and doctrinal study. He also had the heart of a pastor on display in his hymns. Steele was unable to represent either of these pastoral aspects in her hymnody.

34. Watson, *English Hymn*, 202.

35. Breed, *History and Use*, 152–53.

Beddome's Hymns as Baptist

Baptist hymn writers embraced the welcome presence of Watts's hymnody but they almost immediately set out to fill in the gaps for Baptist ecclesiology and theological distinctive. Hymns to accompany the ordinances were in great need. Keach introduced hymn singing to his congregation by singing a hymn after the Lord's Supper in the practice of the Lord, on the night he instituted the Supper (Matt 26:30; Mark 14:26). Hymns for baptism were essentially non-existent until Baptists wrote them to reflect their Biblical view and practice. Part of the role to supplement Watts was to add the types of hymns that he did not write, or simply to add the theological distinctives of a Baptist perspective.[36] Beddome wrote 39 hymns for baptism, indicating the vast need for such hymns. Consider this hymn under the heading "Baptism Divinely Honoured:"[37]

> The Father, and the Son,
> And Holy Ghost unite,
> To shed a lustre o'er
> This great mysterious rite;
> To Jordan's stream an honour's given,
> By Christ the Lord of earth and heaven.
>
> 'Twas there he found a grave and rose again to view;
> And now to us he shows
> The way we should pursue;
> Buried with him, with him we rise,
> To endless bliss above the skies.
>
> The Father by a voice,
> Distinguished his Son;
> Behold the Spirit too
> Does his obedience crown;
> To the eternal sacred Three,
> Immortal praise and glory be.

36. Rippon's Collection of Watts includes 25 hymns under the subject heading of "The Lord's Supper." There are none of Watts' hymns for baptism as Watts was a Paedobaptist. See *Psalms and Hymns.*

37. Beddome, *Hymns*, #597.

Beddome's view of the table was rooted in the *1689 London Confession* as a real presence view.[38] As such, he believed that Christ manifested his presence at the table for believers to enjoy and benefit from. Not in the elements, as Catholics would advance by their view of transubstantiation. Nor somehow around the elements as in Luther's view of consubstantiation. But still much more real than a Zwinglian view of symbolism only. At the table Christ is present in a special manner "for their spiritual nourishment, and growth in him."[39] Here are two examples of hymns demonstrating this doctrinal conviction:

> Oh for a glimmering sight
> Of my expiring Lord!
> Sure pledge of what yon worlds of light
> Will to the saints afford. . . .
>
> May I behold him in the wine,
> And see him in the bread.[40]
>
> Come then, my soul, partake,
> The banquet is divine:
> His body is the choicest food,
> His blood the richest wine.
>
> Ye hungry starving poor
> Join in the sweet repast;
> View Jesus in these symbols given,
> And his salvation taste.[41]

Beddome and his Baptist contemporaries also supplemented Watts's hymns with two additional categories of emphasis that were indicative of their emerging priorities as a group of churches: 1) theological exposition and instruction; and 2) a warming heart for evangelism and ultimately missions. While Beddome is noteworthy on both types, the first of these might be considered his area of prolific expertise.

This new category of hymn writing, which could be referred to as "homiletical," would be refined to an exemplary degree by the pen of

---

38. For more on this view of the table see Davis, *Worship and the Reality of God*.

39. *Second London Confession* 30.7, 272. For more on the real presence of Christ at the table in Baptist practice see Haykin, "His Soul-Refreshing Presence."

40. Beddome, *Hymns*, #672.

41. Beddome, *Hymns*, #669.

Beddome. In this approach to hymn writing, the text was intended to provide "a summary—perhaps memorable—of the interpretation and application of Scripture in the sermon."[42] This is somewhat in the style of Keach,
but more likely directly connected to what he learned from Bernard Foskett.
Motivated by his pastoral desire to give his people the best response to his
sermon both in the corporate worship service and then in the unceasing "all
of life" service of worship (Rom 12:1), Beddome wrote a hymn each week to
correspond to his sermon. Baptists have for centuries been concerned with
the best response hymn for the sermon of the day. Baptist hymnals since this
time period often have robust sections of "hymns to follow the sermon."[43]
While these hymns became overtly evangelistic in the late nineteenth and
twentieth centuries (e.g., addressed to the unbeliever present in worship),
they were initially a vehicle for believers to respond with devotion to the
exhortation just received, and to provide a mnemonic device by which the
sermon's main points could be recalled for application in life that week.

Horton Davies describes Beddome as an, "indefatigable sermon sum-
marizer in verse" and hymns such as his as a "very pedagogical understanding of the function of a hymn, as almost a jingle by which to sum up the
message of the sermon."[44] He attributes this to the Baptists' fidelity to the
letter of the Bible as well as its spirit. At the same time he derides them
since this makes it difficult for them to "take lyrical flight." The concern for
Calvinistic doctrinal precision marks the heightened intent of Baptists of
this age to understand rightly the truth of scripture and then "get it right" in
the worship service.

J. R. Watson cautions against considering Beddome merely, "predictable, homiletic, or boring." He notes that while at times this judgment is
just, he employs a "clarity of line and simplicity of image" that earns himself
a significant place among eighteenth-century hymn writers.[45] If Beddome
had a primary aim for his hymn writing, it appears that it was to provide
his congregation with the best means of summarizing the Biblical truths
contained in his message each week. Every pastor longs for better ways to

42. Music and Richardson, "*I Will Sing*," 21–22.

43. Benson writes regarding Rippon's *Selection*: "This book of 588 hymns was conceived in the interest of the 'Hymn after the Sermon.' It continued to expand until it
reached 1174 hymns by 1844. "When we remember that these were an appendix to
'Watts entire' we become aware of the lengths to which the homiletical conception and
use of hymns naturally leads. Well had Rippon feared, in introducing his original 588
hymns 'that after the sermon there will be many Subjects sought for in vain, both in this
Appendix [*Selection*], and in Dr. Watts'" (Benson, *English Hymn*, 144).

44. Davies, *From Watts and Wesley*, 136.

45. Watson, *English Hymn*, 202.

help his people apply the message to their lives. Beddome was compelling his people through hymnody to retain the main ideas of Sunday's sermon and to apply it Monday through Saturday.

James Montgomery (1771–1854) commends Beddome as a "writer worthy of honour both for the quality and quantity of his hymns." He writes:

> His compositions are calculated to be far more useful than attractive, though, on closer acquaintance, they become very agreeable, as well as impressive, being for the most part pithy. A single idea—always important, often striking, and sometimes ingeniously brought out, not with a mere point at the end, but with the terseness and simplicity of the Greek epigram—constitutes the basis of each piece.

The precision of his effort is seen in what Montgomery cites next. "Many of these were composed as supplementary applications of texts, or the main topics of his sermons."[46] He was not writing generally for universal use. He was writing specifically for local church use. And not just any local church— *his* local church. The same people whose weddings he was officiating; whose family gatherings he was attending; whose sickbeds he would be praying at; and one day whose funerals he would be presiding over. He wanted to know that he had done everything he could do to shepherd them well—for more than five decades!

A second category emerging among Baptists and a most compelling aspect of this new age in hymn writing reflects the first rays of the sun rising on the modern missions' movement. Though Beddome's tenure at Bourton-on-the-Water began a half century before the movement officially started with the founding of the Baptist Missionary Society in 1792, the end of his ministry passed the torch. Initially he is a "voice crying in the wilderness" for a new application of Particular Baptist doctrine. His hymns were not just seeking to move the heart of the worshipers. They were also seeking to send the gospel beyond the sanctuary to those outside the walls by moving the Christian's hands and feet out into the world. Beddome was one of the first to write a missionary hymn in English. "Ascend thy Throne, Almighty King" was published long before the BMS was formed.[47]

> Ascend thy throne, almighty King,
> And spread thy glories all abroad;
> Let thine own arm salvation bring,
> And be thou known the gracious God.

46. Montgomery, "Introductory Essay," xvii.
47. Beddome, *Hymns*, #705.

Let millions bow before thy seat,
Let humble mourners seek thy face,
Bring daring rebels to thy feet,
Subdued by thy victorious grace.

O let the kingdoms of the world
Become the kingdoms of the Lord;
Let saints and angels praise thy name,
Be thou through heaven and earth adored.

Consider also the "commission language" related in these two hymns regarding baptism:

Jesus, the Lord of heaven and earth,
To whom all creatures owe their birth
Sends forth his edict and command,
Through every nation, every land—

Let men of high and low degree
Repent of sin, believe in me,
Then to the sacred stream repair,
And be with speed baptised there.[48]

Also,

Ere Christ ascended to his throne,
He issued forth this great command
Go preach my gospel to the world,
And spread my name through every land.

To men declare their sinful state,
The methods of my grace explain,
He that believes and is baptised,
Shall everlasting life obtain.[49]

Through such hymns, Beddome was preparing the way for the Baptist mission endeavors associated with the name of William Carey. A second hymn, "Let party names no more," is another indication that a new day of reaching across economic, class, national, and ethnic boundaries was dawning.[50]

48. Beddome, *Hymns*, #595.
49. Beddome, *Hymns*, #596.
50. Beddome, *Hymns*, #638.

Let party names no more
The Christian world o'erspread;
Gentile and Jew, and bond and free,
Are one in Christ their head.

Among the saints on earth,
Let mutual love be found;
Heirs of the same inheritance,
With mutual blessings crowned.

Thus will the church below
Resemble that above;
Where streams of pleasure ever flow,
And every heart is love.

Music and Richardson believe this is one of Beddome's finest texts, based upon Galatians 3:28 and listed under the heading "Communion of Saints."[51] David R. Breed concludes, "Nothing could be more indicative of the dawn of the new era than these two hymns ["Ascend Thy Throne" and "Let Party Names No More"], especially when taken together. The spirit of the one is the spirit of the other—brotherhood and the world for Christ."[52]

Conclusion

As mentioned above, Louis Benson considers the activity of Beddome, Steele and others during this time "the golden age of Baptist hymnody."[53] This was emphasized initially by the quality of their hymns and later by the proliferation of their hymnals. The "Bristol Collection" was published in 1769 and is considered the first Baptist hymnal ever published. John Ash and Caleb Evans, both students at Bristol Academy under Foskett where Beddome had also been trained, published this collection of 412 hymn texts. Baptist writers including Joseph Stennett, Anne Steele, Samuel Stennett, and Daniel Turner contributed texts in addition to non-Baptists Watts, Doddridge, Addison, Cowper, and the Wesleys. Beddome contributed 13 texts to this collection.[54] John Rippon, another son of the Bristol Academy,

---

51. Music and Richardson, "*I Will Sing*," 39.

52. Breed, *History and Use of Hymns*, 151.

53. Benson, *English Hymn*, 215.

54. Music and Richardson, "*I Will Sing*," 27–28.

prepared his famous *Selection* for publication in 1787.[55] It is reported that Beddome offered "above 500 hymns" to Rippon for consideration, indicating his esteem for Rippon and what he intended to accomplish. However, only forty-two were selected for inclusion in the first edition and twenty more were added in subsequent editions. Rippon's *Selection* "brought to a wider public the works of many Baptist hymnists, who provided nearly a third of the texts.[56] Charles Haddon Spurgeon used fifteen of Beddome's hymns in his *Our Own Hymn-Book* (1883) for his London congregation almost a century later, demonstrating the persistence of popularity of many of Beddome's hymns.[57]

It is possible that Beddome's hymns were even more popular in the United States than in England.[58] When his *Baptist Catechism* was finally published in the United States in 1849, J. L. Reynolds writes in the Introduction, "The author of this work, Benjamin Beddome, is known to the denomination, in this country, chiefly by means of his excellent hymns. To those who are familiar with the effusions of his poetical genius, and who are conscious of having derived spiritual benefit from them, some further account of the author and of his writings will doubtless be acceptable."[59] Were Beddome to know of the effect of his hymns almost a century after they were written, he certainly would have been pleased. Though written for his own church, to know that his offerings to the little flock at Bourton-on-the-Water were affecting believers for their spiritual good throughout the British Isles and even across the Atlantic Ocean would surely have been a demonstration of wondrous grace. "Such wondrous grace demands a song!"

55. Rippon, *Selection of Hymns.*

56. Music and Richardson, "*I Will Sing*," 53.

57. Spurgeon, *Our Own Hymn-Book.*

58. Forty-one of Beddome's hymns were selected for Stow and Smith, *Psalmist* (1843); forty-six for *Baptist Psalmody* (1851); and thirteen for the *Baptist Hymn Book* (1871).

59. Reynolds, "Introduction," 3.

6

Benjamin Beddome and the Modern Question

The Witness of His Sermons

Jason C. Montgomery

THE YEAR THAT BENJAMIN Beddome began his studies for the ministry in the West of England at the Baptist Academy in Bristol, there was a theological fire that was ignited in the East, in the area known as Northamptonshire. The year was 1737, and the Congregational minister of the Independent church in the small rural village of Rothwell, Matthias Maurice, had set his hand to pen and paper to produce a manuscript that was sure to gain the attention of many. His work was known as *A Modern Question Modestly Answer'd*, in which he posed a question and provided a corresponding answer that struck a nerve that was to bring about a transformation in the English Calvinistic churches that was unanticipated, to say the least.[1]

For the remaining years of the century, this question would be at the forefront of the minds of many as they wrestled with the simple issue it raised. How men answered Maurice's question would clearly put them on one side of the issue or the other. The question? Simply put, Maurice sought an answer to the question of whether or not it was "the duty of unconverted sinners, who hear the gospel, to believe in Christ."[2] To many contemporary

---

1. Maurice, *Modern Question*. All references in this work to the *Modern Question* come from this edition.

2. Maurice, *Modern Question*, 4.

ears, this question seems almost like a moot point, but not so to the ears which initially heard the trumpet blast of Maurice. Bearing a strong resemblance to the title of the book, the issue as it spread throughout the land, became known simply as the "modern question."[3]

It is the intention of this chapter to make use of the issue raised by Maurice, in order to assess the preaching of English Particular Baptist Benjamin Beddome. The modern question shaped much of the preaching in the period during the ministry of Beddome in the eighteenth century, especially in Calvinistic circles. The relationship between Beddome's preaching and the modern question will be considered in a desire to persuasively demonstrate that Beddome in his preaching would have answered emphatically in the affirmative, holding that it was the duty of all who heard the gospel to believe in Christ. This expository conviction of Beddome is to be delineated so as to help the reader understand and appreciate Beddome's preaching as representative of a strain of evangelical preaching among the Particular Baptists of eighteenth-century England.

This subject will be addressed by first examining the surrounding context of Beddome which gave rise to the modern question itself, with a specific look at the stimulating work of Maurice. Second, the life and labor of Benjamin Beddome will be considered with a focus on a representative sampling of his gospel-saturated and invitational preaching. Third, and finally, an analysis of Beddome's preaching against the modern question itself will be presented to substantiate the claim that Beddome's preaching was thoroughly evangelical in nature.

The Modern Question in Eighteenth-Century England

The subject of the modern question will set a helpful backdrop for the examination of Beddome's preaching. Beddome was a highly respected leader among the Calvinistic Baptist preachers in the eighteenth century, and the modern question was front and center among the Calvinistic Baptists, especially their pastors, and growingly so as the century progressed. It would have been virtually impossible to remain neutral on the issue during this period. To understand the pressing nature of this subject, two issues in particular should be considered—the rise of the modern question itself, with

---

3. In this work, the "modern question" will be referred to in two distinct ways. When referring directly to the work of Matthias Maurice we will designate it as a shortened form of the book title as *A Modern Question* or simply *Modern Question*. However, when we are referring to the issue brought to the fore by the publication of *A Modern Question* in general, we will designate it as the *modern question*.

a specific look at Maurice's work, followed by a theological analysis of the question itself as understood by Maurice and company.

The Rise of the Modern Question

To trace the rise of the modern question, we must travel to Rothwell (Rowell), about five miles to the west of Kettering, a town that would become well known in the history of eighteenth-century Particular Baptists, as the home of the ministry and labours of Andrew Fuller. In 1714, Matthias Maurice, a Welshman, was called to Rothwell to replace another Welshman, Richard Davis.[4] It seemed, according to Geoffrey Nuttall, that "when Maurice came to Rothwell, he was to all appearance, exactly the man to carry on Davis's High Calvinist tradition."[5] When Nuttall used "High Calvinist" he meant what we intend by hyper-Calvinist. As many have found, defining hyper-Calvinism can be a difficult endeavour. Peter Toon in the *New Dictionary of Theology* offered the following helpful definition:

> It is a system of theology framed to exalt the honour and glory of God and does so by acutely minimizing the moral and spiritual responsibility of sinners. It puts excessive emphasis on acts belonging to God's **immanent being**—the immanent acts of God, eternal justification, eternal adoption, and the eternal covenant of grace. It makes no meaningful distinction between the secret and revealed will of God, thereby deducing the duty of sinners from the secret decrees of God. It emphasizes irresistible grace to such an extent that there appears to be no real need to evangelize; furthermore, Christ may be offered only to the elect.[6]

Iain Murray, in *The Forgotten Spurgeon*, stated that

> Hyper-Calvinism in its attempt to square all truth with God's purpose to save the elect, denies that there is a universal command to repent and believe, and asserts that we have only warrant to invite to Christ those who are conscious of a sense of sin and need. In other words, it is those who have been spiritually

---

4. For the ministry of Richard Davis and the part he played in the rise of the modern question see Nuttall, "Northamptonshire," 101–23.

5. Nuttall, "Northamptonshire," 108.

6. Toon, "Hyper-Calvinism," 324. Toon further cited Curt Daniel noting that hyper-Calvinism is "that school of supralapsarian 'five-point' Calvinism which so stresses the sovereignty of God by over-emphasizing the secret over the revealed will of God and eternity over time, that it minimizes the responsibility of sinners, notably with respect to the denial of the use of the word 'offer' in relation to the preaching of the gospel."

quickened to seek a Saviour and not those who are in the death of unbelief and indifference, to whom the exhortations of the Gospel must be addressed. In this way a scheme was devised for restricting the Gospel to those who there is reason to suppose are elect.[7]

These definitions can be summarized in the following positions:

1.   It is in the supralapsarian school in relation to the decrees of God, where the decree to save has logically preceded the decree to create. One might say that all hyper-Calvinists were supralapsarians, but not all supralapsarians were hyper-Calvinists.

2.   In hyper-Calvinism there is an overemphasis on the secret will of God's decree over against his revealed will in the Scripture to a point that the revealed will is interpreted in light of the secret.

3.   In this light, the responsibility the church has to the lost is restricted to the elect and the warrant for faith and the duty the lost have to believe in the gospel are interpreted in light of God's secret purposes.

Peter Toon provides a two-fold summary of the above positions stating that for the hyper-Calvinist there is "no purpose . . . served in offering the grace of Christ to all in the preaching of the gospel . . . [and] it is not the duty of sinners who hear the Gospel to repent of their sins and believe on Christ for the forgiveness of sins."[8]

Now, the abandonment of hyper-Calvinism would not be a transition Maurice would make lightly and it would not come without great cost. But with great cost often comes great gain. As Roger Hayden has noted, "controversy opened when Matthias Maurice, the successor of Richard Davis at Rothwell, wrote *A Modern Question Modestly Answer'd*, [in] 1737."[9] By the time of the publication of his work, Maurice had been in Rothwell for over twenty years and "the propriety of inviting the unconverted to trust Christ was becoming a divisive issue with paedobaptist . . . churches."[10] Although Maurice had come to Rothwell sharing the convictions of Davis, by 1737, these convictions had changed. Maurice's *Modern Question* is structured around four major sections: 1) Introduction: Clarification of Issue and Statement of Thesis, 2) Argumentation for Thesis in Thirty Biblical Texts,[11]

7.   Murray, *Forgotten Spurgeon*, 47.

8.   Toon, *Emergence of Hyper-Calvinism*, 129.

9.   Hayden, *Continuity and Change*, 186.

10.   Brown, *English Baptists*, 73.

11.   Maurice lays out the following order of texts as lines of evidence in support of

3) Proposing and Answering of Ten Objections, and 4) Concluding Exhortations to Those Who Answer in the Negative.

In the opening paragraph of his work, Maurice begins by noting in an opposing format what he is not seeking to do in his work, and opposing that with what he is seeking to accomplish. He wrote:

> It must be observed that this question does not consider what power, or what inclination unconverted sinners have to obey any part of the law of God; but only what according to that law is their duty? Neither is it here asked whether it is their duty to give their assent to the report, and grant that all that is said in the Gospel is true; nor what power the fallen sons and daughters of Adam have to work themselves up into that faith? But whether God does by his Word make it the duty of unconverted Sinners, who hear the Gospel preached or published, not only to believe Christ, but to believe in Christ? Any person surely, who lays aside all affectation of singularity, and sincerely and unfeignedly makes the Bible the rule of his faith, must say, that God does by his Word plainly and plentifully make it the duty of unconverted sinners, who hear the Gospel, to believe in Christ. This I affirm, and aiming at the Glory of Christ, and the establishment and comfort of godly, honest minds, this I shall prove, by producing some of the many, very many portions of Scripture which bear their testimony thereunto.[12]

Regarding the affirmative side of his presentation, with this opening statement Maurice's intention is clear. To begin, he is asking what, according to the law, is the duty of the unconverted. This is crucial to note for it demonstrates why it is fitting and proper to call an unbeliever—un-awakened/unregenerate—to repentance and faith. Men apart from Christ stand under the law of God. This is not to say that all men, even saved men, do not stand in some relation to the law of God. All self-respecting Calvinists would have agreed with the tenets of the *Savoy Declaration of Faith* which stated that the "moral law doth forever bind all" and furthermore that the moral law remains, even for the believer, "as a rule of life."[13]

---

his position: Ps 2:10–12; 4:2–5; Prov 1:20–23; 8:1, 4, 5, 10, 32, 33; 9:1–6; Eccl 12:1, 13; Is 1:18; 27:5; 55:1–2, 3, 7, 22; Ez 33:11; Mi 6:8; Mt 3:2, 3, 8; 11:28–30; 22:2–4; 23:37; 27:37–40; 28:19–20; John 6:27–29; 7:37; 12:36; 16:8–9; Acts 2:38; 3:19; 8:22–23; 16:31; 17:30; Rev 14:6–7.

12. Maurice, *Modern Question*, 3–4.

13. Renihan, *True Confessions*, 137–38. We have cited here from the *Savoy* due to it being the "official" confession of the Independent/Congregational churches.

Furthermore, the law can be rightly summed up under the two great commandments of loving God and loving men. Maurice sees in the command to love God, the implication of the duty of faith. He makes this argument in the second section of his work, where he brings out various lines of Scriptural evidence to support his thesis. For his 29th argument in favour of the *modern question*, Maurice selects as his text Matthew 22:37–40 where Jesus says: "You shall love the Lord your God with all your heart and with all your soul and with all your mind. This is the great and first commandment. And a second is like it: You shall love your neighbour as yourself. On these two commandments depend all the Law and the Prophets."[14] From this Maurice deduces the following observations: [NL 1–6]

1. God commanding perfect Love.

2. In his Law we learn not what we are able to do, but what we ought to do.

3. Jesus Christ is the Lord Jehovah, and therefore Love to him with all our Heart and Soul is his Due.

4. Without Faith in him it is impossible to love him.

5. As the Command to love Christ must oblige us to the use of all the means absolutely necessary thereto, so it must oblige us to faith; without which 'tis impossible to please God.

6. The commandment obliging me to love my neighbour as myself, obliges me to love myself; and therefore to believe in Christ.[15]

Finally, Maurice is asking, if God makes it the duty of unconverted sinners who hear the Gospel preached/published, not only to believe Christ, but to believe in Christ. The issue is not simply getting people to consent to the truthfulness of the gospel. Hyper-Calvinists were often content to expound upon doctrine and leave it at that. Baptist historian Joseph Ivimey notes of John Brine that "he contented himself with what he considered clear statements of doctrinal truth, without making any application of his subjects."[16] For Maurice and his growing band of evangelically minded Calvinists, this simply would not do. Men needed to be pressed, persuaded, and encouraged not simply to believe Christ, but to believe in Christ.

---

14. Unless otherwise indicated, all Scripture quotations are from the English Standard Version, 2011.

15. Maurice, *Modern Question*, 20–21.

16. Ivimey, *History of the English Baptists*, 3:269.

A Mini-Theology of the Modern Question

Having examined the rise of the modern question, we need to draw our thoughts together regarding this explosive eighteenth-century issue in some summary fashion. What can be said of the theology of the modern question? The following five-point rubric is offered which will serve us well later in our evaluation of the preaching of Beddome.

Priority of Revealed Will Over the Will of Decree

First, whereas hyper-Calvinism interpreted the revealed will of God in light of the secret will, modern question advocates did not. The advocates of the modern question, led by the example of Maurice himself, gave priority to the will of God revealed in the Scriptures. Repeatedly Maurice drew the attention of his readers to the clear teaching of the Scriptures. In fact, he stated in the beginning that he sought to prove his thesis "by producing some of the many, very many portions of Scripture which bear their testimony thereunto."[17] He followed this up at the end of his work, stating that "Tho' some have thoughtlessly and too suddenly took up that Notion, yet let them now in the presence of God impartially compare it with the Scriptures, some texts whereof I briefly produced, as persons willing to submit their souls to the revealed will of God, and they will see that it is a pernicious dangerous error."[18] The "Notion" that some had taken up was the notion that all men who hear the preached word need not believe in Christ. This "Notion" Maurice believed was clearly negated by the clear teaching of the revealed will of God found in the Scriptures. Thus, modern question advocates sought to leave the secret things to the Lord and live by the light that God had given in his Word.

This is in full keeping with the Reformed tradition. As Toon notes that, generally speaking, "Reformed divines in England and on the continent carefully distinguished between the secret and the revealed will of God and refused to deduce the duty of minister and people from anything but the revealed will of God."[19] Thus, for example, John Calvin in his *Institutes of the Christian Religion* stated:

> Moses has beautifully expressed both in few words: "The secret things," says he, "belong unto the Lord our God: but those things which are revealed belong unto us and to our children."

17. Maurice, *Modern Question*, 4.

18. Maurice, *Modern Question*, 31.

19. Toon, *Emergence of Hyper-Calvinism*, 143–44.

We see how he enjoins us, not only to devote our attention to meditations on the law of God, but to look up with reverence to his mysterious providence. This sublime doctrine is declared in the book of Job, for the purpose of humbling our minds. For the author concludes a general view of the machine of the world, and a magnificent dissertation on the works of God, in these words: "Lo, these are parts of his ways: but how little a portion is heard of him!" For which reason, in another place he distinguishes between the wisdom, which resides in God, and the method of attaining wisdom which he hath prescribed to men. For after discoursing concerning the secrets of nature, he says that wisdom is known only to God, and "is hid from the eyes of all living." But a little after he subjoins, that it is published in order to be investigated; because it is said to men, "Behold the fear of the Lord, that is wisdom." To the same purpose is this observation of Augustine: "Because we know not all that God does concerning us by an excellent order, we act solely in good will according to the law."[20]

The Moral Law Demands Faith

Second, the modern question affirmed that faith in Christ was a duty implied in the summation of the moral law, to love both God and neighbour. Maurice brought this out clearly in his work by way of addressing various objections and answers to the modern question. Objection seven read, "But unto all moral obedience it is granted the children of men are called, especially those who have the written law, the commandment makes it their special duty to obey."[21] Thus the objector grants that men are called to keep God's moral law, and this is especially so when men have the law of God in written form. This objection comes straight out of Romans where the Gentiles have the moral law of God written on their hearts, but the Jews are even more accountable, possessing the law written down on tablets of stone. With this, the objector thinks he has a great argument, and with much of it, Maurice would agree.

However, consider his reply, "And (that being so) wherever the Gospel is preached and heard, faith in Christ is a moral duty, and repentance towards God is a moral duty; there the moral law requires that faith. The eternal moral law of God is every way perfect. Christ has not given a new

---

20. Calvin, *Institutes of the Christian Religion*, 213.

21. Maurice, *Modern Question*, 24.

law to his Church, distinct from that."[22] Maurice turns the objector's argument back on him, pointing out that the call given in the gospel to repent and believe, are given by Christ as commands. And furthermore, it must be noted, that Christ is not giving a new law. This is reminiscent of James who reminds the church that "there is only one lawgiver and judge" (Jas 4:12). In other words, the law of God and the law of Christ are not two different things. So, believing in Christ is not a command to which a man is called to respond, until it comes to him. But once the gospel is revealed to him, the command rests upon him unmistakably as a moral duty. Yet still, it is a moral duty of the law as such, being the law of God, that is the moral law, and not some new law given by Christ disconnected from the moral law of God.[23]

Lack of Power Does Not Equate to Lack of Duty

Related to this is a third theological point addressing the objection often made by hyper-Calvinists that "man is weak, and has no power to obey, therefore why should he be commanded?"[24] Maurice responded, "Tho' man has lost his power, God has not lost his authority; nor is the law of God disannulled: Besides, tho' man has lost his power, he has not quite lost his reason; therefore to deal with him by precepts, prohibitions and promises, is the most agreeable way."[25] Maurice, in his fifth coupling of objections and answers, stated:

> Objection: If he was commanded only to perform moral natural acts, it might seem more agreeable; but you say he is commanded to perform spiritual acts, which are not in his power.
> Answer: And pray what power has he to perform moral, natural acts? The Scripture says he is without strength, Rom 5:6 and Paul says that he, after conversion, was not sufficient to think any thing, and therefore not a moral, good thing, 2 Cor 3:5. But when God inclines the heart, in his strength, persons perform the one or the other; and seeing it pleases him, why should not he make use of commands to incline the heart to good acts of any kind?

22. Maurice, *Modern Question*, 24.

23. This is a fascinating point that Maurice is trying to highlight. A much more detailed and clear presentation of it however, is given by Alverey Jackson in his work *The Question Answered*. The reader is directed to the next footnote touching on Jackson's work for the full text of Jackson's argument.

24. Maurice, *Modern Question*, 23.

25. Maurice, *Modern Question*, 23.

With this, Maurice shuts the door on this objector. Faith is indeed required as a duty, even if man lacks power in an unregenerate state. A lack of power (which is true of all men), does not necessitate a lack of duty.

Saving Faith and Repentance the Duty of All

Fourth, the faith to which the non-elect are exhorted in the Scripture, is the same faith to which the elect are exhorted—saving, believing faith, in Christ and in Christ alone. The fact that they (the non-elect) do not have it (saving faith), does not negate the truth of their being called to it. It will simply not do, as hyper-Calvinists affirm, to reduce the kind of faith and repentance to which the non-elect are called, to be simply some form of common faith and legal repentance.[26] Andrew Fuller himself would later discover this truth as well. As he noted:

> Those exhortations to repentance and faith, therefore, which are addressed, in the New Testament, to the unconverted, I supposed to refer only to such external repentance and faith as were within their power, and might be complied with without the grace of God. The effect of these views was, that I had very little to say to the unconverted; at least, nothing in a way of ex-hortation to things spiritually good, or certainly connected with salvation.[27]

Faith and Repentance both Gift and Duty

Finally, faith and repentance are to be seen as both blessing/gift and duty. The hyper-Calvinist view of this is seen in John Brine, who wrote, "if re-pentance and faith are to be taken as 'Conditions of Life,' one would have salvation or justification by works."[28] But this is a false dichotomy, and we do not have to choose between one or the other. Curt Daniel notes here that hyper-Calvinists see "faith is a gift. Therefore, faith cannot be a duty, for duty is works."[29] Though this sounds straightforward enough, it should not be embraced too quickly. Thus, Daniel has stated: "True Reformed theology

---

26. The work of Peter Toon cited throughout this paper, *Emergence of Hyper-Calvinism*, is an excellent resource for these typical hyper-Calvinist distinctions, especially chapter 7 on "Man, His Sin, and Salvation."

27. Ryland, *Work of Faith*, 37.

28. Garrett, *Baptist Theology*, 93.

29. Daniel, *History and Theology*, 90.

argues that it is not inconsistent for the same thing to be both a duty and a gift. As Augustine said, 'Demand what thou willst, O Lord, and give what thou demandest.' And he does."[30]

Benjamin Beddome: Messenger, Method, and Message

When the firestorm of the modern question began to spread in Northamptonshire, Benjamin Beddome was just out of his teen years, safely tucked away in the evangelical confines of the West, enrolled as a new student at the Bristol Baptist Academy. The hyper-Calvinism that found such ready soil in the East, would not find such a prepared place to take root in the West. Particular Baptist life in the West was rich and full. Its heritage stretched back to the glory days of the seventeenth century and the evangelically based *Second London Baptist Confession of Faith of 1689.*[31] Under the leadership of gospel-men like John Beddome, Benjamin's father, pastor of the Pithay Church in Bristol, and Bernard Foskett, tutor at the Bristol Baptist Academy and pastor of the Broadmead Church, the theology advocated by Maurice would not have been opposed, even if the issue had been raised, which apparently, it was not.

According to Roger Hayden, in the West there had been a "sustaining among Particular Baptists (of) an evangelical Calvinism which was unashamedly founded upon the *1689 Confession.*"[32] Along this line, Thomas R. McKibbens noted in his work on Baptist preaching that "the Broadmead Baptist Church in Bristol became synonymous with a great tradition of an educated and evangelical preaching ministry. Broadmead's influence far exceeded its size, for through the graduates of the Bristol Baptist College the church reached, and still reaches, remote parts of the world with the gospel."[33] This was Beddome's heritage. This was the air Beddome breathed throughout the early days of his life. It was sweet, it was Christ-saturated, it was evangelical, and in the familiar terminology of this work, it was "modern."

---

30. Daniel, *History and Theology of Calvinism,* 90.
31. Gaydosh, *Baptist Confession of Faith.*
32. Hayden, *Continuity and Change,* 181.
33. McKibbens, *Forgotten Heritage,* 30

Messenger

As the years passed and the firestorm grew in the East, Beddome found himself in what Robert Hall Jr. referred to as "village retirement" in Bourton-on-the-Water.[34] This retired life began in the year 1740 when he was called to the church to serve on probation. He did this for the next three years, officially becoming the pastor of the Bourton congregation in 1743. This would be Beddome's sole pastorate for the remaining years of his life. He served in Bourton without interruption for a total of 55 years.

Beddome is the picture of faithful, persevering, provincial ministry. The eminent Baptist statesman Robert Hall Jr., whose ministry spanned the close of the eighteenth century and on into the next, said of Beddome after his passing, in a recommendation he was asked to give toward the compilation of Beddome's many hymns in 1818, that

> Mr. Beddome was on many accounts an extraordinary person. His mind was cast in an original mould; his conceptions on every subject were eminently his own; and where the stamina of his thoughts were the same as other men's . . . a peculiarity marked the mode of their exhibition. Favoured with the advantages of a learned education, he continued to the last to cultivate an acquaintance with the best writers of antiquity, to which he was much indebted for the chaste, terse, and nervous diction, which distinguished his compositions both in prose and verse. Though he spent the principal part of a long life in a village retirement, he was eminent for his colloquial powers, in which he displayed the urbanity of the gentleman, and the erudition of the scholar, combined with a more copious vein of attic salt than any person it has been my lot to know.[35]

With a brilliant mind, a sound and evangelical education, a well-rounded literary palette, and skillful prose, all coupled together with a heart for Christ, Beddome was amply supplied with many gifts useful for a life of ministry among God's flock in the country. He had a reputation, according to Hall, for powerful yet refined speech, gentle manners of sophistication, scholarly intellect, and a charming wit to boot. It is no wonder that Thomas Brooks, the pastor of Bourton-on-the-Water in the nineteenth century, in writing a history of the church, looked back on the days of Beddome and referred to him as that "eminent man."[36]

34. Beddome, *Hymns*, vi.
35. Beddome, *Hymns*, v–vi.
36. Brooks, *Pictures of the Past*, 21.

Method

Benjamin Beddome was highly regarded not simply as a man and minister, but also as a preacher. The same Robert Hall Jr. who had such high praise for his person, had high praise for his preaching as well. He notes in the same hymn book recommendation that

> As a Preacher, he was universally admired for the piety and unction of his sentiments, the felicity of his arrangement, and the purity, force, and simplicity of his language; all which were recommended by a delivery perfectly natural and graceful. His printed discourses, taken from the manuscripts which he left behind him at his decease, are fair specimens of his usual performances in the pulpit. They are eminent for the qualities already mentioned; and their merits, which the modesty of the author concealed from himself, have been justly appreciated by the religious public.[37]

One place this universal admiration was certainly seen was in associational life. Beddome was a highly respected leader in the Midland Association. The policy for the Association was to have men preach no "oftener than once in three years."[38] However, Benjamin Francis, pastoral friend of Beddome and writer of his obituary, noted that from 1743 to 1789, Beddome preached no less than "17 times in 46 years" which upon close "examination it will appear, in the instance of Mr. Beddome, that this [policy] has not always been strictly adhered to."[39]

This same reputation also extended to the churches, both his own and many others.

Francis records "how acceptable his labours were to the churches, when he could be prevailed on to visit them, has long been known at Abingdon, Bristol, London, and in the circle of the Midland Association."[40] Thus from the East (London) to the West (Bristol) and everywhere in between (Abingdon and the Midlands), Beddome's reputation was secure as a brother of great use to the churches. He was like "the brother" in the Apostle Paul's second letter to the church in Corinth, "who is famous among all the churches for his preaching of the gospel" (1 Cor 8:18).

---

37. Beddome, *Hymns*, vi–vii.
38. Rippon, "Rev. Benjamin Beddome," 325.
39. Rippon, *Baptist Annual Register*, 2:325.
40. Rippon, *Baptist Annual Register*, 2:322.

In preaching, he was a man gripped by the text. Frequently in his sermons, he would exhort his congregation to give attention to "my text."[41] Exhorting his congregation and pressing truth upon them from Proverbs 3:15 on the supreme value of wisdom that is worth their every pursuit he proclaimed,

> "Riches make to themselves wings," honour is an empty puff of air, knowledge vanisheth, desire faileth; nay, the fashion of this world, and everything in it, passeth away; but the wisdom spoken of in *my text*, that is, internal vital religion, is a permanent and abiding principle, an incorruptible seed, a well of water that springeth up to everlasting life; it rises superior to all opposition, and will outlast the wreck of time and the ruins of the creation. O, then, let us get this wisdom; and, with all our gettings, get understanding![42]

An anecdotal story is told of his preaching of an occurrence at a minister's meeting in Gloucestershire, recounted by Benjamin Francis:

> After public service began, his natural timidity, it seems, overcame his recollection. His text and his discourse, for he did not preach by notes, had left him; and in the way from the pew to the pulpit, he leaned his head over the shoulder of the Rev. Mr. Davis, pastor of the place, and said, "Brother Davis, what must I preach from?" Mr. Davis, thinking he could not be at a loss, answered, "Ask no foolish questions." This afforded him considerable relief. He turned immediately to Titus 3:9. "Avoid foolish questions;" and he preached a remarkably methodical, correct, and useful discourse on it.[43]

While this is probably not the recommended method for sermon preparation or delivery, there are at least two points on which Beddome must be commended. The man knew he needed a text; and he sought to preach from that text. Francis recorded of him, regarding his commitment to the text of Scripture in preaching, that he "being a good textuary, and admitting that scripture is the best interpreter of scripture, his proofs were given with an accuracy concerning the sword of Goliath, 'There is none like it,' or equally suitable, through all the sacred volume."[44] He had by that point in his life, reached a deep level of mastery of the Scripture. "Indeed," Francis noted:

41. Beddome, *Sermons*, 93.

42. Beddome, *Sermons*, 93. Emphasis added.

43. Rippon, *Baptist Annual Register*, 2:320.

44. Rippon, *Baptist Annual Register*, 2:321. It is worthy of noting, that the *Oxford English Dictionary* defines a "textuary" as one who is an "expounder . . . one well

sermonizing was so much his forte, that at length when knowledge had received maturity from years, and composition was
familiarized by habit, he has been known, with a wonderful
facility of the moment, to sketch his picture at the foot of the
pulpit stairs, to colour it as he was ascending, and, without turning his eyes from the canvas, in the same hour, to give it all the
fit of a master.

On August 7, 1776, at the ordination service of John Sutcliff, one of the
men credited with the formation of the Baptist Missionary Society toward
the end of the century, Benjamin Beddome was present. Though "he had
been strongly urged to take part in the ordination service . . . he declined
. . . [but] was prevailed upon to preach in the evening."[45] Of note, one of
the members of the congregation that evening was the evangelical Anglican
minister of Olney, John Newton, writer of the celebrated hymn *Amazing
Grace*. Later that night Newton would write in his dairy of Beddome: "He is
an admirable preacher, simple, savoury, weighty."[46]

Message

The Apostle Paul said of his preaching that he "did not come proclaiming
. . . the testimony of God with lofty speech or wisdom, (rather he) decided
to know nothing . . . except Jesus Christ and him crucified" (1 Cor 2:1–2).
Could such be said of the preaching of Beddome? What characterized the
preaching of the man from the village of Bourton-on-the-Water?

His efforts at preaching, according to Benjamin Francis, were "unremitted and evangelical."[47] Francis went on to note of Beddome that "in his
preaching he laid Christ at the bottom of religion as the support of it, placed
him at the top of it as its glory, and made him the centre of it, to unite all
its parts, and to add beauty and vigour to the whole."[48] One might rightly
say that Christ was the sum and substance of the preaching of this beloved
brother. This summation bodes well for the following examination of Beddome's preaching against the *Modern Question* of Maurice specifically and
against the *modern question* itself more generally.

---

acquainted with and ready at quoting texts." Francis aptly uses such a term to describe
Benjamin Beddome.

45. Haykin, *One heart and One Soul*, 120.
46. Haykin, "Benjamin Beddome," 1:167.
47. Rippon, *Baptist Annual Register*, 2:320.
48. Rippon, *Baptist Annual Register*, 2:321.

An Analysis of Beddome's Preaching On the Theology of the Modern Question

Reaching back to the discussion of the modern question, it is at this point that some sort of comparative analysis must be made. What do we learn of Beddome's preaching regarding his postulated response to the modern question? The approach here will be to take the treatment of the modern question and superimpose it as a grid onto the preaching of Beddome.

Priority of Revealed Will Over the Will of Decree

Beddome was one who boldly and freely offered the gospel of Christ, full of grace, to all the Lord brought under his ministry, calling all without reservation to trust in the mercy and grace offered in that very preached word. Once in preaching to his congregation extoling the triumph of mercy over judgment from James 2:13, he declared the hopeful words that, "One sin deserves judgment, that is, the eternal wrath and displeasure of God; but mercy extends to many, nay, numberless sins. Our sins are like the sands; God's mercy like the sea, that covers those sands. Our sins rise to heaven; God's mercy is above the heavens. Great mercies follow great provocations; multiplied mercies, multiplied provocations."[49] At this point, turning to all under the sound of his voice, he called upon them to embrace several "duties" from the text, one of which was "to trust in" mercy.[50] Making it clear just what it was they were to trust in, he clarifies regarding mercy that "it is the proper object of trust, and makes God so."[51]

This general call to trust in the mercy of Christ, provided freely in the gospel to all who would trust in it, was not characteristic of the preaching of hyper-Calvinism at all. Free offers of grace (and mercy) were frowned upon at best, if not simply openly denied. This can be seen most clearly in the principle text of many hyper-Calvinists of the day by Joseph Hussey, a Congregational minister in Cambridge. Simply in the title to Joseph Hussey's book, *God's Operations of Grace, but No Offers of Grace*, there is indication of a denial that preachers of the gospel were to offer grace indiscriminately to all. In part, this was driven by their understanding of the relationship between God's will of decree, or his secret will, versus his revealed will.[52] Advocates of the modern question disagreed, as did Beddome. Beddome

49. Beddome, *Sermons*, 33.

50. Beddome, *Sermons*, 33.

51. Beddome, *Sermons*, 33.

52. Hussey, *God's Operations*.

was guided in his life and ministry by the revealed will of God, leaving the will of God's decree to God himself. This is evident from even a cursory examination of Beddome's extant sermons. Further, Beddome's position on the will of God is evident from statements such as the one he made in his sermon on "The Divine Providence," asserting that "It is not the absolute decrees, but the righteous laws of God, that are to determine our conduct; we are to be guided, not by his secret, but his revealed will."[53]

Beddome also wrote *A Scriptural Exposition of the Baptist Catechism*, in which he first states the question and answer from the catechism, followed by an elaboration on the answer in the form of a Scriptural exposition:

> Q. 44. What is the duty that God requireth of man?
>
> A. The duty, which God requireth of man, is obedience to his revealed will.
>
> Hath God revealed his will? Yes. He hath showed his word unto Jacob, his statutes and his judgments unto Israel (Ps 147:19). Hath he revealed it plainly? Yes. So that he may run which readeth it (Heb 2:2). And fully? Yes. I have not shunned to declare to you the whole counsel of God (Acts 20:27). Should we therefore seek to be acquainted with it? Yes. Lead me in thy truth and teach me (Ps 25:5). Is obedience to God's revealed will a duty? Yes. And now, O Israel, what doth the Lord thy God require of thee, but to walk in his ways (Deut 10:12). Is it the duty of all? Yes. Give ear all ye inhabitants of the world, both low and high, rich and poor (Ps 49:1–2). But especially of the redeemed? Yes. Ye are bought with a price, therefore glorify God in your body, and in your spirit, which are God's (1 Cor 6:20). And is it their whole duty? Yes. Let us hear the conclusion of the matter, fear God and keep his commandments, for this is the whole duty of man (Eccl 12:13).[54]

Clearly it is the revealed will of God, to be found in the Scripture alone that is to define the duty of the believer. But what of God's decrees? Beddome addresses this point in his exposition of question/answer ten from the catechism, asking and answering the question, "Should we be curious to know the divine decrees? No. For secret things belong to God (Deut 39:29)."[55] Just to make it clear he goes on: "Are God's precepts then, and not his decrees,

53. Beddome, *Sermons*, 49.

54. Beddome, *Scriptural Exposition*, 87–88.

55. Beddome, *Scriptural Exposition*, 23.

the rule of our conduct? Yes. Things which are revealed belong unto us and to our children (Deut 29:29)."[56]

Moral Law Demands Faith

In establishing the position of the modern question that the moral law itself demanded faith, Maurice had made use of Matthew 22:37–40 where Christ had summarized the requirements of God's moral law in two points: love of God and love of neighbour. From this text Maurice built a six-fold exegetical argument, which, though he may use somewhat modified verbiage, Beddome, in a sermon "On the Obedience of the Heart" from Proverbs 3:1, stands in agreement with at every point.[57]

First, Beddome places stress on the need for all men to keep the commandments of God from the heart, which is necessary due to the fact that being the commandments of God "they call for the greatest respect."[58] To the matter of how one is to hold this respect for them Beddome writes, "We must not only peruse them, endeavour to understand them, and have them so deeply impressed upon our minds as not to forget them, but keep them; and it is not every kind of keeping that will be pleasing to God, or profitable to ourselves; but our hearts must keep them."[59] This, by casual observation, leaves one with a great problem; Beddome notes the heart lacks a "vital principle," and to make matters worse, it contains "on the contrary, a bias toward that which is evil."[60] Thus to borrow from Maurice, God commands perfect love, and to this end we stand under a great obligation and a great deficiency at the same time. This fact, emphasizing Maurice's second argument from the text of Matthew's gospel record, we ought to love God, but in fact are not able to do so.

Third, fourth, and fifth, Maurice exhorts us to love Christ (this is implied in the command to love God—since Christ is God), to understand that faith is absolutely necessary to obeying the command to love Christ, and finally, to love Christ by faith in order to please Christ. With these points in mind note the following lengthy, but important, statement from Beddome:

> [The heart] must be *opened to receive the Lord Jesus Christ.* The same faith that opens the heart to Christ does also fit it for, and

56. Beddome, *Scriptural Exposition*, 23.
57. Beddome, *Sermons*, 428–34.
58. Beddome, *Sermons*, 428.
59. Beddome, *Sermons*, 428.
60. Beddome, *Sermons*, 429.

incline it to, every good work; thus we read of the obedience of faith; and that charity which is the bond of perfection, and the fulfilment of the whole law, is said to be the fruit of faith unfeigned. The *heart that is shut against Christ* will be open to temptation; whereas, *the heart that is open to Christ* will be shut against temptation. Till *Christ is received into the heart* there cannot be, when *Christ is received into the heart* there cannot but be, a conformity to God in the life; for he is there as a spring of action as well as the hope of glory. The more firmly we rely upon his atoning sacrifice, the more readily we shall submit to his kingly authority. In a word, *without faith in Christ, as the grand medium of our access to, and acceptance with God, it is impossible to serve him in that manner which he requires.* Hence, when the blessed Redeemer had been *instructing his disciples to forgive their offending brother not only seven, but seventy times seven, which seems rather to lie an act of charity* than of faith, instead of saying, "Lord, increase our charity," or love, they say, "Lord, increase our faith;" for as *the forgiveness recommended is the immediate fruit of love, so a holy sanctified love proceeds from faith*: and the stronger our faith is the more fervent and disinterested will our love be.[61]

Consider the points of emphasis italicized in the quotation. First, corresponding to Maurice's third point regarding loving Christ, Beddome speaks of the heart (the seat of affection/love) as that which must "be opened to receive" Christ, or be "open to Christ."[62] The heart of man that is open to Christ and receives Christ, is the heart of a man who loves Christ.

Second, Beddome sees the heart of man as simultaneously commanded to do what it must do, and what it cannot do. Thus, he states that "The pleasure of duty, and our perseverance in duty, both depend upon a gracious change wrought in the heart."[63] This is the duty of loving God, loving Christ and persevering in it, in order to "be pleasing to God."[64] How will this be accomplished? It is at this point that Beddome points to the astounding New Covenant promise of God from the prophets of old to grant men a new heart for that very purpose.

The Scriptural logic for Beddome (and Maurice) is as follows: 1) the duty to love God rests on all men, 2) this is a law that one ought to fulfill, but has no power for it and every power against it working within, 3) Christ,

61. Beddome, *Sermons*, 431–32. Emphasis added.
62. Beddome, *Sermons*, 431–32.
63. Beddome, *Sermons*, 429.
64. Beddome, *Sermons*, 428.

being God, is ever worthy of this love, and 4) in order for this love to find a home in one's heart, one needs a new heart, that will usher forth in a loving expression of faith in Christ alone. Without this "faith in Christ as the grand medium of our access to, and acceptance with God, it is impossible to serve him in that manner which he requires."[65] Or as Maurice says in his fifth point, alluding to Hebrews 11:6, without faith it is impossible to please him.

All of this leads to Maurice's sixth and final point of loving one's neighbour—a point with which Beddome fully concurs. This concurrence is seen where Christ declares that in order for his disciples to fulfill the moral obligation of loving their neighbour—seen in the noble act of forgiving "their offending brother not only seven, but seventy times seven"—they must have not their love increased, but rather their faith. For, Beddome adds, "the forgiveness recommended is the immediate fruit of love, so a holy sanctified love proceeds from faith: and the stronger our faith is the more fervent and disinterested will our love be"

Lack of Power Does Not Equate to Lack of Duty

Attention is now focused on a third theological conviction of those who held an affirmative position concerning the modern question under the rubric: Lack of power does not equate to lack of duty. One text that seems to be quite the favourite of Beddome in gospel exposition is Matthew 23:37: "O Jerusalem, Jerusalem, the city that kills the prophets and stones those who are sent to it! How often would I have gathered your children together as a hen gathers her brood under her wings, and you were not willing." For Beddome this text "exhibits a striking continuation of the sublime and pathetic. It opens to us, as it were, the very heart of the Redeemer; so that in discoursing upon it, the orator has an excellent opportunity of employing his eloquence, and the heaven-instructed minister, anxious for the good of souls, of showing the greatest warmth and affection."[66] Beddome seems to convey the pathos of Christ in relation to the lost. At the same time however, as he is entering into their struggles in sin, understanding their hardness of heart, and sympathizing with their inability to come to Christ on their own, he will not lower the bar on the requirement of the duty of faith in the Saviour.

Beddome reminds his hearers in the simplest terms in this message that "it is bad to turn a deaf ear to God's ministers."[67] He himself identified

65. Beddome, *Sermons*, 432.
66. Beddome, *Sermons*, 184.
67. Beddome, *Sermons*, 185.

with Christ, whom he saw the text picture "as a preacher of righteousness, lamenting the little success that attended his ministrations."[68] Here Beddome noted is to be observed Christ's:

> compassionate heart; for the text certainly implies, that if their prejudices had been removed, and they had come to him, they should not have been cast out; if they had acknowledged him as the Messiah, it would have prevented their temporal ruin; and if they had believed in him as such, their eternal destruction. This naturally brings to our minds that most affectionate declaration to the church at Laodicea, "Behold! I stand at the door and knock; if any man hear my voice, and open the door, I will come in to him, and sup with him, and he shall sup with me."[69]

Here, is found another of Beddome's favourite preaching texts, Revelation 3:20. A rich text displaying, for Beddome, Christ's heart for the lost. Beddome clearly sees this text in the framework of evangelism—calling sinners to repentance and faith in him, opening the door to him that he might come in, and that he might be present where once he was not welcome.

Beddome's next words in his message are noteworthy in light of the modern question.

> These words [referring to Rev 3:20 previously quoted] however, as well as those of my text, do not imply that Christ, as God, doth determine the salvation of those that are finally lost; but that Christ does all that can be done, without subduing the obstinacy of the human will, and takes such methods with impenitent sinners as will leave them finally without excuse. He calls them, not to satisfy the justice of God, or do anything to procure an interest in that satisfaction which he has made; but that they would seriously consider their lost and miserable condition without him, believe his doctrines, obey his precepts, and receive what he freely bestows; that if not weary and heavy laden, they would seek to be so; and if weary and heavy laden, they would come to him for rest.[70]

Here Beddome portrays Christ as setting forth the free offer of the gospel, full of grace and mercy for men to come and take. There is in this ministration of Christ to the lost a call to "receive what he freely bestows."

Nevertheless, the text states clearly, they "were not willing." In fact, Beddome notes here, "We have set before us in these words the stubbornness

68. Beddome, *Sermons*, 187.

69. Beddome, *Sermons*, 187.

70. Beddome, *Sermons*, 187–88.

and perverseness of those to whom Christ had discovered so tender a regard."[71] Furthermore, nothing seems able to convince them to come. Beddome notes that "All the opposition that Christ meets with arises from a perverse will; and till its corrupt bias is removed, miracles will not convince, nor threatenings affright, nor promises allure."[72] This is not to say that miracles are not to be worked, or that threatenings are not to be used, or even that the promises of the gospel are not to be set forth. However, men in this condition of unwillingness prefer "shadows to substantial felicity, thereby discovering both their ingratitude and folly."[73]

What is at the heart of the problem? Beddome notes two things keeping men from the duty of coming to Christ in full trust.

> 1. There is a natural weakness in the will, so that it cannot of itself incline to that which is spiritually good. Its bias is towards evil. It prefers the service of Satan and the pleasures of sin, to the favour of God and eternal happiness; and the more pure and precious any discovery of God is, the more it is disrelished by the carnal mind. "How weak is thine heart!" says God to Israel of old; and the same may be said to all sinners now. The strength of their lusts is owing to the weakness of their hearts.
>
> 2. Besides this weakness, there is a bitter enmity. "The carnal mind is enmity against God;" his law and his gospel, his holiness and his grace. *As men cannot do what they ought, by reason of impotency, so they will not do what they can, through stubbornness and obstinacy.* They are in bondage, and they choose to be so.[74]

Beddome clearly affirms, as can be seen, men in and of themselves lack power, but at no time does he lessen in the least their moral obligation to receive the word about Christ. In this Beddome's Calvinism can be seen, but it is of the orthodox version, and not the heterodox "hyperism" of many. His Calvinism was fully in accord with the modern question on this matter.

Saving Faith and Repentance the Duty of All

Fourth, examination must be made regarding the duty of saving faith and repentance being placed upon all who hear the gospel. The key term here is "saving" as it relates to faith and repentance. As alluded to in the

71. Beddome, *Sermons*, 188.

72. Beddome, *Sermons*, 188.

73. Beddome, *Sermons*, 188.

74. Beddome, *Sermons*, 188–89.

examination of the mini-theology of the modern question, hyper-Calvinists had no problem stating that Christ called all to faith and repentance, as long as distinction was made regarding the nature of said faith and repentance. Hyper-Calvinists distinguished between two types of faith—common and saving, and two types of repentance—legal and evangelical. John Brine, who, when confronted with the question as to "whether 'evangelical Repentance' and 'Special Faith' are indeed the 'Duties of all who hear the Gospel,'" responded "with a resounding 'No.'"[75]

This distinction was not necessarily the problem, for the distinction between these types of faith and repentance have a long history in the Reformed tradition. For example, even Calvin distinguishes between legal and evangelical repentance in his *Institutes of the Christian Religion*. He writes:

> Others, perceiving this word to have various acceptations in Scripture, have mentioned two kinds of repentance: and, to distinguish them by some character, have called one legal; in which the sinner, wounded by the envenomed dart of sin, and harassed by the fear of Divine wrath, is involved in deep distress, without the power of extricating himself: the other they style evangelical; in which the sinner is grievously afflicted in himself, but rises above his distress, and embraces Christ as the medicine for his wound, the consolation of his terrors, and his refuge from all misery.[76]

Beddome himself also made this distinction, especially in regard to repentance at various places in his preaching. Most pointedly in a sermon from Joel 2:14, Beddome carefully stated this distinction and unmistakably pointed to the kind of repentance God required of men for true life. He expressed his thoughts as follows:

> With respect to repentance, or turning to God. There is what is called a legal repentance, or distress of mind arising from the terrors of the law, or the dread of punishment; and though it is not such a repentance as accompanies salvation, not being mixed with faith and love, yet temporal judgments have sometimes been averted, and temporal blessings enjoyed, where this humiliation has taken place. Such was the case with one of the wicked kings of Israel: Seest thou how Ahab humbleth himself before me? Because he humbleth himself before me, I will not bring the evil in his days. Similar to this is Daniel's address to Nebuchadnezzar: O king, let my counsel be acceptable unto

75. Garrett, *Baptist Theology*, 93.

76. Calvin, *Institutes of the Christian Religion*, 596.

thee! Break off thy sins by righteousness, and thine iniquities by shewing mercy to the poor, if it may be a lengthening of thy prosperity. He does not assure him that this will be the issue, but intimates the probability of it. However, all this is distinct from that repentance which is unto life, and which we have principally in view. This is properly called evangelical, and flows from a principle of divine life in the soul. And though it is the work of the Holy Spirit to produce it, yet he deals with us as rational creatures, using suitable motives and encouragements in order to lead us to repentance, and therefore it becomes us to attend to them. Amongst various other motives, the hope of forgiveness is one of singular importance, and which the scriptures do not fail to urge. Let the wicked forsake his way, and the unrighteous man his thoughts; and let him return unto the Lord, and he will have mercy upon him, and to our God, for he will abundantly pardon.[77]

Thus, there is a distinction to be made, but the difference is in the application. Hyper-Calvinists believe that all God calls the non-elect to is a legal repentance and a common faith. Not so for Beddome and the advocates of the modern question. The next theological distinction will take this further in demonstrating how saving faith and repentance can be both duty and gift at the same time. But first, more needs to be heard from Beddome regarding the duty that all men are under when the gospel comes to them.

Perhaps the clearest statement regarding the modern question is to be found in his sermon on John 6:29, "This is the work of God, that ye believe on him who he hath sent" (KJV). It is in this text, that Beddome finds strong affirmation of the duty of men to whom the gospel is revealed, to believe its message. Beddome stated:

Whether faith in Christ is a duty required of all who live under the gospel dispensation, the most stupid and thoughtless, unaffected and unconcerned, has been disputed; however, that those to whom God has revealed the truth are under an indispensable obligation to receive it, which is one branch of saving faith, has been acknowledged by all. Hence, Christ tells the Scribes and Pharisees, "Unless ye believe that I am he, ye shall die in your sins:" but thus Simon Magus believed; nay, thus the devils believe, who at the same time tremble.

A reverential regard to the gospel, as every way worthy of God, is also confessed to be an universal duty; and the want of

77. Beddome, *Twenty Short Discourses*, 2:88–89.

it, and, more especially, a direct opposition to it, is supposed to involve men in guilt, and expose them to punishment.

Nor do any deny, that when a real conviction of sin has taken place, and persons being quickened by the grace of the Spirit have a deep sense of their danger and misery, it is their duty to fly with all possible speed to the hope set before them in the gospel. "Come unto me," says Christ, "all ye that labour and are heavy laden, and I will give you rest."[78]

Though Beddome does not refer to this issue explicitly as the modern question, with all that is swirling around him in the eighteenth century, as we have seen above, he is unmistakably pointing to the issue. Beddome begins here acknowledging the "disputed" issue regarding "whether faith in Christ is a duty required of all who live under the gospel dispensation." By the "gospel dispensation" it seems clear from other uses of this term, especially places where he contrasts the "gospel dispensation" with the "legal dispensation," he intends to refer here to the new covenant age embracing and following from the time of the incarnation of Christ.[79]

Having effectively side-stepped the "dispute" he prefers to dwell on what he sees as more sure ground and state his position on the matter. He points to his conviction by coming at this issue from three distinct angles. **First, he notes those who have had the truth of the gospel "revealed" to them.** These are the people with whom the modern question is directly concerned. The modern question is not concerned with the issue of the destiny of the un-evangelized. Rather, the advocates of the modern question, as well as Beddome, are focused upon those who by the provision of God, now know the gospel. Beddome clearly states here that these, knowing the gospel, "are under an indispensable obligation to receive it" and further, that this kind of receiving is an expression of "saving faith." This directly puts him at odds with the hyper-Calvinist position which would agree that all men who have the gospel revealed to them are called to believe it, but not with saving faith, which is restricted to the elect alone. To make the matter unmistakable, that it is saving faith he believes is the duty of these to whom the gospel has been made clear, he points to three groups who have had the gospel revealed to them, and are now being held to account for not believing. He points to the Pharisees, Simon Magus, and the demons—who all clearly understood who Christ claimed to be in the gospel, refused to believe it, and were subsequently judged for their rejection of him.

78. Beddome, *Sermons*, 164–65. All quotations throughout this section will be taken from these pages unless otherwise noted.

79. See Beddome, *Sermons*, 56, 77, 120, for comparative material.

Second, Beddome then changes his angle, looking at this from the issue of how men should respond to the gospel, again that is, men who have had the gospel revealed to them. Beddome states they should have for it a "reverential regard" that is "worthy of God." This reverential regard for the gospel is furthermore a "universal duty." Additionally, lacking it or being actively opposed to the gospel involves men "in guilt, and expose(s) them to punishment." This the hyper-Calvinists also deny. No greater judgment is incurred for a non-elect individual who rejects the gospel according to the hyper-Calvinist. Beddome disagrees, strongly.

Third, and finally, Beddome affirms (what all affirm—even the hyper-Calvinist) that "when a real conviction of sin has taken place, and persons being quickened by the grace of the Spirit have a deep sense of their danger and misery, it is their duty to fly with all possible speed to the hope set before them in the gospel." With this the modern question advocates and the hyper-Calvinists shared some common ground.

Beddome's concluding exhortation to those without Christ in his congregation was to be soberly received. He exhorted them, "Go to him, then, O sinner, and cry for this faith; pleading his mercy, and thy necessity."[80] Beddome saw Christ as full of mercy, and men, as full of need. This last word by Beddome also serves as a strong lead-in to our final point of comparison between Beddome and Maurice's *Modern Question*.

Faith and Repentance both Gift and Duty

Those who affirmed the modern question, along with the Baptist from Bourton, affirmed the Scriptural truth that faith and repentance are both gift and duty. Beddome touches on this issue at several points in his sermonizing, but nowhere more powerfully than in a sermon based on 2 Cor 5:20.[81] There we find the Apostle Paul pleading with the Corinthian assembly, "We implore you on behalf of Christ, be reconciled to God."

This glorious reality of reconciliation can be observed from several vantage points that will help bring out the gift/duty aspect of this final theological point. First, consider the work of God in the work of reconciliation. In his sermon Beddome points to the conversion of a sinner in reconciliation requiring the

> necessity of divine change, (and) not a change of the conduct
> only, but of the inward frame and temper of the mind. This must

80. Beddome, *Sermons*, 168.
81. Beddome, *Twenty Short Discourses*, 1:119–27.

be effected by the almighty power of God. The conversion of
a sinner is a greater miracle than the dividing of the sea, the
making Jordan to stand on heaps, the casting down of the walls
of Jericho, or raising the dead body of Lazarus. Not only everything without, but everything within opposes it.[82]

Second, in addition to the work of God, Beddome points in his sermon
to Christ. He concludes pointing to Christ's reconciling work: "How much
are we indebted to the Lord Jesus Christ, without whom this reconciliation
never would, nor ever could have taken place! His blood laid a foundation
for it; his grace brings it about."[83]

The third element involved in the reconciliation of sinners to God is
the work of Christ's ambassadors, his "royal messengers, who derive their
authority and receive their commission from him. To him they look for
direction, and would faithfully discharge the trust he reposes in them."[84]
Beddome notes that in this ministry of reconciliation, God is pictured as
courting sinners, and the chief means by which he does this courting is
through his ministers, whose "chief business . . . that which employs their
heads, their hands, their tongues, their hearts, is to carry on the great work
of reconciliation."[85] In order to bring about the reconciliation of sinners to
God, Christ commissions his ambassadors with a four-fold task:

1. In order to sinners' reconciliation to God, it is necessary for ministers
   boldly to declare, and faithfully to open the natural enmity of their
   hearts against him.

2. Ministers are further to teach and assert, that though the ground-work
   of our reconciliation was laid in the eternal counsels of God, yet that
   it is actually brought about in time, by the effectual operations of the
   divine Spirit.

3. Christ's servants are likewise to declare, that there is need of a farther
   reconciliation in those who are already reconciled to God.

4. Ministers are faithfully to denounce the terrible judgments of God
   against those who live and die unreconciled to him.[86]

He adds the way these ambassadors are to carry out this work: 1) with perfect unanimity, 2) with warmth and affection, 3) with spiritual power and

82. Beddome, *Twenty Short Discourses*, 1:124.
83. Beddome, *Twenty Short Discourses*, 1:124.
84. Beddome, *Twenty Short Discourses*, 1:116.
85. Beddome, *Twenty Short Discourses*, 1:117–18.
86. Beddome, *Twenty Short Discourses*, 1:118–122.

authority, and 4) with meekness [and] gentleness.[87] Further they must use "all the means of persuasion. 'We beseech you.' We use no coercive measures; we do not endeavour to frighten but draw you to your duty."[88]

This last word moves us to our final element in the work of reconciliation. Beddome notes that we clearly have a "duty" in this work.[89] In another sermon on "Encouragements to Hope," Beddome, noting the work of God in this effort, fully lays a great weight on the shoulders of those needing to close with Christ. He says, "Though it is the work of the Holy Spirit to produce it, yet he deals with us as rational creatures, using suitable motives and encouragements in order to lead us to repentance, and therefore it becomes us to attend to them."[90]

Interestingly, the Independent hyper-Calvinist Joseph Hussey made use of the same text from 2 Cor preached on here by Beddome. In his work Hussey emphatically declared that he found in 2 Cor 5:20, "no invitation [or] earnest exhortation to accept of Christ in the sinner's first reconciliation to him." And John Brine was of the conviction that to say that "evangelical repentance and special [saving] faith" are "the duties of the unregenerate" is tantamount to embracing "Arminianism."[91] Beddome, along with the advocates of the modern question, disagreed with both men.

Conclusion

Matthias Maurice clearly staked his ground in 1737 with his publication of *A Modern Question Modestly Answer'd*, and had Benjamin Beddome known Maurice, it ought to be abundantly clear, he would have gladly stood with him on the same ground in a spirit of solidarity. This chapter has sought to make use of the issue raised by Maurice to assess the preaching of English Particular Baptist Benjamin Beddome and to demonstrate his affirmation of the theological principles that infused the modern question in the eighteenth century.

Charles Haddon Spurgeon, commenting once on hyper-Calvinist preaching, remarked, "permit me to say I do not believe in the way in which some people pretend to preach the Gospel. They have no Gospel for sinners as sinners, but only for those who are above the dead level of sinner-ship

---

87. Beddome, *Twenty Short Discourses*, 1:124.
88. Beddome, *Twenty Short Discourses*, 1:124.
89. Beddome, *Twenty Short Discourses*, 1:124.
90. Beddome, *Twenty Short Discourses*, 1:186.
91. Hussey, *God's Operations of Grace*, 322; Ryland, *Life and Death*, 5.

and are technically styled sensible sinners."[92] He added in this particular sermon entitled the "Parable of the Good Samaritan":

> Like the priest in this parable, they see the poor sinner, and they say, "He is not conscious of his need, we cannot invite him to Christ." "He is dead," they say, "it is of no use preaching to dead souls." So they pass by on the other side, keeping close to the elect and quickened, but having nothing whatever to say to the dead, lest they should make out Christ to be too gracious and His mercy to be too free.[93]

Beddome had a gospel for sinners as sinners. Beddome preached a gospel that exalted the gracious, free mercy of Christ. Beddome offered a gospel that called all who heard it to repentance and faith in the one and only one who was mighty and willing to save, the Lord Jesus Christ. In a hymn given the title "The Freeness of the Gospel," Beddome penned these words to be taught to and sung by his congregation, for whose souls he faithfully laboured over five decades in the Midlands of England, with an affection fixed on Christ, and a heart devoted to rescuing sinners with the free gospel of Jesus.

> How free and boundless is the grace
> Of our redeeming God;
> Extending to the Greek and Jew,
> And men of every blood!
>
> The mightiest king and meanest slave
> May his rich mercy taste;
> He calls the beggar and the prince
> Unto the gospel feast.
>
> None are excluded thence, but those
> Who do themselves exclude;
> Welcome the learned and polite,
> The ignorant and rude.
>
> Come then, ye men of every name,
> Of every rank and tongue;
> What you are willing to receive,
> To you it doth belong.

92. Spurgeon, "Parable of the Good Samaritan."
93. Spurgeon, "Parable of the Good Samaritan."

Come without money, without price,
The rich provision share;
Fear not that you will be refused,
For such are welcome here.[94]

94. Beddome, *Hymns*, #373.

Bibliography

Primary Sources

Addicott, Len L. G. Champion, and K. A. C. Parsons, eds. *Church Book: St Andrew's Street Baptist Church, Cambridge 1720–1832*. London: Baptist Historical Society, 1991.

Altingius, Jacobus. *Methodus Theologiae didacticae*. Amsterdam, 1687.

Ames, William. *The Marrow of Theology*. Translated by John Dykstra Eusden. Grand Rapids, MI: Baker, 1997.

Arminius, Jacobus. *Opera theologica*. Leiden: Godefridum Basson, 1629.

The Baptist Catechism. Revised by Paul King Jewett. Grand Rapids: Baker, 1952.

Brakel, Wilhelmus à. *The Christian's Reasonable Service*. Vol 1. Translated by Bartel Elshout. Morgan, PA: Soli Deo Gloria, 1992.

Beddome, Benjamin. "Christ Manifested to the Soul." In *Sermons Printed from the Manuscripts of the Late Rev. Benjamin Beddome*, 119. London: William Ball, 1835.

———."Christ the Subject of Prayer." In *Sermons Printed from the Manuscripts of the Late Rev. Benjamin Beddome*, 237. London: William Ball, 1835.

———. *Hymns Adapted to Public Worship, or Family Devotion*. London: n.p., 1818.

———. "Letter of proposal from Benjamin Beddome (1717–1795) to Anne Steele (1717–1778), 23 December 1742." *Angus Library and Archives*. http://theangus. rpc.ox.ac.uk/?media-bank-object=letter-of-proposal-from-benjamin-beddome-1717-1795-to-anne-steele-1717-1778-23-december-1742.

———."Memoir." In *Sermons Printed from the Manuscripts of the Late Rev. Benjamin Beddome*, ix–xxiv. London: William Ball, 1835.

———. *A Scriptural Exposition of the Baptist Catechism*. 1776. Reprint, Birmingham, AL: Solid Ground, 2006.

———. *Sermons Printed from the Manuscripts of the Late Rev. Benjamin Beddome*. London: William Ball, 1835.

———. "'Tis God the Spirit Leads." *Hymnary.org*. https://hymnary.org/text/tis_god_the_spirit_leads

———. *Twenty Short Discourses adapted to Village Worship*. 8 vols. London: J. W. Morris/Burton, Smith, and Co., 1807–1825.

————. *Twenty Short Discourses Adapted to Village Worship or the Devotions of the Family.* Vols. 1–3. 2nd ed. Dunstable: J.W. Morris, 1807–1809.

————. *Twenty Short Discourses Adapted to Village Worship or the Devotions of the Family.* Vol. 4. 4th ed. London: R. Clay, 1822.

————. *Twenty Short Discourses Adapted to Village Worship or the Devotions of the Family.* Vol. 5. 5th ed. London: W. Simpkin and R. Marshall, 1833.

————. *Twenty Short Discourses Adapted to Village Worship or the Devotions of the Family.* Vol. 6. 5th ed. London: W. Simpkin and R. Marshall, 1834.

————. *Twenty Short Discourses Adapted to Village Worship or the Devotions of the Family.* Vols. 7–8. London: Samuel Burton, 1825.

Beddome, Benjamin, Jr. *Tentamen philosophico-medicum inaugurale de hominum varietatibus et earum causis.* Leiden: P. van der Eyk and D. Vygh, 1777.

Boston, Thomas. *Human Nature in Its Fourfold State.* 1720. Reprint, London: Banner of Truth Trust, 1964.

————. *An Illustration of the Doctrines of the Christian Religion, Comprehending a Complete Body of Divinity.* Vol. 1. Aberdeen: G. and R. King, 1848–52.

Braunius, Johannes. *Doctrina Foederum sive Systema Theologiae didacticae et electicae.* Amsterdam: Abraham van Someren, 1691.

Bucanus, Gulielmus. *Institutiones theologicae seu locorum communium christianae religionis.* Geneva: Samuelis Chouet, 1648.

Bulkeley, Peter. *The Gospel-Covenant.* London: Thomas Parkhurst, 1674.

Calvin, John. *Institutes of the Christian Religion.* Edited by John T. McNeill. Translated by Ford Lewis Battles. Philadelphia: Westminster, 1960.

————. *Opera Quae Supersunt Omnia.* Edited by Johann-Wilhlem Baum, et al. Brunsvigae: C. A. Schwetschke et Filium, 1863–1889.

Charnock, Stephen. "The Necessity, the Nature, the Efficient, and the Instrument of Regeneration." In *The Complete Works of Stephen Charnock,* edited by Thomas Smith, 7–335. Vol. 3. Edinburgh: James Nichol, 1865.

Cocceius, Johannes. *Summa theologiae ex Scriptura repetita* in *Opera omnia theologica, exegetica, didactica, polemica, philologic.* Vol. 7. Amsterdam: Janssonius-Waesberge, Boom & Goethals, 1701–1706.

The Colonial Church and School Society. *Psalms and Hymns, compiled from the Most Approved Collections, and Adapted for Public, Social, and Private Use.* London: Seeleys, Fleet Street, and May, 1860.

Dutton, Anne. *A Letter against Sabellianism.* London: M. Lewis, 1764.

Edwards, John. *Veritas Redux: Evangelical Truths Restored.* London: Robinson, Lawrence & Wyat, 1707.

Fuller, Andrew G. "The Calvinistic and Socinian Systems Examined and Compared, as to Their Moral Tendency." In *Controversial Publications,* edited by Joseph Belcher, 108–242. Vol. 2 of *The Complete Works of Andrew Fuller.* Harrisonburg, VA: Sprinkle, 1988.

————. *The Complete Works of the Rev. Andrew Fuller.* 3 Vols. Edited by Joseph Belcher. 1845. Reprint, Harrisonburg, VA: Sprinkle, 1988.

————. "The Deity of Christ." In *Miscellaneous Expositions,* edited by Joseph Belcher, 693–704. Vol. 3 of *The Complete Works of Andrew Fuller.* Harrisonburg, VA: Sprinkle, 1988.

————. *The Gospel Worthy of All Acceptation*. In *The Works of Andrew Fuller*, edited by Andrew Gunton Fuller, 150–90. 1801. Reprint, Carlisle, PA: Banner of Truth Trust, 2007.

Gill, John. *An Answer to the Birmingham Dialogue Writer: Part 1 and 2*. In *A Collection of Sermons and Tracts*, by John Gill, 107–61. Vol. 2. London: George Keith, 1773.

————. *The Cause of God and Truth*. Grand Rapids: Baker, 1980.

————. *A Complete Body of Doctrinal and Practical Divinity*. In *The Collected Writings of John Gill* [CD-ROM]. Paris, AR: Baptist Standard Bearer, 2007.

————. *The Doctrine of the Trinity, Stated and Vindicated*. 2nd ed. London: G. Keith and J. Robinson, 1752.

Hall, Robert. "Recommendatory Preface." In *Hymns Adapted to Public Worship, or Family Devotion*, by Benjamin Beddome, v–viii. London: n.p., 1818.

Heidegger, Johann Heinrich. *Corpus theologiae christianae . . . adeoque sit plenissimum theologiae didacticae, elenchticae, moralis et hisoricae systema*. Vol. 1. Zurich: Typis Joh. Henrici Bodmeri, 1700.

Henry, Matthew. *The Complete Works of the Rev. Matthew Henry*. Edinburgh/London/Dublin: A. Fullarton and Co., 1853.

————. *A Scripture-Catechism, in the Method of the Assemblies*. London: T. Parkhurst, 1703.

Hiller, Thomas. "The Doctrines of Grace. Circular Letter of the Midland Association." In *The Baptist Annual Register* 1, edited by John Rippon, 37–42. London: n.p., 1793.

Ivimey, Joseph. *A History of the English Baptists*. London, 1811. Vol 1.

Keach, Benjamin. *The Breach Repair'd in God's Worship, or Singing Psalms, Hymns, and Spiritual Songs proved to be an Holy Ordinance of Jesus Christ*. London: n.p., 1691.

Leigh, Edwards. *A Treatise of Divinity*. London: William Lee, 1646.

The London Baptist Confession of Faith, Thirty-Two Articles of Christian Faith and Practice with Scripture Proofs, Adopted by the Ministers and Messengers of the General Assembly which Met in London in 1689. London: n.p., 1689.

Maresius, Samuel. *Collegium theologicum, sive Systema breve universae Theologiae, comprehensium octodecim disputationibus*. Geneva: n.p., 1659.

McGlothlin, W. J. *Baptist Confessions of Faith*. Philadelphia: American Baptist Society, 1911.

Montgomery, James, ed. *Christian Psalmist; or Hymns Original and Selected*. Glasgow: Chalmers and Collins, 1825.

Newman, William. *Rylandiana: Reminiscences Relating to the Rev. John Ryland, AM*. London: George Wightman, 1835.

Owen, John. *A Discourse Concerning The Holy Spirit*. Vol. 3 of *The Works of John Owen*. Edinburgh: T. & T. Clark, 1862.

Priestley, Joseph. *Reflections on Death*. Birmingham: J. Belcher, 1790.

"Recent Deaths: Mr. R. Cooper." *Baptist Magazine* 40 (1848) 428.

Rippon, John. *Baptist Annual Register 1798, 1799, 1800, and Part of 1801: Including Sketches of the State of Religion Among Different Denominations of Good Men at Home and Abroad*. Vol. 2. London: n.p., 1801.

————. *A Brief Memoir of the Life and Writings of the Late Rev. John Gill, DD*. Reprint, Harrisonburg, VA: Gano, 1992.

————. "Rev. Benjamin Beddome, A.M. Bourton-on-the-Water, Gloucesteshire." *Baptist Annual Register* 2 (1794–1797) 314–26.

————, ed. *The Psalms and Hymns of Dr. Watts with Dr. Rippon's Selection*. London: n.p., 1787.

————, ed. *A Selection of Hymns from the Best Authors, Intended as an Appendix to Dr. Watts's Psalms and Hymns*. London: Thomas Wilkins, 1787.

Robinson, Robert. *Posthumous Works of Robert Robinson*. Harlow: Benjamin Flower, 1812.

————. *Select Works of the Rev. Robert Robinson*. Edited by William Robinson. London: J. Heaton & Son, 1861.

————. *Seventeen Discourses of Several Texts of Scripture; Addressed to Christian Assemblies in villages near Cambridge. To which are added, Six Morning Exercises*. New ed. Harlow: Benjamin Flower, 1805.

————. *Two Original Letters by the Late Mr. Robert Robinson*. London: J. Marsom, 1802.

Spurgeon, Charles H. "The Parable of the Good Samaritan." October 5, 1862. *Christian Classics Ethereal Library*. http://www.ccel.org/ccel/spurgeon/sermons08.xliv.html.

————, ed. *Our Own Hymn-Book: A Collection of Psalms and Hymns, for Public, Social, and Private Worship*. London: Passmore and Alabaster, 1883.

Stennett, Joseph, II. *The Christian Strife for the Faith of the Gospel*. London: Aaron Ward, 1738.

Synopsis purioris theologiae, disputationibus quinquaginta duabus comprehensa ac conscripta per Johnnem polyandrum, Andream Rivetum, Antonium Walaeum, Antonium Thysiu. 1625. Edition sexta, curavit et praefatus est Dr. H. Bavinck. Leiden: Donner, 1881.

Theodosia [Anne Steele]. *Poems on Subjects Chiefly Devotional*. 2 vols. London: Buckland, Ward, and Pine, 1760.

Turner, Daniel. "Spiritual Darkness: Letter from the Rev. D. Turner of Abingdon to the Rev. Mr. Beddome of Bourton." *Baptist Magazine* 7 (1815) 9–14.

Turretin, Francis. *Institutes of Elenctic Theology*. Edited by James T. Dennison Jr. Translated by George Musgrave Giger. Phillipsburg, NJ: P&R, 1994.

————. *Institutio theologiae elencticae*. Vol. 1. 1679–1685. New ed. Edinburgh, 1847.

van Mastricht, Petrus. *Theoretico-practica theologia, qua, per capita theological, pars dogmatica, elenchtica et practica, perpetua successione conjugantur, praecedunt in usum operas, paraleipomena, seu skeleton de optima concionandi method*. Amsterdam: Henricus & Theodorus Boom, 1682–1687.

Vermigli, Peter Martyr. *Loci Communes*. London: Thomas Vautrollerius, 1583.

————. *Philosophical Works: On Relation of Philosophy to Theology*. Edited and translated by Joseph C. McLelland. Peter Martyr Library 4. Kirksville, MO: Truman State University Press, 1996.

Wallin, Benjmain. *The Eternal Existence of the Lord Jesus Christ Considered and Improved*. London: n.p., 1766.

Watts, Isaac. *The Psalms of David Imitated in the Language of the New Testament, and apply'd to the Christian state and worship*. London: Clark, Ford, and Cruttenden, 1719.

Witsius, Joh. *De Economia Foederum Dei cum Hominibus*. Basel: Rudolph Im-Hoff, 1739.

Wendelin, Marcus Friedrich. *Christianae theologiae libri duo*. Hanover: Wechelianis, Schleichii & de Zetter, 1734.

Wollebius, Johannes. *Compendium theologiae christianae*. Amsterdam: Aegidium Janssonium Valckenier, 1650.

Zanchius, Girolamo. *Opera theologicorum, tomus quartus.* Geneva: Samuelis Crispini, 1617–19.

Secondary Sources

Aalders, Cynthia Y. *To Express the Ineffable: The Hymns and Spirituality of Anne Steele.* Eugene, OR: Wipf and Stock, 2009.

Arnold, Richard. "A 'Veil of Interposing Night:' The Hymns of Anne Steele (1717–1778)." *Christian Scholar's Review* 18.4 (1989) 371–87.

Aulén, Gustaf. *Christus Victor: An Historical Study of the Three Main Types of the Atonement.* Translated by A. G. Herbert. London: SPCK, 1970.

Bauckham, Richard J. "The Role of the Spirit in the Apocalypse." *Evangelical Quarterly* 52 (1980) 75–77.

Beeke, Joel, and Mark Jones. *A Puritan Theology: Doctrine for Life.* Grand Rapids, MI: Reformation Heritage, 2012.

"Benjamin Beddome." *Hymnary.org.* http://www.hymnary.org/person/Beddome_Benjamin?sort=desc&order=Instances.

Benson, Louis F. *The English Hymn: Its Development and Use in Worship.* Philadelphia: Presbyterian Board, 1915.

Berkhof, Louis. *The History of Christian Doctrines.* 1937. Reprint, Edinburgh: Banner of Truth, 2002.

Betheridge, Alan. *Deep Roots, Living Branches: A History of Baptist in the English Western Midlands.* Leicester: Troubador, 2010.

Brackney, William H., ed. *Baptist Life and Thought: 1600–1980. A Source Book.* Valley Forge, PA: Judson, 1983.

Bray, G. L. "Trinity." In *New Dictionary of Theology,* edited by Sinclair B. Ferguson, et al., 691–94. Downers Grove, IL: InterVarsity, 1988.

Breed, David R. *The History and Use of Hymns and Hymn-Tunes.* Chicago IL: Fleming H. Revell Co., 1903.

Brooks, Thomas. *Pictures of the Past: The History of the Baptist Church, Bourton-on-the-Water.* London: Judd & Glass, 1861.

Broome, J. R. *A Bruised Reed: The Life and Times of Anne Steele, Together with Anne.* Harpenden, England: Gospel Standard Trust, 2007.

Brown, Raymond. *The English Baptists of the Eighteenth Century.* London: Baptist Historical Society, 1986.

Bush, Russ, and Tom Nettles. *Baptists and the Bible.* Nashville, TN: Broadman and Holman, 1999.

Champion, L. G. "Robert Robinson: A Pastor In Cambridge." *Baptist Quarterly* 31 (1985–1986) 241–46.

Clipsham, Ernest F. "Andrew Fuller and Fullerism: A Study in Evangelical Calvinism: The Development of a Doctrine." *Baptist Quarterly* 20 (1963) 99–114.

Cramp, J. M. *Baptist History: From the Foundation of the Christian Church to the Close of the Eighteenth Century.* London: Elliot Stock, 1871.

Cross, Anthony R. *Useful Learning: Neglected Means of Grace in the Reception of the Evangelical Revival among English Particular Baptists.* Eugene, OR: Pickwick, 2017.

Culross, James. *The Three Rylands: A Hundred Years of Various Christian Service.* London: Elliot Stock, 1897.

Daniell, David. *William Tyndale. A Biography*. New Haven, CT: Yale University Press, 1994.

Daniels, Richard. *The Christology of John Owen*. Grand Rapids: Reformation Heritage, 2004.

David, John Jefferson. *Worship and the Reality of God: An Evangelical Theology of Real Presence*. Downers Grove, IL: InterVarsity, 2010.

Davies, Horton. *From Watts and Wesley to Martineau, 1690–1900*. Vol. 2 of *Worship and Theology in England*. Grand Rapids, MI: Eerdmans, 1996.

Dix, Kenneth. "'Thy Will Be Done': A Study in the Life of Benjamin Beddome. *Bulletin of the Strict Baptist Historical Society* 9 (1972).

Dixon, Philip. *"Nice and Hot Disputes": The Doctrine of the Trinity in the Seventeenth Century*. London/New York: T. & T. Clark, 2003.

Eadkins, Joanna. "The Beddome Family: John Beddome." http://www.gwydir.demon.co.uk/jo/genealogy/beddome/john.htm.

Edmondson, Stephen. *Calvin's Christology*. Cambridge: Cambridge University Press, 2004.

Fairchild, Hoxie Neale. *Religious Trends in English Poetry*. Vol. 2 of *English Hymns of the Eighteenth Century: An Anthology*. Edited by Richard Arnold. American University Studies 4.137. New York: Peter Lang, 1991.

Farley, Benjamin Wirt. *The Providence of God*. Grand Rapids, MI: Baker, 1988.

Garrett, James Leo. *Baptist Theology: A Four-Century Study*. Macon, GA: Mercer University Press, 2009.

Garrigou-Lagrange, Reginald. *De deo uno: Commentarium in primam partem S. Thomae*. Paris: Desdee, 1938.

———. *God, His Existence and His Nature: A Thomistic Solution of Certain Agnostic Antinomies*. Vol. 2. Translated by Bede Rose. 5th ed. St. Louis: Herder, 1941.

———. *Predestination: The Meaning of Predestination in Scripture and the Church*. Rockford, IL: Tan, 1998.

Hanson, R. P. C. *The Search for the Christian Doctrine of God: The Arian Controversy, 318–381*. Grand Rapids, MI: Baker, 2005.

Hayden, Roger. *Continuity and Change: Evangelical Calvinism Among Eighteenth-Century Baptist Ministers trained at Bristol Academy, 1690–1791*. Didcot, Oxfordshire: Baptist Historical Society, 2009.

———. "The Contribution of Bernard Foskett." In *Pilgrim Pathways: Essays in Honor of B. R. White*, edited by William H. Brackney and Paul Fiddes, 189–206. Macon, GA: Mercer University Press, 1999.

———. "This Failure of the Past Is Having an Effect Today." *Baptist Times* 7237 (1989) 4.

———. "The Particular Baptist Confession 1689 and Baptist Today." *Baptist Quarterly* 32 (1987–1988) 408–9.

Haykin, Michael A. G. "Benjamin Beddome (1717–1795)." In *The British Particular Baptists, 1638–1910*, edited by Michael A. G. Haykin, 166–83. Vol 1. Springfield, MO: Particular Baptist, 1998.

———. "Benjamin Beddome (1717–1795): His Life and His Hymns." In *Pulpit and People: Studies in Eighteenth-Century Baptist Life and Thought*, edited by John H. Y. Briggs, 93–111. Milton Keynes: Paternoster, 2009.

———. "'Glory to the Three Eternal': Benjamin Beddome and the Teaching of Trinitarian Theology in the Eighteenth Century." *Southern Baptist Journal of Theology* 10.1 (2006) 72–85.

————. "'His Soul-Refreshing Presence': The Lord's Supper in Baptist Thought & Experience in The 'Long' Eighteenth Century, With Particular Reference to Anne Dutton & John Sutcliff." Institute for Christian Worship Lectures, February 2008. https://www.academia.edu/3131537/his_soul-refreshing_presence_the_lords_supper_in_baptist_thought_and_experience_in_the_long_eighteenth_century.

————. *One Heart and One Soul, John Sutcliff of Olney, His Friends and His Times.* Darlington: Evangelical, 1994.

————, ed. *The British Particular Baptists: 1638–1910.* 3 vols. Springfield, MO: Particular Baptist, 2003.

Heppe, Heinrich. *Reformed Dogmatics: Set Out and Illustrated From the Sources.* Edited by Ernst Bizer. Translated by G. T. Thomson. Grand Rapids, MI: Baker, 1978.

Hodge, Charles. *Systematic Theology.* Vol. 2. Peabody, MA: Hendrickson, 1999.

Howson, Barry H. "Hanserd Knollys (c. 1598–1691)." In *British Particular Baptists: 1638–1910,* edited by Michael A. G. Haykin, 38–63. Vol. 1. Springfield, MO: Particular Baptist, 1998.

Hughes, Graham W. *With Freedom Fired. The Story of Robert Robinson, Cambridge Nonconformist.* London: Carey Kingsgate, 1955.

Ivimey, Joseph. *A History of the English Baptists.* 4 vols. London: Isaac Taylor Hinton/ Holdsworth & Ball, 1811–1830.

James, Sharon. *In Trouble and In Joy.* Darlington: Evangelical, 2009.

Julian, John. *A Dictionary of Hymnology: Setting Forth the Origin and History of Christian Hymns of All Ages and Nations.* London: John Murray, 1907.

Kelly, J. N. D. *Early Christian Doctrines.* Peabody, MA: Prince, 2007.

Kidd, Thomas S. *The Great Awakening: The Roots of Evangelical Christianity in Colonial America.* New Haven, CT: Yale University Press, 2007.

Letham, Robert. *The Holy Trinity: In Scripture, History, Theology, and Worship.* Phillipsburg, NJ: P&R, 2004.

Love, W. DeLoss. *Samson Occom and the Christian Indians of New England.* Boston, MA/Chicago, IL: Pilgrim, 1899.

Lumpkin, William L. *Baptist Confessions of Faith.* Valley Forge, PA: Judson, 1959.

MacLachlin, H. John. *Socinianism in Seventeenth-Century England.* Oxford: Oxford University Press, 1951.

Martin, Hugh. *Benjamin Keach (1640–1704): Pioneer of Congregational Hymn Singing.* London: Independent, 1961.

McBeth, H. Leon *The Baptist Heritage.* Nashville, TN: Broadman, 1987.

McGuckin, John Anthony. *St. Cyril of Alexandria and the Christological Controversy: Its History, Theology, and Texts.* Leiden: Brill, 1994.

————. *The Westminster Handbook to Patristic Theology.* Louisville, KY: Westminster John Knox, 2004.

Muller, Richard A. *Calvin and the Reformed Tradition: On the Work of Christ and the Order of Salvation.* Grand Rapids, MI: Baker, 2012.

————. *Christ and the Decree: Christology and Predestination in Reformed Theology From Calvin to Perkins.* Durham, NC: Labyrinth, 1986.

————. *Dictionary of Latin and Greek Theological Terms.* Grand Rapids, MI: Baker, 1985.

————. "*Fides* and *Cognitio* in Relation to the Problem of Intellect and Will in the Theology of John Calvin." *Calvin Theological Journal* 25 (1990) 207–24.

————. "Jonathan Edwards and the Absence of Free Choice: A Parting of Ways in the Reformed Tradition." *Jonathan Edwards Studies* 1.1 (2011) 3–22.

————. *Post Reformation Reformed Dogmatics: The Rise and Development of Reformed Orthodoxy, ca. 1520 to ca. 1725.* 4 vols. Grand Rapids, MI: Baker, 2003.

————. "The Spirit and the Covenant: John Gill's Critique of the Pactum Salutis," *Foundations* 24 (1981) 4–14.

————. "Toward the Pactum Salutis: Locating the Origins of a Concept." *Mid-America Journal of Theology* 18 (2007) 11–65.

————. *The Unaccommodated Calvin: Studies in the Foundation of a Theological Tradition.* Oxford: Oxford University Press, 2000.

Music, David W., and Milburn Price. *A Survey of Christian Hymnody.* Carol Stream, IL: Hope, 1999.

Music, David W., and Paul A. Richardson. *"I Will Sing the Wondrous Story": A History of Baptist Hymnody in North America.* Macon: Mercer University Press, 2011.

Naylor, Peter. "John Collett Ryland: 1723–1792." In *The British Particular Baptists: 1638–1910,* edited by Michael A. G. Haykin, 184–201. Vol. 1. Springfield, MO: Particular Baptist, 1998.

————. *Picking Up a Pin for the Lord: English Particular Baptists from 1688 to the Early Nineteenth Century.* London: Grace Trust, 1992.

Nettles, Tom J. "Benjamin Keach (1640–1704)." In *British Particular Baptists: 1638–1910,* edited by Michael A. G. Haykin, 94–131. Vol. 1. Springfield, MO: Particular Baptist, 1998.

————. *By His Grace and for His Glory: A Historical, Theological and Practical Study of the Doctrines of Grace in Baptist Life.* Cape Coral, FL: Founders, 2006.

————. *Teaching Truth, Training Hearts: The Study of Catechisms in Baptist Life.* Amityville, NY: Calvary, 1998.

Nuttall, Geoffrey F. "George Whitefield's 'Curate': Gloucestershire Dissent and the Revival." *Journal of Ecclesiastical History* 27 (1976) 382–84.

————. *The Holy Spirit in Puritan Faith and Experience.* 2nd ed. Chicago: University of Chicago Press, 1992.

Oliver, Robert. *The Chapels of Wiltshire and the West.* Vol. 5 of *The Strict Baptist Chapels of England.* London: Fauconberg, 1968.

Osborne, Thomas M. "Thomist Premotion and Contemporary Philosophy of Religion." *Nova et Vetera* 4 (2006) 607–32.

Ott, Heinrich. *Die Antwort des Glaubens.* 3rd ed. Stuttgart and Berlin: Kreuz Verlag, 1981.

Pelikan, Jaroslav. *The Emergence of the Catholic Tradition (100–600).* Vol. 1 of *The Christian Tradition: A History of the Development of Doctrine.* Chicago: University of Chicago Press, 1971.

————. *Reformation of Church and Dogma (1300–1700).* Vol. 4 of *The Christian Tradition.* Chicago: University of Chicago Press, 1984.

Placher, William C. *The Domestication of Transcendence: How Modern Thinking about God Went Wrong.* Louisville, KY: Westminster John Knox, 1996.

Roberts, R. Philip. *Continuity and Change: London Calvinistic Baptists and The Evangelical Revival 1760–1820.* Wheaton, IL: Richard Owen Roberts, 1989.

Robinson, Henry Wheeler. *The Life and Faith of the Baptists.* London: Methuen and Company, 1927.

Routley, Erik. *I'll Praise My Maker: A Study of the Hymns of Certain Authors Who Stand In or Near the Tradition of English Calvinism 1700–1850.* London: Independent, 1951.

Seeberg, Reinhold. *Text-Book of the History of Doctrines.* Translated by Charles E. Hay. 2 vols. Grand Rapids, MI: Baker, 1952.

Sell, Alan P. F. *Christ and Controversy: The Person of Christ in Nonconformist Thought and Ecclesial Experience, 1600–2000.* Eugene, OR: Pickwick, 2011.

Sherman, Robert. *King, Priest, and Prophet: A Trinitarian Theology of Atonement.* New York: T&T Clark, 2004.

Smith, Karen. "The Liberty Not to Be a Christian: Robert Robinson (1735–1790) of Cambridge and Freedom of Conscience." In *Distinctively Baptist: Essays on Baptist History. A Festschrift in Honor of Walter B. Shurden,* edited by Marc A. Jolley with John D. Pierce, 151–70. Macon, GA: Mercer University Press, 2005.

Stokes, William. *The History of the Midland Association of Baptist Churches, From Its Rise in the Year 1655 to 1855.* London: R. Theobald/Birmingham: John W. Showell, 1855.

Torbet, Robert G. *A History of the Baptists.* 3rd ed. Valley Forge, PA: Judson, 1963.

Trueman, Carl R. *The Claims of Truth: John Owen's Trinitarian Theology.* Carlisle, Cumbria: Paternoster, 1998.

Underwood, A. C. *A History of the English Baptists.* London: Kingsgate, 1947.

van Asselt, Willem J. "Christ's Atonement: A Multi-Dimensional Approach." *Calvin Theological Journal* 38.1 (2003) 52–67.

van Asselt, Willem J., et al., eds, *Reformed Thought on Freedom: The Concept of Free Choice in the History of Early-Modern Reformed Theology.* Grand Rapids, MI: Baker, 2010.

Vaughn, J. Barry. "Benjamin Keach." In *Baptist Theologians.* Edited by Timothy George and David S. Dockery. Nashville, TN: Broadman, 1990.

Walker, Austin. *The Excellent Benjamin Keach.* Dundas, ON: Joshua, 2004.

Watson, J. R. *The English Hymn: A Critical and Historical Study.* Oxford: Clarendon, 1997.

Weaver, Rebecca H. *Divine Grace and Human Agency: A Study of the Semi-Pelagian Controversy.* Patristic Monograph Series 15. Macon, GA: Mercer University Press, 1996.

White, Barrington R. *The English Baptists of the Seventeenth Century.* History of the English Baptist 1. 2nd ed. Didcot, Oxfordshire: Baptist Historical Society, 1996.

Williams, Rowan. *Arius: Heresy and Tradition.* Grand Rapids, MI: Eerdmans, 2001.

Young, Doyle L. "Andrew Fuller and the Modern Mission Movement." *Baptist History and Heritage* 27 (1982) 17–27.

Unpublished Materials and Archives

Bourton-on-the-Water Church Book 1719–1802. Angus Library, Regent's Park College, Oxford University.

The Circular Letter of the Western Association. 1776.

Newton, John. *Diary (1703–1805).* Princeton University Library, Princeton, NJ.

Purdy, Thomas. "Letter to John Sutcliff." April 11, 1775. Sutcliff Papers, Angus Library, Regent's Park College, Oxford University.

Theses

Ascol, Thomas Kennedy. "The Doctrine of Grace: A Critical Analysis of Federalism in the Theologies of John Gill and Andrew Fuller." PhD diss., Southwestern Baptist Theological Seminary, 1989.

Carmichael, Joseph Van. "The Hymns of Anne Steele in John Rippon's *Selection of Hymns:* A Theological Analysis in the Context of The English Particular Baptist Revival." PhD diss., Southern Baptist Theological Seminary, 2012.

Hayden, Roger. "Evangelical Calvinism among Eighteenth-century British Baptists with Particular Reference to Bernard Foskett, Hugh and Caleb Evans and the British Baptist Academy, 1690–1791." PhD diss., University of Keele, 1991.

Holmes, Derrick. "The Early Years (1655–1740) of Bourton-on-the-Water Dissenters who later constituted the Baptist Church, with special reference to the Ministry of the Reverend Benjamin Beddome A.M. 1740–1795." Unpublished Certificate in Education Dissertation, St. Paul's College, 1969.

Oliver, Robert William. "The Emergence of a Strict and Particular Baptist Community among the English Calvinistic Baptists 1770–1850." PhD diss., London Bible College, 1986.

Park, Hong-Kyu. "Grace and Nature in the Theology of John Gill (1697–1771)." PhD diss., University of Aberdeen, 2001.

Timmons, Aaron J. "The Cause of Christ and Truth: Arguments for the Deity of Christ in the Anti-Socinian Writings of John Gill, Dan Taylor, and Andrew Fuller." ThM thesis, Southern Baptist Theological Seminary, 2008.

White, Jonathan Anthony. "A Theological and Historical Examination of John Gill's Soteriology in Relation to Eighteenth-Century Hyper-Calvinism." PhD diss., Southern Baptist Theological Seminary, 2010.